With all my love & best wishes for a complete recovery this time.

Happy Christmas just you & I together.

Nanni

Nowt so queer as folk

A book of reminiscence about Yorkshire and Yorkshiremen

Derrick Boothroyd

ISBN 0 903 775 03 4

Published and printed in Great Britain by
Watmoughs Limited Idle Bradford West Yorkshire **BD10 8NL;**
and London

'All the world's queer except thee and me—and even tha's a bit queer.'

—A Yorkshire husband speaking to his wife

Contents

Part two—The Yorkshire Post

Part three—The World of Wool

Part four—Yorkshire Cricket

Part one—Shoddy Saga

Where there's muck there's brass

People who do not live there are apt to be disparaging about Batley, a town of some 50 000 inhabitants set in a valley in the middle of an urban sprawl bounded to the north by Leeds and Bradford and to the south by Halifax and Huddersfield. A former colleague of mine always used to refer to it as "the sun trap of the north", an ironic comment on the smoke which used to billow out of the mill chimneys and hang over the place like a shroud. In neighbouring Dewsbury they crack the old joke about the birds having to fly backwards in Batley to keep the soot out of their eyes. In Morley they say there is only one thing that can be done with Batley and that is to fill it in. Perhaps the ultimate in denigration was the comment of a Russian-born film producer, Sergei Nolbandov, who came to Batley on location during the filming of my novel *Value for Money*. He stood on the heights of Hanging Heaton and gazed down in awe at the panorama of Batley spread out before him in all its murky glory. "Wonderful!" he said enthusiastically. "The nearest approach to hell I've ever seen!"

But that was twenty years ago. Today Batley is quite different. To say it is but a shadow of its former self would be a misuse of words because in many respects it is more resplendent than ever before. The market square is still cobbled and still dominated by the gothic bulk of the town hall, the public library and Zion Methodist chapel—commonly known as Shoddy Temple. But these buildings are memorials to the industrial might of Batley no longer. They are soot-blackened no more. A transformation has been wrought by sand blasting. Their colour is now that of natural stone. They look as if they had been built in the last fortnight, not over a century ago. And although the effect is pleasing to the eye and aesthetically beyond reproach it is in a way a mockery. The town which for over a century has traded on the maxim of "Where there's muck there's brass" has been cleaned out of existence—and as an old Batelian I cannot help but regret it.

Not that the cleaning up of the public buildings is the only transformation which has occurred in Batley in recent years. There have been others just as fundamental. Batley's famous shoddy mills have almost all disappeared, victims of the great contraction and decline of the wool textile industry which has driven the small family firms remorselessly out of business.

Some of the mills have been pulled down to make way for housing and shop developments. Others have suffered an even sadder fate. They have been converted into modern, streamlined factories turning out such things as kitchen furniture, electronic equipment, plastic goods, birthday cards and, of all things, ladies' panties. Fox's biscuit works is now the largest employer of labour in the town and although working conditions are very much pleasanter than they were in the old shoddy mills I suspect that every time a packet of biscuits comes off the conveyor belt a shoddy manufacturer turns in his grave in nearby Batley cemetery. That Batley should have come to this!

Shoddy has been Batley's chief claim to fame ever since it was first manufactured by a man called Benjamin Law in 1813. He found that if old clothes made of wool were ground down the resulting fibrous mass (shoddy) could be mixed with virgin wool and re-manufactured into new cloth. The effect of this was dramatically to reduce the price of wool clothes and bring them within the means of the working man and woman for the first time in history. Until this discovery they had usually worn fustian—a thick, twilled cotton cloth usually dyed in a dark shade. From 1813 onwards there was a gradual move to wool and the attire of the workman became indistinguishable from that of his master. This represented a social revolution of some significance and although shoddy has nowadays many competitors in the shape of man-made fibres it is surprising that Batley has had so little recognition of this outstanding contribution to social history.

The rags which go into the making of shoddy today come from two sources—discarded clothing which is known as "old rags" and tailors' clippings which come under the designation "new rags". The rags are collected by tatters, housed in marine stores and sold to the rag merchants who sort them into dozens of different grades and sell them to the shoddy manufacturer. The shoddy manufacturer grinds them down in rag grinding machines and the resulting shoddy is graded and sold to the woollen manufacturer, who mixes it with virgin wool and proceeds to spin the blended material into yarn and weave the yarn into cloth. The cloth so produced is not of as high quality as that produced exclusively from virgin wool because the fibres from the rags have been subject to wear. But, as every Batley man will tell you, high grade shoddy is often superior to low grade virgin wool.

Shoddy was first made from soft rags such as knitted garments and stockings. Later a man called Samuel Parr produced a type of shoddy by grinding up hard rags made of woven cloth. When he tried to sell this new style shoddy to the cloth manufacturers he was told it would not go—it was too hard for the machines. Parr, however, was determined. "It mun go", he insisted, mun being Yorkshire dialect for must. So, eventually, it did and shoddy from hard rags has been known to this day as mungo. Shoddy itself, on the other hand, has bowed to modern euphemism and, by order of the shoddy manufacturers' association, is now known as reclaimed wool—another change which would make the old-time shoddy manufacturers a little restless in their graves.

The use of shoddy in the Batley woollen mills developed rapidly after Law's discovery and ushered in a period of great expansion. The power loom had not come into use in the Batley area until 1790 and in 1813 there were only two or three mills in the town, the bulk of cloth manufacture still being a cottage industry. Those mills there were in existence were known as company mills, several manufacturers having banded together to share the heavy cost of building the mills and equipping them with power looms and spinning machinery. By 1850, however, there were thirty mills in the town, most of them substantial three-storey buildings accommodating several hundred workpeople.

It took a couple of wars to bring Batley's industrial expansion to its peak—the Crimean War of 1854 and the Franco-Prussian War of 1870. Shoddy cloth was ideal for army uniforms and was also used for blankets, and Batley's prosperity knew no bounds. The mills worked night and day on army contracts and, in the latter war, supplied both sides with strict neutrality!

Batley in the 1850s and '60s was a microcosm of Victorian England—a town of great industry and enterprise but also of extremes of wealth and poverty. Assisted by income tax at a few pence in the pound the manufacturers, many of whom had little education and some of whom had to sign their cheques with a cross, made vast fortunes. They built themselves large mansions in Upper Batley and equipped themselves with carriages and pairs and all the other appurtenances of wealth.

The mill workers did not fare so well. They worked from six in the morning until six at night, six days a week, for wages ranging from 6s to 40s a week according to their degree of skill, and they lived in an industrial slum—in long rows of drab back-to-back terrace houses consisting of one room up and one down with twenty or more people sharing a privy down the street. Even the children worked, being employed as half-timers in the mills. This meant that they worked in the mill from six in the morning until twelve noon and spent the afternoon at school. They usually worked as pieceners and received between 1s 9d and 8s 6d a week.

The manufacturers competed with each other in their display of wealth just as they competed in business and every house that was built in Upper Batley was a little bigger and more grandiose than the last. They were, however, all designed by the one local architect, a man called Hanstock, and as his professional experience was confined to mills and chapels the houses he erected were not things of outstanding beauty. What chiefly distinguished one from another was the shape of the tower—for nearly all Hanstock's houses had towers.

The story is told of one wealthy manufacturer who could neither read nor write whose sole instruction to Hanstock was to build a house in every way superior to John Smith's down the road. "And what about aspect?" enquired the architect. "Aspect?" repeated the perplexed manufacturer. "Has John Smith got an aspect?" "Well yes, of course he has. Every house must have an aspect." "Aye well, then," came the reply, "if John Smith's got one aspect tha mun give me three." Another story is told of another manufacturer who built a house with four reception rooms and fifteen bedrooms but always had his meals in his shirt sleeves in the kitchen!

Mill chief aged 102

The biggest and best known firm in Batley, J T & J Taylor Ltd, is still in existence on a small scale but is now part of the textile business empire of Lord Kagan, the Gannex raincoat chief, and no member of the Taylor family is connected with it. Nor does it produce the type of cloths which made it famous.

The Taylor saga really begins toward the end of the eighteenth century when Batley was a rural village dotted with the cottages of the handloom weavers, of whom Abraham Taylor was one. Abraham manufactured a coarse kind of woollen cloth and sold it a piece at a time over the counter at Leeds cloth market. In those days wool was carded and spun by hand, one bobbin at a time on the spinning wheel. This job was done by the female members of the family while the male members did the weaving upstairs. Abraham lived until 1808 and in his time the rotary carding machine came into use as well as the various forms of spinning machines known as the jenny, the billy, the tommy, the horse and the mule. These developments paved the way for Abraham's son, Thomas, to become a maker of fine cloth and first a shareholder and then one of the earliest proprietors of a complete woollen mill.

It was his sons, John, Thomas and Joshua, who founded the firm of J T & J Taylor in 1845. In the partnership agreement John contributed £400, Thomas £80 and Joshua £60. The agreement was very much a home-made document and laid down among other things that "no one shall at any time buy or sell any commodity and pocket a profit himself" and that "no speculation (except very trifling) shall be gone into previous to the approval of two of the partners". For some odd reason an eight-day clock was included in the partnership assets.

The three brothers remained partners for the rest of their lives and in 1852 bought Blakeridge mill which was to become the biggest in Batley. Later the firm bought several other mills in the town and at their peak employed 1 500 people. This was when the mills had come under the control of Joshua's son, Theodore C Taylor, the greatest of the Taylors and undoubtedly Batley's most famous son. He lived to the great age of 102 and directed the firm personally almost up to the day of his death in 1952.

Theodore was among a variety of other things a keen local historian and left many records relating to the history of Batley in general and the Taylor firm in particular. A book "One hundred years: records, recollections and reflections" was published in 1946 and gives vivid descriptions of his life and times.

He recalls his grandfather, Thomas, sitting and smoking his long churchwarden clay pipe in the Blakeridge mills house. "He always wore a one-coloured cloth suit, drab on weekdays, black on Sundays. It consisted of tail coat, cut square with large gamekeeper pockets, waistcoat and breeches with buttoned leggings. Overall, except on Sundays and holidays, he wore a blue linen apron and round his neck, besides the old fashioned stand-up linen collar, a blue and white spotted stock and out of doors always an enormous silk hat."

He also recalled his grandmother. "She was tall and fair and on weekdays wore a print dress and a white frilled cap. She always had one or two maids who slept out. All the washing and baking were done at home and jam was made, butter churned and beer brewed. She probably made her own matches, candles and soap. She certainly made at home all her family's underclothes and when her children were young their outer garments as well. With eight children to clothe and care for she must have had her hands full. She was a devoted churchwoman and saw that her children learned their catechism and collects and attended service at Batley parish church."

The family link with Batley parish church was not to endure —for strictly business reasons. The Taylors transferred their religious loyalties to the Congregational church. It all concerned the passage of dye water from the Blakeridge mill dyehouse to Batley beck. On its way the water passed through the vicar's garden and as it had rather an obnoxious colour and smell the vicar took a very dim view of it. He resolved either to stop the water or, alternatively, to extract a very high price from the firm for its continuance.

Taylors maintained that they had ancient rights in the matter and refused to agree to the vicar's terms. The vicar thereupon issued a writ and it is recorded that Thomas Taylor's last visit to the parish church was with the vicar's writ in his pocket. The vicar subsequently won the case and the firm had to discontinue dyeing at Blakeridge. No member of the family ever stepped inside Batley parish church again.

In his book Theodore traces the history of woollen manufacturing in Batley from the days when it was purely a cottage industry, carried on by the clothiers and their families, to the advent of steam power towards the end of the eighteenth century. "Steam power", he writes, "developed the factory system and the clothier became the manufacturer. It is a verbal curiosity that whereas the word manufacturer means a maker by hand it was only as handwork declined that the term manufacturer replaced the term clothier. No single clothier was rich enough to build or own a complete factory so at Batley, as at other places, several of them clubbed together to build a mill and buy machinery and the 'company mill' as it was called came into being. Most Yorkshire mills of the first forty years of the nineteenth century were company mills to which each manufacturer sent his wool to be carded and spun."

Although the whining of the spinning wheel was not heard in Batley clothiers' cottages after the early years of the nineteenth century there were no power looms in the local mills until well on into that century. "The thud of the treadle and the clack of the picker against the shuttle were, until well after 1866, the work music in many Batley homes. The company mills were at first only carding, spinning and fulling mills. Cloth continued for some time longer to be woven and finished in the clothiers' homes."

Theodore entered the business in 1866 and he records that in the "art and mystery" of cloth making a good deal of humbug was included. There were particularly strange proceedings in milling and finishing. "There was the concocting, for instance, from repulsive ingredients of a strange brew for the 'lecking' or soaking of cloth before milling. Every Tuesday morning a Birkenshaw pig breeder delivered a load of pigs' excreta with which to 'dose' the cloth before milling and each manufacturer then had what was called an 'old wesh barrel' on wheels, horse drawn to people's houses to collect human urine which was also an ingredient in the pre-milling process."

Another mysterious practice was the "sprouting" of beer on the ends of pieces of cloth to neutralize the effect caused by the various processes. The sprouter filled his mouth with ale which he sprayed over the cloth. Theodore recalls that the head finisher who did this job had once been addicted to the bottle but had become a keen Methodist and teetotaller. "As an ex-drinker," Theodore comments, "it must have been very trying to him to eject the too-welcome liquid but no doubt the firm's weekly bills for 'sprouting' must have been much smaller than before!"

The hours of work when Theodore entered the business in 1866 were sixty a week, 6 am to 6 pm with short periods off for meals on Mondays to Fridays and 6 am to 2 pm on Saturdays, the closing of the mills on Saturday afternoon having been recently introduced and regarded as a big concession by the operatives. And when extra time was necessary it was not uncommon for operatives to work until 8 pm on four nights and work right through the night on Friday until 2 pm on Saturday —a total of eighty hours a week.

Theodore's conscience was offended by the social injustice of the times and it was this which prompted him to become one of the pioneers of profit sharing with his employees. His brother, Arthur, and his cousin, John, who were his partners at the time were strongly opposed to such a scheme and in 1892 Theodore offered to buy them out of the business to enable him to put his profit-sharing ideas, which had grown very strong, into practice.

He could not finance the deal himself but he obtained support from a private bank. He records how he spent an anxious time in the banker's "sweating room" seeking to convince two partners of the bank that his profit-sharing scheme was a practicable proposition. "I fully explained my profit-sharing scheme and they said 'And so you are proposing to give the management of your business to your workpeople?' I replied that so long as I borrowed anything from them I should keep control myself. This must have satisfied them for so long as I required to borrow they showed remarkable confidence in me." Although the loan was soon paid off Theodore was to keep that control for the next sixty years. Throughout that time the profit-sharing scheme was in operation and the staff and workpeople received more than £3 000 000.

Under Theodore's dynamic direction the business went from strength to strength and markets were developed all over the world. Theodore did not devote his energies entirely to woollen manufacturing, however. He had a keen interest in politics and in the "khaki election" of 1900 was elected as Liberal MP for the Lancashire division of Radcliffe-cum-Farnworth, a neighbouring constituency of Winston Churchill's at Oldham. Theodore was in the House of Commons for eighteen years and played a prominent part in the suppression of the opium trade between India and China.

Theodore so long outlived his generation that I knew him quite well, heard him speak at many functions and interviewed him on several occasions. He was a small man with a dome-shaped head, almost bald, lean, ascetic features, very piercing eyes seen through steel rimmed spectacles and a grey moustache and neat beard. He spoke in cultured English with no Yorkshire intonation and pronounced it crisply and incisively.

I was present at one of his last public meetings in Batley in 1949 when, at the age of nearly ninety-nine, he spoke for half an hour or more to a crowded audience in Batley town hall in support of Max Ramsden, the Conservative candidate in a celebrated Batley by-election. It was a courageous thing for a prominent Liberal to do but he was so strongly opposed to Socialism that he felt his action was justified.

I wrote in the *Yorkshire Post* as follows: "A ninety-eight-year-old Liberal stepped on to Max Ramsden's Conservative platform at Batley town hall tonight and delivered one of the most forceful indictments of Socialism that has been heard in the campaign. Mr Taylor, who had travelled forty miles from his home in Grassington, stood and spoke for half an hour in a firm, clear voice that could be heard in every part of the densely packed hall. An overflow audience in the nearby court-room had the speech relayed to them. He brought applause from the audience by his remorseless logic and laughter by his witty asides. 'I suppose you expect something very antiquated from me' he began. 'I am reminded of the meetings I used to speak at in the old days before the franchise was conferred on the working man. I am here tonight because I am a life-long Liberal and I believe in freedom.'

"He went on to speak of private enterprise. Was it wrong that through hard work and self denial a man should save a little money and start a business? It was said the worker had no chance to rise but the town of Batley had given many proofs of how false it was to talk about a privileged class. 'The men who made the woollen trade of this district did not belong to a privileged class and nor did their successors. During my long life I have seen more than one carding overlooker become a wealthy manufacturer and I have seen a country farmer's boy become the proprietor of several mills. Where is the privilege there? The privilege is to those who work the hardest'."

But although Theodore was a great benefactor to his employees he was, like most of the early Batley manufacturers, a great autocrat. He ruled his mill with a rod of iron and struck terror to inspire respect. Everybody from the deputy managing director to the office boy regarded him with awe and answered summonses to his presence with trepidation. He insisted on knowing about everything that was going on at the mills and all the major decisions and many of the minor ones were taken by him alone. He called in his deputy managing director one day and asked him why a certain matter had not been referred to him. He was told that the matter was considered to be a comparatively minor one and not worthy of reference to him. But the deputy managing director was told bluntly that his decision was a wrong one and before ending the interview Theodore delivered this Parthian shot: "Kindly remember in future, Mr . . . , that as long as there is breath left in this body and a brain in this head that brain will direct and control the activities of this business."

My father did business with the head of the rag department at Taylors and was told many stories by him of Theodore's autocratic and at times almost sadistic behaviour. He did not restrict himself to instructing his staff on how the business should be run. He also gave them instruction on how their private lives should be conducted. The head of the rag department, whom I will call Brown, was very keen on horse racing and always took a day off to attend the St Leger at Doncaster. Theodore, who was bitterly opposed to all forms of gambling, must have heard about this peccadillo and the day before the St Leger was due to be run he summoned Brown to his office. "I am arranging a meeting of departmental heads tomorrow, Brown", he informed him. "I trust you will be able to be present?" Brown swallowed uneasily and replied that as a matter of fact he had arranged to take the day off as he had rather an important private engagement. "That is unfortunate", said Theodore. "A family wedding or something of that nature?"

"Well no Mr Taylor, not exactly . . ."

"But it's something you can't postpone?"

"Er . . . yes. I'm afraid it's not possible to postpone it."

Theodore put the fingers of his hands together and pierced Brown with a remorseless stare. "You aren't by any chance going to Doncaster tomorrow are you Brown?" he demanded.

Brown mumbled that as a matter of fact he had fleeting thoughts in that direction.

Theodore's expression changed to one of horrified amazement. "You mean to sit there, Brown, and tell me that you are proposing to miss a meeting of departmental heads of this business to go to a race meeting? You'll be telling me next that you actually intend to back some of the horses."

Brown assured him that he had never dreamt of such a thing. It was purely the spectacle that appealed to him. But in view of the departmental meeting he would, of course, forsake that pleasure on this occasion.

Theodore was a hard taskmaster and was more lavish with his criticism than with his praise. Brown told how at one of these meetings of departmental heads he felt confident that for once in his life Theodore would hold him up to the others as an example of excellence. The matter under review was the stocks position. There had been a big fall in the price of wool and Theodore was conducting a searching enquiry into the foresight shown by his managers. "I am confident," he said, "that all your stocks will be low and that you will have anticipated the current fall in values—it has, after all, been clearly indicated for some time. But let us look at the exact position."

He turned to the wool buyer first. "Now," he said, "how much wool have we in stock valued at current prices. £1 000 perhaps?"

The wool buyer looked distinctly uneasy. "Well no Mr Taylor, I'm afraid it's not quite as low as that. I would say about £3 000."

"£3 000", exclaimed Theodore, so sharply that the wool buyer almost jumped out of his chair. "You have allowed the stocks to remain at £3 000 after all the warnings we have had of a fall. That doesn't sound very far sighted to me, gentlemen. Not very far sighted at all."

He turned to the head of the noils department and expressed similar dissatisfaction with his stock position and then, with the same result, to the shoddy stock manager.

Meanwhile Brown was sitting preening himself as he awaited Theodore's praises, for the rag stock position was excellent. With good judgement and a little luck he had reduced his stocks to negligible proportions.

"Now, Brown", said Theodore, having castigated every other manager in the room, "what value of rags are we currently carrying?"

Perhaps Brown was a little too sure of himself, a little too smug in his manner. "The rag stock has been reduced to no more than £500, Mr Taylor", he said proudly.

Theodore gave him one of his most piercing looks. "Well that's just £500 too much, Brown, isn't it? And now, perhaps, we can turn our attention to the next item on the agenda, gentlemen . . ."

Theodore's private life was not free of tragedy and while his only son died at the age of four he lost both his wife and his elder daughter in the flu epidemic after the First World War. He married for a second time in 1920 and spent most of the remainder of his life in his country house at Grassington at the head of Wharfedale. Up to almost the end of his life he travelled two or three days a week to the mills at Batley—a round trip of eighty miles—and controlled the business as closely as ever. Always a religious man he used latterly to pass the time in his chauffeur-driven Daimler reciting hymns.

His hundredth birthday in August, 1950, put the spotlight of publicity upon him more brightly than ever before and in addition to countless newspaper interviews he gave a radio talk on the BBC entitled "One hundred years". The centenary was marked by a trip to Blackpool for every employee and Theodore was photographed doing the palais glide with some of the mill girls on the floor of the Winter Gardens ballroom.

My last meeting with the old man was some months after his hundredth birthday when he attended the fifty-ninth annual meeting of employees at Blakeridge mill. I wrote in the *Yorkshire Post* of that occasion as follows:

"Has he come?" I heard a blue-faced newspaper photographer ask a man at the door of a Batley mill canteen on Saturday morning as he struggled in with his heavy artillery of bags, flash bulbs and cameras.

"Come?" replied the man, as though the suggestion that he might not have come was an affront to his personal pride. " 'Course he's come. He's been here two hours."

"Oh," said the photographer, "I thought the frost might have put him off. It's bitterly cold this morning."

The man at the door displayed pity and condescension.

"Nay lad," he said gently, "it would take more than a bit of frost to put him off coming here."

Of course it would! Everyone in Batley knows that. He would have left his Grassington home promptly at 8 am and for the last hour or so would have been going through his speech with his secretary making alterations and additions. Any moment now he would be coming into the canteen where so many of his thousand workpeople were assembled—a small, dynamic figure with a white beard and a heavy black overcoat, who would hurry down the room and take his place before the desk on the flower-banked platform. How otherwise could the fifty-ninth annual meeting of the employees of J T & J Taylor Ltd, cloth manufacturers, conceivably begin?

I imagine the photographers expected Mr Theodore Taylor to sit muffled up with a rug and a hot-water bottle and gaze benevolently down on the audience while the other directors conducted the meeting. What else could a man aged one hundred be expected to do?

But there again everyone in Batley could have enlightened them. It was the other directors who sat back and listened. Mr Taylor opened the meeting and closed the meeting. He announced the year's dividends. He presented prizes to his younger employees for their prowess at the technical college and he enjoined each of them to "keep it up and you will reach the top"; "work hard and you will get on"; or "keep trying and you will succeed". And for half an hour, without pause, he stood with his hands firmly on the desk and talked about the history of the firm, the principles of cloth manufacture, the road to success in business and a good many other subjects.

There was this on running a business: "It is for the customers to say what they want and for the manufacturers to make it. If a man never attempts what appears to be impossible he will never accomplish what is possible. Don't be daunted by difficulties. Take them as a challenge to your manhood. In business life it is better to have tried and failed than never to have tried at all. Don't seek any easy job. For a first-rate man there is no easy job. Easy jobs make inferior men."

Then there was his philosophy for old age: "If we have a firm religious faith the best is yet to be. I can't understand how any old man can ignore the fact that death is soon coming. But common prudence dictates that the future life should be provided for. The old man should still be looking forward. It seems to me that as we grow older we should be valuing more and more the realities of life and thinking less of the appearances. What are the realities of life? Not titles, wealth and power but the love of, and the love by, those dear to us. Poor indeed is the man for whom no one cares. Rich indeed is the man who has helped to make others happy by his Christian faith and who can calmly contemplate the future."

Theodore died peacefully in October, 1954, and was buried in Batley cemetery on a site overlooking the nearby Blakeridge mills which for eighty-six years had been so great a part of his life.

Creditors present portraits in oils

Like J T & J Taylor the firm of G & J Stubley Ltd employed some 1 500 workpeople at its peak and established a world-wide reputation for its cloths. It is one of the tragedies of the wool textile industry that these great firms—and many more like them in other parts of the West Riding of Yorkshire—have disappeared in the last ten years or so due primarily to the inability of the family-run firm to finance its business as it had been doing very successfully for over a century.

There are several reasons for this but the main one is probably the extortions of the modern tax collector, who takes so much from a company's profits that sufficient is not left in the business to pay the very heavy cost of keeping the machinery efficient and up to date. In the days when these firms were built up by enterprising entrepreneurs such as the Taylors and the Stubleys the tax on profits was negligible and they were able to plough back the great bulk of them into the business .Today the rate of corporation tax is 52 per cent. Another reason for the decline of the textile family business is that the optimum size of a production unit equipped with the latest machinery is far too large today for a family business to handle. Unless he is highly specialized the day of the small operator in the wool textile industry is over. It is the big public companies with ample resources behind them who are alone able to trade profitably today.

Stubleys was founded in 1850 by two brothers, George and James, on a joint capital of £300. Coming of homely stock they started their working lives in the Batley mills as pieceners, labouring from six in the morning until seven at night with the exception of Saturdays when work ceased at 4 30 pm. Each drew a wage of 1s 6d a week. Promotion soon came and the boys were elevated to the job of scribbling feeders at 4s a week. Later they fed the carders at 5s and eventually became fettlers at 12s. Having become the family breadwinners because of their father's death in a mill accident the two of them had to devise ways and means of augmenting their mill earnings and did a variety of jobs in their spare time.

James was fortunate enough to secure a spinner's job at Hick Lane mills (which his firm was later to own) and he came to be regarded as one of the finest spinners in the district. George did not advance so far but they were both able to save and when they had accumulated £150 each they decided to set up in business on their own. In 1850 they acquired a plot of land in an area unsalubriously named Bottoms on the banks of Batley beck—the town did not possess a river.

They erected a modest two-storey building and began as commission spinners, their equipment consisting of two sets of carding machinery and mules. They soon found, however, that there was not enough commission spinning to keep the machinery running continuously and the brothers turned their attention to the weaving of blankets and cloths. The first pieces were disposed of with difficulty, having to be hawked from town to town before eventually being sold to a customer at Barnsley, twenty miles away.

In 1854 they had a stroke of good luck—if the outbreak of the Crimean War can be so described. The fledgling firm decided to try and get some government contracts and eventually was given its first big chance in the shape of a large government contract for army blankets. They responded to the challenge and for a while the mill ran at full pressure. Before the order was completed, however, the war ended and in their inexperience the brothers had not protected themselves under the formal contract for such a contingency. The government had no scruples in cancelling the contract and the brothers were left with a huge stock of unsaleable army blankets on their hands.

They struggled on but to add to their problems they found themselves in a severe post-war slump in which failures were an everyday occurrence. In common with many much longer established and wealthier firms they were swept off their feet and had no alternative but to meet their creditors.

The creditors, recognizing that the failure was not of their making, treated the partners with generosity and made it possible for the firm to carry on. Fifteen years later, in 1872, their faith in the Stubley brothers was justified. Every creditor was paid in full and they were so delighted that they arranged a special dinner to mark the occasion and presented George and James with their portraits in oils "as a tribute to their characters".

Trade improved after the post-Crimean slump, and the advent of a Liberal government together with the implementation of a free trade policy restored the fortunes of the textile industry. With Cobden's commercial treaty of 1860 between England and France, and the resulting opening up of continental markets to the English manufacturers, the Stubley brothers perceived and exploited a golden opportunity. They developed extensively their connections in France, Germany, central and eastern Europe and the Balkans and this business became the nucleus of the world-wide activities which eventually developed. Some years later, in 1878, George and James were awarded a gold medal for their products at the Paris Universal Exhibition. From that time onwards the firm was acknowledged to rank as one of the largest and most important in the heavy woollen district.

James died in 1896 and George in 1908, a year after the purchase of Hick Lane mills at which James had begun his career as a spinner. The new chairman was John Stubley, eldest son of James. He followed in his father's footsteps so far as energy and enterprise were concerned and in 1903 he went to Canada and blazed a trail for the extensive North American trade which was built up the following year. John died in 1911 and was succeeded by his brother, David, who lived until 1934. It was he who escorted King George V and Queen Mary round Bottoms mill in 1912. The outbreak of the First World War two years later marked the beginning of a period of tremendous activity in the mills and millions of yards of khaki serge and greatcoat cloth and hundreds of thousands of army blankets were turned out.

The firm survived the slump of the early post-war years and also the long slump of the 1930s and once again was put into top gear by the outbreak of the second world war in 1939. More millions of yards of khaki cloth and blankets were produced as well as heavy woven aeroplane felt and special jungle blanket material. After the war the mills' resources were applied to the manufacture of cloths for export to North America and a big trade with both Canada and the United States was soon built up. By now, however, the writing was on the wall for family businesses in the textile industry and the firm was put into voluntary liquidation by the fourth generation of Stubleys to be connected with it.

Paid his rates in copper

Another leading firm in Batley for many years was Charles Robinson & Co Ltd of Victoria and Park Lane mills who also employed over 1 000 people. The founder was one of the most colourful characters Batley has ever produced. Known everywhere as Charlie he was the son of a small farmer and after a very sketchy education started work at the age of thirteen in the warehouse of Park Lane mills, then occupied by John Skelsey & Co.

Charlie married young and was then earning £1 a week, just enough to enable him and his wife, Jane, to live in a tiny cottage bordering on the parish churchyard. His wife was a servant at the home of Colonel Benjamin Sheard in Upper Batley—one of the leading families in the town—and Charlie's ambition was probably fed by Jane's stories of the luxuries of life at the top. "I'll own Park Lane mills myself before I've finished" he is said to have told his young bride.

He started out on his own with tiny capital dealing in what were known as fents, nooks and bribes. He quickly showed an immense capacity for hard and persistent work, combined with perseverance and a dogged will to succeed, and eventually he prospered sufficiently to rent room and power at New Branch mills, Batley, and started as a woollen manufacturer in partnership with his brother-in-law, Ingham Nussey. On

9 August 1883, they went to a machinery manufacturer to buy their first looms with a joint capital of £40. They outlined their plans to the machinery maker and asked him to trust them. They would pay for the looms out of their profits. The machinery maker was impressed by their earnestness and sold them twelve looms on receipt of a deposit of £40. "You'll have to work hard, think on", he told them.

Work hard they did. Ingham Nussey recalled many years later that "Many a score nights we never went to bed and many a score nights we couldn't sleep when we did for wondering where the money was to come from to pay the rent and the operatives' wages, or where the orders were to come from to keep the machinery running. It was a long time before we began to make money and the mill became our own."

Eventually, however, the mill became too small for them and they took the bold step of acquiring the very much larger Victoria mills which happened to be empty. Many people said Charlie—who was the dominant partner—had overreached himself but he set to work with his customary zeal as a salesman and secured substantial orders. He then turned his attention to equipping the mills with the most modern machinery he could find and the business grew remarkably quickly. A few years later Charlie fulfilled his life's ambition by buying Park Lane mills to cope with all the orders which were now flowing in from all over the world. He concentrated on heavy cloths containing large quantities of shoddy and it was said in Batley that Robinson's was the only mill in the district which could "make summat out of nowt".

He was by this time a wealthy man and having built himself a large house in Upper Batley he proceeded to indulge his love for animals, which he had acquired on his father's farm. He began by establishing a model stud farm at Arthington, where he bred hackneys which were to earn world-wide renown. He was a most successful exporter and had the distinction of breeding a National Society winner. Even with the farm his business instincts had to express themselves and he sold hackneys very profitably in many parts of the world, particularly in Spain and South America. He also developed his interests in sheep and cattle and despite the calls of woollen manufacturing found time to pay regular visits to the cattle markets in the West Riding. He was known to get up very early and buy hundreds of heads of cattle and sheep before turning up at the mill for his day's work. He eventually moved his home from Batley to Harrogate and died at Rossett Grange aged 72.

Charlie was a big, powerful fellow and had an aggressive manner to match his somewhat formidable appearance. Down at his mills, like Theodore Taylor, he struck terror to inspire respect. He always worked hard himself and expected his employees to do the same. He would not tolerate inefficiency and men were set on and sacked with remorseless regularity. He had a reputation as a hard taskmaster. He had only to see a man wasting his time to dismiss him on the spot.

But his aggression was matched by a ready sense of humour and he told the story against himself of seeing a man standing idly in the mill yard. "What's tha think tha's doing?" he asked him. The man looked at him steadily. "Waiting Mr Robinson, just waiting." "Waiting", repeated Charlie vociferously. "If that's all tha has to do tha'd better get thi cards and get out. We've no place for waiters here."

"Tha means I'm sacked?", said the man.

"Aye", said Charlie, "tha's sacked."

The man continued to eye him steadily. "But tha can't sack me, Mr Robinson", he said dourly.

"Oh can't I?", replied Charlie. "Just tha tell me which department tha works in and tha'll soon see if I can sack thee."

The man smiled wryly. "I don't work here at all, Mr Robinson. I'm a foreman at Taylors waiting for a parcel. And, by God, I'm glad I am an' all."

He also told of the employee he had sacked who came to try and persuade him to give him his old job back. He told him a sorry tale. "I've been through hell since I left here, Mr Robinson," he told him, "sheer hell."

"Oh aye", replied Charlie unimpressed. "And did tha see any manufacturers i' hell then?"

"No Mr Robinson, I can't say I did. But I did see a sack with thy name on it."

"Tak thi coit off and get back to work, lad", he was told. "Tha's got a sense of humour if nowt else."

Charlie was once asked by an acquaintance if he would provide a job at his mills for his son. He told him to send the lad along to see him. Charlie opened the interview abruptly by asking him if he had brought a "character" with him—by which he meant a reference. The young man said he hadn't. "I take no one on at this mill without a character", said Charlie, "so tha'd better set to and get thissen one from thy headmaster or somebody. And tha mun be back wi' it in half an hour." The lad duly returned after half an hour and Charlie glared at him.

"Now, tha's got thissen a character has tha?"

"No, Mr Robinson, I haven't" the lad replied. "But I've got thine and I've just called back to say I'm not coming."

Charlie's aggressiveness was combined with a high degree of emotionalism. He was a very religious man and went to Hick Lane Wesleyan chapel every Sunday. And he was often so moved by a hymn or a prayer that tears would roll down his face. This was a side of his character of which he was apparently a little ashamed and he made up for it by being more than usually aggressive at the mill next morning. His employees knew all about his chapel histrionics and the word would go round the mill early on Monday morning "Watch out this morning, lads, t'boss has been roaring again in chapel."

He had an abrupt manner with travellers and his interviews with them were said to go like this:

Traveller: "Morning."

Charlie: "Morning."

Traveller: "Owt?"

Charlie: "Nowt."

Traveller: "Morning."

Charlie: "Morning."

Sometimes—not often—a traveller got the best of him. Knowing that Charlie would bargain him down to the last penny a shoddy salesman offered him a little used type of shoddy at 1s a pound—his price was in fact 9d.

"How much?" asked Charlie.

"A bob to you, Mr Robinson."

"Aye, well then, I'll cap thee. I'll gi' thee 9d."

"And I'll cap thee, Mr Robinson", came the reply. "I'll take it."

Like many of the manufacturing fraternity Charlie was a complete individualist and a firm believer in *laissez faire.* He had no time at all for anyone who interfered in any way with his business activities. He was indeed a law unto himself and was constantly at loggerheads with the Batley corporation over the rating assessments for his mills which he considered extortionate. To show his displeasure at what in his opinion was a totally unjustifiable rate increase he decided to pay his bill in copper and had it put in sacks and conveyed in one of the mill's horse-drawn wagons to the office of the borough treasurer, Mr G N Lumb. There was consternation as the sacks were carried in but Mr Lumb was equal to the occasion and refused to accept the money on the grounds that it was not legal tender. Charlie refused to move it and there it stayed overnight. The following day Mr Lumb had it returned to the mill.

Charlie, however, refused to pay any other way and the matter eventually came before the magistrates, who made an order that the rates should be paid in legal tender. The case aroused tremendous interest in the town and it was some time before Charlie capitulated and sent a cheque.

Mr Lumb ran into him in the street some time later and said affably that now the matter was settled he hoped there were no hard feelings. "I had a job to do, Mr Robinson, and I hope you won't think any the worse of me for doing it." Charlie eyed him coldly. "I couldn't, Mr Lumb", he said tersely and walked on.

Although he liked singing hymns in chapel there was no artistic side to Charlie's character and he cared nothing for literature or music. Nor had he much of an eye for beauty. He was an intensely practical man and saw everything in practical terms. He once went to Switzerland with a party of friends and was so unimpressed by the grandeur of the mountain scenery that he was impatient to get back to Batley before he had been there a couple of days. He was for ever saying that he did not know how the mill would be getting on without him. Eventually one of his friends was moved to protest. They were all admiring a particularly striking precipice. All, that is, except Charlie, who was sitting on a rock writing a letter to his mill manager with his latest instructions. "Can't you forget that damned mill of yours for half an hour and admire the view Charlie?", his friend protested. "Just look at that precipice! Isn't it marvellous! Doesn't it inspire you?"

Charlie looked at it without enthusiasm. "Aye", he said reflectively, "it's a fair drop is that. We could just do wi' that down at our mill. Make a wonderful tip for our ashes."

Dedicated and ruthless businessman as he was Charlie was always very generous by nature and when he became wealthy made frequent big donations to local charities. He gave large sums to Batley hospital and paid for the installation of electricity there. He also gave substantial support to several of the town's chapels and in one of them installed an organ. He was a shy philanthropist, however, and spurned all publicity. In all good faith one of the two local newspapers reported one of his donations to charity and Charlie was so incensed about it that he went to see the editor and threatened him with the direst penalties should he ever report such an occurrence again. He was also a generous benefactor to individuals down on their luck and he was known to have helped many of his employees who were in trouble, including some of those whom he had previously sacked.

There are no longer any characters like Charlie Robinson to be found in Batley because the world of today no longer provides the right environment for their growth. And the mills which he ran so successfully have long since closed down. In the flowery columns of obituary devoted to him in the local papers in 1929 appeared this tribute: "Mr Robinson was a gentleman of remarkable force of character. In fact he was a dual character, possessing indomitable perseverance, a keen business instinct, a ruthless disregard for business obstacles, a rough and ready method of dealing with employees and yet apart from the workaday life no man exhibited a broader sympathy, a kindlier disposition or a more tender regard for those in pain or sickness, while his private benefactions were almost boundless. The poor and needy have lost a good friend and many local charities a generous but unostentatious supporter."

Picnics in clothes basket for thirteen children

Charles Robinson exemplified the aggressive Yorkshireman, blunt in speech and somewhat overbearing in manner. John Joseph Jubb, a contemporary of his, represented the diffident, self-effacing Yorkshireman who likes to stand back and let other people take the limelight. John Joseph's father, John

Jubb, was, however, very prominent in the public life of Batley and was elected as the first mayor of the town when it received its first charter of incorporation in 1869. John Joseph found himself propelled into municipal life by his father in spite of his own reluctance and in 1884 his father proudly watched him installed as mayor. The Jubbs remain the only father and son to hold that office in Batley's history.

The Jubbs were shoddy manufacturers, John Jubb founding the firm at Phoenix mills. John was a shrewd businessman and made a great deal of money—some of which he spent in building one of the biggest houses in Batley, Blenheim House, which today is a freemasons' lodge and comfortably accommodates a couple of hundred people at dinner dances. But John Joseph did not inherit his father's business acumen and the firm foundered in the slump immediately following the First World War, after which John Joseph lived comfortably off his capital for the rest of his life.

He was productive enough in his private life, however, and fathered thirteen children, all of whom reached old age apart from one, Joseph, who was killed in action with the Leeds Pals in 1916. The Jubb family was the Swiss Family Robinson of Batley and the fifteen of them, including father and mother, were reputed to go and watch cricket matches taking a picnic tea with them in a clothes basket!

John Joseph was a most hospitable man and my father, who as a young man was a close friend of his son, Joseph Jubb, said that the dining room table at Blenheim House was never bare from one week to another. It was constantly laden with hams, tongues, chickens and other foodstuffs for the entertainment of the hordes of visitors brought to the house by the thirteen children. Visitors could also help themselves to an inexhaustible stock of drinks, champagne included, and some of them apparently stayed at the house for weeks without John Joseph always being aware of it. He met one young man in the dining room one day and greeted him by saying it was a long time since he had seen him. "How do you mean Mr Jubb?" was the reply. "I've been staying here a fortnight."

John Joseph's birthday was 6 November and every year was celebrated with a big house party, a bonfire and one of the best displays of fireworks ever to be seen in the district. He was equally open-handed in his public life and his mayoralty was marked by more lavish entertaining at the town hall than ever before or since. He was mayor in 1887, the golden jubilee of Queen Victoria, and the celebrations in Batley were almost on a scale to compete with those at Buckingham Palace!

None of the thirteen children was very industrious although it was an exaggeration to say, as some people did, that not one of the lot of them had done a decent day's work in his life. The view that they were spoiled from the cradle onwards by their indulgent father was probably nearer the truth. When the eldest announced that he was intending to get married John Joseph said to him "And what d'you think you're going to keep a wife on?" To which the reply was "Nay, father, you've coped with thirteen of us all these years—another one's not going to make any difference is it?"

Despite his gregariousness and liking for company John Joseph had a rather mournful appearance and manner and was something of a hypochondriac. Whenever anyone asked him how he was he would shake his head sadly and proceed to give a detailed account of his latest symptoms and the nature of the affliction they probably indicated. "I'm not at all well today I'm afraid", he would say. "I've got some peculiar pains in the bottom of my stomach. I reckon it's gallstones I'm in for."

In addition to Blenheim he had a house at Scarborough and spent a lot of time there during the summer. His favourite activity was to sit at the end of the stone pier fishing with a rod and line and he did this for hours on end. He was always conveyed to the pier in the carriage and pair which he kept at Scarborough (he had another in the stables at Blenheim House) and the carriage was always waiting for him at the entrance to the pier when the day's sport was over.

John Joseph had some unusual eccentricities and one of them was a desperate fear of storms. He was quite terrified by thunder and lightning and in his later years this terror became so great that he chose the most unusual way of avoiding it. He is reputed to have had an organ installed in his cellar and whenever thunder was about he would retire there and drown the noise of it by banging away on the organ until the storm had subsided.

The local paper reports his death at Scarborough in 1929 with the same flowery phrases it had earlier used for Charles Robinson and readers were given every possible detail about him and a list of his thirteen children, whom they had married and what offspring had been produced. The report ended abruptly: "The funeral took place on Wednesday. The coffin was of unpolished oak with brass mounting. The grave was lined with white lilac."

Even more flowery, however, was the vicar's encomium. "We cannot allow the body of this good man to pass from this hallowed church", said the vicar, "without saying how beautiful is the fragrance of the life that is spent in public service—a wonderful life, three times mayor of his own municipality and son of the first mayor of Batley. A man always ready to sacrifice himself for the public good, a splendid example for us of the younger generation. Would to God there were many more such as he! Here on this lovely June afternoon, in the most beautiful cemetery in England, the most beautiful God's acre, with birds singing and the fragrance of glorious May blossom, surely we thank God for the example of such a life and we also take courage by all that we know about him."

A parsimonious pair

Not all the old Batley manufacturers were as generous and hospitable as John Joseph Jubb. Some indeed were downright parsimonious and two whom I will call Schofield, John Thomas and his son John Henry, were among them. They ran a prosperous shoddy business and although they both left large sums of money when they died they did not exhibit any signs of affluence during their lifetime, and competed with each other in frugality. Neither would spend a shilling if sixpence would do and both qualified for the calumnious jingle which is said by southerners to be the motto of all Yorkshiremen: "Hear all, see all, say nowt; eat all, sup all, pay nowt; and if ever tha does owt for nowt allus do it for thissen."

They were inseparable companions and used to have lunch together at the Co-op cafe in Commercial Street and often had bitter arguments as to whose turn it was to pay the bill. John Thomas usually clinched the matter by saying John Henry would have to pay as he hadn't got any money with him.

The cafe was a somewhat austere establishment providing a

set three-course meal at a fixed price. This was considered far too dear by both of them and to reduce the bill they would order half portions of potatoes and half portions of green vegetables. John Thomas always had a glass of milk with his lunch and he considered that to be too expensive also. One day he and his son were having lunch with other shoddy men when John Thomas sipped his milk and complained that it did not taste too fresh. One of the shoddy men, knowing how parsimonious he was, thereupon seized the glass and before the horrified eyes of both of them proceeded to drain the contents at one draught. "Can't taste owt wrong wi' it at all" he commented returning the empty glass to John Thomas. Needless to say he did not order another!

John Thomas was an acquaintance of my grandfather and in the very early days of motoring invited him and my grandmother to go to Scarborough for the day with him and his wife. They set off from Batley and before they had got to Leeds nine miles away one of the tyres burst and they had to summon assistance from a garage. The bill for a new tyre duly fitted was £5 10s. It was at that point that John Thomas discovered that he had only £2 in his wallet. He had to borrow the remainder from my grandfather and also borrow the cost of meals and other expenses of the outing, including another breakdown on the way back, this time due to mechanical trouble. My grandfather waited for the return of his money for many years and eventually wrote it off as a bad debt!

My father knew a man who worked at their mill in a managerial capacity for many years and his tales of the Schofields' parsimony were numerous. The manager, whom I will call Smith, had to spend six weeks in hospital at one period and when he told John Henry he would have to go into hospital John Henry was most helpful. "We'll pay you your full salary, of course", he told him. They did—for two weeks. Then they knocked him down to half salary and for the final two weeks paid him nothing.

Sometime after this incident Smith was offered another job at more money and handed in his resignation. But he was one of the main pillars of the establishment and John Henry would not hear of him leaving and made a counter offer including a bonus which, he was promised, would make him better off than the job he had been offered. So Smith decided to stay and at John Henry's insistence wrote to the other firm at once turning the job down. Smith thereupon asked for a written contract but John Henry would not hear of it. "I never like signing things" he said. "Besides what do you want a contract for? Don't you trust me?" Put like that Smith could not persist but he was to rue his action for the bonus part of the agreement was never forthcoming. Smith eventually took it up with John Henry and the explanation he was given was that a much more substantial provision had been made for him in his will. Smith expressed incredulity and a few days later John Henry produced his will and showed him the provision in black and white. Delighted by this Smith worked with a will for years and when John Henry eventually died waited hopefully for his legacy. When it did not come he approached John Henry's solicitors and asked them about it. They explained that a codicil had been inserted some years previously nullifying the bequest.

John Henry was, however, a very shrewd businessman and had a reputation for "making a profit out of owt." Smith had experienced his tactics once when in the early days of radio John Henry said he did not think much of the new invention and would let him have his "apparatus" for less than it had cost him—namely £20. Smith went over to John Henry's home to collect the radio and he had it all parcelled up for him together with some spare valves which, he explained, he was throwing in free because they were no use to him without the set. When Smith got the set home and assembled it he could not get a sound out of it. He complained to John Henry whose reply was "Well it were all right when it left here. Tha must have rattled it." Smith had to get a radio engineer to put it right at a cost of £8 and when he suggested to John Henry that he should make some contribution to the cost of the repairs the manufacturer replied "All right, then, I will if you insist. But, mind you, I'm not throwing t'valves in at that price—I shall want another £4 for them."

"I'm t'boss here now!"

For sheer money making ability Batley's annals contain no one to top Harry Fenton, whose fortune from shoddy cloth manufacturing and speculation of one sort and another was said to run at its peak into several millions. Fenton was one of the thrusting, aggressive, buccaneering types of Yorkshireman who will stop at nothing to achieve their ends—however trivial some of these ends may be. Quite early on in his career Fenton paid a large amount of money for a magnificent house in Scarborough. He went to a big firm of decorators in Leeds and demanded to see "t'manager"—it was one of his rules of business that he dealt with "principals only". The manager duly received him and Fenton told him of his extensive requirements. "And I want the whole job finishing by next weekend" he stipulated.

The manager, not enamoured by his aggressive manner, said he was afraid that would be quite impossible. It would require twenty men to complete such a job by next weekend and he had not got them available.

"How many do you employ?" asked Fenton.

The manager replied that that was hardly a relevant question. The firm had many other orders in hand. It was not a question of how many he employed but how many he could spare.

"I'm telling you I want it finished by next weekend" Fenton insisted. "Send every man you've got. I don't care what it costs."

But the manager was adamant and Fenton left in a blustering rage. His next step was typical. He contacted the owners of the decorating firm and put in a bid for the business which they could not refuse. As soon as the contracts were signed—and this was arranged very quickly—he returned to the shop and demanded to see the manager once again. "Now then", he greeted him, "I'm t' boss here now and I want every man you've got over at my house at Scarborough tomorrow."

The job was duly completed within a week.

Residing in Scarborough evidently gave Fenton social aspirations and he decided to join a rather snobby local golf club. He applied for membership but to his fury was turned down. He reacted in the usual way. He bought the land which the club had leased and informed the captain of the club that unless he was made a member immediately he intended giving the club notice to quit. Apparently he was duly elected but never visited the club in his life.

There was a tragic end to the Fenton story. His business collapsed in the slump of the early 1920s and he was reduced to penury. But even worse than that he was charged with fraud and appeared in the dock at the Old Bailey. The case aroused tremendous interest in the heavy woollen district before Fenton, who proved to be just as shrewd in the witness box as he was in business, secured his acquittal.

I used Harry Fenton as the model for my other novel based in Batley, *Shoddy Kingdom.*

Other manufacturer characters

Batley has bred many other manufacturers whose activities and eccentricities merit recording. There was Joseph Newsome, founder of one of the few woollen manufacturing firms still surviving. He was a very religious man and a pillar of St Mark's church in Dewsbury. He carried his religious principles into the sphere of woollen manufacturing and would not do business with travellers who were dissenters. It was said that one or two artful and not high-principled dissenters succeeded in doing business with him by equipping themselves with Church of England prayer books and appearing to be engrossed in them when it came to their turn to go in and see him.

There was John Whittaker, a pioneer of the rag trade, said to be the first man to use oil on rags which greatly facilitated grinding them into shoddy. Whittaker was renowned as a dandy and always wore a tall top hat and a swallow-tailed coat. He was totally uneducated and when he started in business could neither read nor write. This naturally embarrassed him when it came to signing his name with a cross on cheques and he eventually paid a guinea to be taught how to write his signature.

There was Sam Parr, the originator of mungo, whose secondary claim to fame was his formidable physical strength. He was reputed to be able to lift up a table on each corner of which a man was sitting. He was also reputed to be able to play with 56 lb weights as though they were marbles!

There were the Talbot brothers, Joseph and Abraham, who were in partnership together as woollen manufacturers but didn't get on privately. Although they lived in large houses opposite each other in Upper Batley they were said never to have spoken a word to each other outside the mill for forty years.

There were the Sheard brothers, Benjamin and George, who ran one of the oldest manufacturing firms in the town, Michael Sheard & Sons. The Sheards were both well educated by their father and represented the cream of Batley society. Benjamin, who had a large house with a tower called Elmwood (now occupied by a member of the Taylor family), was in command of the Batley rifle volunteers which he and others established in 1866 and was always known as Colonel Sheard. George had built for himself an even bigger house—the biggest in Batley in fact. Known as the Woodlands, it is today the Wilton Park museum.

Both the Sheards were generous and gregarious and were renowned for their lavish dinner parties at which champagne was said to be "supped by the bucket". This did not endear them to the teetotal fraternity, always strong in Batley. Colonel Sheard had several sons one of whom, Jamie, was a black sheep of the darkest hue. He was in the habit of taking his father's carriage and pair and disappearing for wild weekends and was often returned in police custody. When his father stopped his allowance he raised money by pawning his mother's diamond rings in Leeds and eventually brought his dissolute life to an end by hanging himself in the stables at Elmwood.

Not all these Batley manufacturer characters belong to the distant past. Some have flourished almost up to the present day. They nearly all come into one of the two main categories of Yorkshiremen—the blunt, thrusting, ostentatious type who always make their presence felt and are impervious to the dislike and sometimes open hostility they generate, and the quiet, diffident, self-effacing, unpretentious types who may be just as shrewd and successful in business but hide their light if not under a bushel then under a bale of shoddy.

Jeddy Fozzard was one of these. He began his career as a rag grinder at one of the shoddy mills and eventually rented a small warehouse and launched out on his own between the two wars with one grinding machine as his sole capital equipment. He extended the business over the years but he was not a tycoon by nature and did not make a fortune. He did, however, make very good profits and he could have lived in a far more expansive style than he did. The trouble was that thrift was so deeply ingrained in him that spending money unnecessarily caused him acute pain and he continued to live in the same humble surroundings throughout his life.

He was not mean; he was frugal—and there is a gulf of difference. He would walk half a mile in the pouring rain to get on a bus at a stop other than the one outside his home because the fare was a penny or two cheaper. He would not buy a newspaper because he could have a look at one for nothing in the reading room of the public library, as he had done during his poverty stricken youth. He scarcely ever took a holiday in his life because he regarded holidays as unjustified self-indulgence. But he had no hesitation in paying the fees for his son to be educated at a public school—he regarded that as money well spent. He died only a few years ago and left a considerable fortune.

Another unpretentious woollen manufacturer of recent vintage was Horace Moorhouse who ran a medium-sized mill on the Morley boundary. He never attempted to emerge from his humble origins and was known to everyone in the mill as 'Orace. He could do any job in the mill as well as any of his employees and quite regularly did it when holidays or illness made it necessary. He was the only man who had mastered the intricacies of the mill crane and when it broke down (which it frequently did) 'Orace had to be called out of the managing director's office to get it working again. He would take off his jacket, roll up his sleeves and get on with it.

Although thrifty by nature 'Orace had a gregarious side and had a weakness for pale ale. He drank large quantities of it in a pub round the corner where everyone knew him and tended to take advantage of his comparative wealth. He had so many hangers on that his weekly bills from the pub were said to be higher than his bills for shoddy at the mill. 'Orace economized by having sandwiches for lunch which he transported in a very battered attache case.

He was once asked by some of his workpeople if they could have a mill trip to Blackpool like other mills in the town. He agreed and said he would go on the trip himself. But it was not an outstanding success. It was the first and last. "It were all 'Orace's fault" one of the workers confided. "He had the coach stop on the way home at every blasted pub between Blackpool and Morley and we arrived home so bloody drunk and so bloody late that t'wives would have nowt to do with us."

But although the district still throws up the odd character or two they are a dying breed. One reason for this is the spread of a uniform system of education which tends to turn out mass produced products rather than individual pieces of craftsmanship. Another reason is that the present age is not adapted to the development of individuality. The influence of the welfare state tends to make us all conventional little cogs in an efficient but rather dull machine. And, of course, crippling taxation and controls of one sort and another nowadays make it quite impossible for a man to build up a business in Batley as he could fifty years ago.

Another reason is the corroding influence of television and other canned amusements which have changed the social fabric of towns like Batley out of recognition. In the period I have been writing about Batley was a very closely knit and highly integrated community in which people depended on each other for their social life and recreation. There were scores of societies in the town, many run by the churches and chapels, which covered a wide range of interests. And people developed their interests and their personalities by taking part in these activities. Today Batley, like the rest of the country, sits glued to the television screen, and because it produces fictitious characters for us like those in Coronation Street we think it's marvellous. In the early part of this century Batley and other mill towns like it in Yorkshire were producing real characters just as diverting as those in the TV serials.

Floral tributes were inscribed

There are few better ways of observing the life of a town than by being a reporter on one of its local papers. You see its life in every aspect—literally from the cradle to the grave.

I had my fill of the grave during my three years on the *Batley Reporter* from 1938 to 1940. About a dozen residents died each week on average and we got a list of them from the cemetery. If the list contained anyone of any importance in the town my two senior colleagues would handle it and the report would begin "We very much regret to report the death which took place at his home on Monday of Mr John Taylor of Mount Pleasant, Batley, who for the past fifty years had been a Sunday school superintendent at Talbot Street Methodist church. . . ." The deaths of those of little importance had still to be briefly reported, however, and they were my province. I would set out with my notebook and go round from one bereaved home to another to get the required information about the deceased—his age, his place of employment, his place of worship and any claims to local fame such as membership of the committee of the working men's club.

The majority of people in Batley were working class and lived in bleak, back-to-back terrace houses with one room downstairs and one or two rooms upstairs. The open coffin was usually lying on the table in the downstairs room, while the relatives sat round it looking appropriately lugubrious.

I thought at first I would be a most unwelcome visitor and even wondered whether I would be exposing myself to the charge of intruding on private grief. But not a bit of it! I could not have been welcomed more warmly.

"Come in and sit you down, lad," the relative answering the door would say when I explained my business. And then, turning to the widow, he would explain "It's the young man from the *Batley Reporter*, Mabel. He wants particulars about our Fred."

The widow would proceed to say what a good husband he had been and how devoted they had been. "We never had a cross word" she would whimper. This information was usually received in respectful silence by the assembled relatives but occasionally there were protests against this stretching of the truth. "Nay, Mabel, don't exaggerate. He were an old bugger at times were your Fred."

I hastily explained at this juncture that I was not wanting to report any judgements on Fred's habits as a husband but merely wanted to know where he had worked, and for how long, and what chapel he had attended. "He were a willeyer at Taylor's all his life and went to Zion chapel" the widow would say. And that was really all there was to say about him. No one could think of much else.

"Would you like to have a look at him?" the widow would ask as I again expressed my sympathy and got up to go. At first I was a bit squeamish and said no thank you, but I soon realized I was disappointing everyone. By not viewing the body I was not entering into the spirit of things. Consequently I changed my approach. I learned to murmur my acceptance of the invitation to view the body and, on viewing it, to pass some trite comment such as "He looks very peaceful". A junior reporter on the other local paper, the *Batley News*, once told me that when he said to a widow how very peaceful her husband looked in his coffin she examined the corpse very closely and said "Aye he does an' all, doesn't he? But he always were a bit slow on t'uptake were Albert, so happen he hasn't tumbled to what's happened to him yet." He also quoted a widow as saying how well her dead husband looked. "It were that day trip to Scarborough last week—did him a world of good" she was said to comment.

Funerals were great events in those days—particularly the big ones. The local papers not only reported the hymns sung, what the minister said in his oration and what type of coffin was used (mahogany with brass handles) but devoted several columns to long lists of the names of all the people attending and what or whom they were representing, and sometimes equally long lists of the inscriptions on all the wreaths. Today's weekly newspaper reporters would call a strike in protest against such labours before the last rites were completed!

There were only three of us at the *Batley Reporter*—the main office of the paper was in Dewsbury—and when there was a funeral of a prominent citizen—a manufacturer, an alderman, a councillor or a justice of the peace—it was a case of all hands on deck. The chief reporter, Maurice Childe, and his second in command, Joe Harrison, really came into their own in reporting funerals and although they professed to hate them I am quite sure they enjoyed them enormously. Standing at the top of the chapel steps with their notebooks and pencils in their hands they were monarchs of all they surveyed. They knew ninety-five per cent of the people attending the funeral and took a professional pride in not having to ask people for their names as the representatives of the other local paper had to do because their men were less experienced. What is more one-hundred per cent of those attending knew Maurice and Joe and were ready to be very obsequious to them to make sure of getting their names in the paper.

"'Morning, Maurice, 'morning Joe", they would all say as

they trooped in, some of them stopping to make quite sure their names and description were noted correctly—particularly if it was a manufacturer's funeral and there were business considerations. "Put t'name of t'firm in Joe, there's a good fellow", they would plead. "And say I'm representing my co-directors an' all".

Some people claimed to be representing half a dozen other people and wanted them and all their firms in the list but Maurice and Joe would not tolerate this and did not hesitate to use their sovereign powers. "I'm sorry, Mr Blackburn", they would say. "We can't have you representing the chairman of the markets, baths and town hall committee as well as all these other people. We shall have to confine the people you're representing to three or four—space is limited you know."

After the service the coffin was carried out of the chapel by the undertaker's men, looking suitably solemn, and put back into the hearse for transport to the cemetery where, as the *Batley Reporter* would subsequently report, "the last sad rites at the graveside were conducted".

There was usually only a small number of people at the graveside because ninety-five per cent of the businessmen, having already made sure of getting their names in the paper, had no further interest in the proceedings. On coming out of chapel they would stand around in groups of four or five waiting for the cortege to get moving so that they could decently return to their mills. Some groups did a little business while waiting—many a ton of rags or shoddy was sold at the bottom of the chapel steps—but most of them discussed the deceased with appropriately gloomy faces.

"How much then?" one man would ask the rest of the group. There would be a short silence while they directed their minds to the matter and then one of them would say decisively "Twenty-five thousand. That's my guess. Twenty-five thousand."

Heads would shake at this and another member of the group would say "I shan't be surprised if it's nearer forty. He made a packet during t'last boom you know. And he spent nowt. Wouldn't even buy you a drink unless it was a shandy." "Aye" another would exclaim, "an' I bet he diddled t'tax to some tune an' all. There were no flies on him. No flies at all."

Southerners may think these coffin-side forecasts of what the deceased's will would be proved for were disrespectful to the dead and evidence of a ruthlessly mercenary mind. But estimating other people's material riches was second nature in Batley and no one ever took it amiss. Indeed far from being appalled by it I am sure the deceased would have been flattered to know that he was being subjected to such a practical and meaningful post-mortem. It would seem to him to be far more apposite than the minister's flowery assessment of his character.

My contribution to the big funeral reports took place at the cemetery, which was rather a remarkable place. Just as the shoddy manufacturers built themselves large mansions in Upper Batley while they were alive their families made provision for large memorials when they died and some of the tombstones could almost be described as miniature Nelson's columns. There was, I suspect, the same competitive spirit at work in death as in life. En masse these phalanxes of soot-blackened tombstones were a formidable sight indeed and when the director of the film *Value for Money*, Ken Annakin, first saw them he aptly described Batley cemetery as being "like a scene from a lurid nightmare".

After the mourners had departed from the graveside and the gravediggers had begun to put the earth back I had to scramble among the wreaths and write down the inscriptions on them—and as there were anything up to fifty of them, some containing several lines of verse, it was quite a time-consuming occupation. The gravediggers were always anxious to help and would often read the inscriptions out to me as I wrote them down. They also educated me on the facts of death. "Do you know why they have brass handles on coffins?" one of them asked me one day. I said I expected it was so that the coffins could be conveniently carried. "Nowt of t'sort" was the reply. "When you are burying one on top of another—say a wife on top of a husband—he may have been in for thirty years. T'brass handles will be all that's left and when we hit 'em we know we've got as deep as we can go without disturbing anyone, if you see what I mean."

Maurice and Joe considered that only funerals of prominent citizens should be covered, as it were, in depth. They considered the funerals of commonplace citizens should be reported but only briefly, stating merely the day the funeral took place, who conducted the service and officiated at the graveside, who were the family mourners and who were the undertakers—provided they were advertisers. If the undertakers were not advertisers they did not get the free publicity of a mention.

It was my job to cover some of these minor funerals in preparation for the great day when I should be entrusted with one of the big ones and as there were three or four interments a day it meant spending a good deal of my time at the cemetery. It was a cold job in winter—and it seemed to be nearly always winter in Batley cemetery—but I developed a friendly relationship with the chief custodian of the cemetery, Fred Burn, and he and I would sit by the fireside in the cemetery lodge toasting our toes until the next cortege was due to arrive.

Fred was by nature a genial, cheerful fellow but he took his job very seriously. He watched his burial figures like a managing director watching his profits and he would become quite depressed if his yearly total fell below the level of the previous year. If on the other hand his figures were ahead of the previous year he would positively glow with satisfaction. "I'm up to 200 and it's only October" he would greet me. "If we have a good three months to end the year with I shall be ten per cent up on last year. Of course, I'll grant you I was helped by those cold spells in January and February. . . ."

Fred was also very knowledgeable on the facts of death and often entertained me with macabre information such as how long it took bodies to decompose in different types of soil. He would often be halfway through a ghoulish story of some exhumation or other when his sharp ear would detect the approach of the cortege for the 2 15 pm funeral and he would immediately leap to his feet and race out to the cemetery gates in order to guide the hearse and accompanying vehicles to the graveside. The first-class graves were easy to find but some of the second class were more difficult—and most of my funerals were second class.

I did not have to bother with the wreaths at these funerals but merely collected a list of family mourners, usually provided by the undertaker. If the undertaker had not got a list I would go a little later to the grand finale of the proceedings which was, of course, the funeral tea, usually held at the Co-op cafe. One had to be very poor indeed to be buried without a funeral tea—and some of the teas I gatecrashed at the Co-op cafe could quite well have been called funeral feasts. There were not only large plates of ham, but cakes, trifle, fruit and various other delicacies. The teas would start in sepulchral silence—due not so much to respect for the deceased as to the difficulty of eating ham and talking at the same time—but once the eating part of the proceedings was over the mourners' sorrows seemed to lift and conversation began to flow. "Well", someone would say, "old Henry wouldn't have wanted us to be miserable would he?" I remember one funeral tea which finished up with a sing-song round the Co-op piano, but that was considered by some to be taking things a bit too far.

I found I was always very welcome at these gatherings and would often be asked to have a plate of ham myself. "Sit yourself down and enjoy yourself, lad", one of the mourners would say. "It's enough to give you your death of cold is yond cemetery."

Southerners do not understand this comparatively light-hearted approach to death in places like Batley and tend to regard it, like the coffin-side speculations on the size of the will, as irreverent and deplorable. Yorkshire people don't see it like this at all. Death in their philosophy is merely the ultimate fact of life and is accepted with the same stoic demeanour as all the other vicissitudes of human existence.

In places like Batley they can even laugh at death and make jokes about funerals. An undertaker once told me of the discussion he had with one Batley man over which cab he should travel in at his wife's funeral. There were no children so the undertaker suggested that he should travel with his mother-in-law. "Nay, not her", was alleged to be the reply. "If you put me in with her it'll right spoil t'day for me."

In Batley they can even look forward to death with a sense of humour. The story is told of a Batley joiner who made a coffin for his own use and kept it in his garage. On his death the instructions were that the brass name plate on his front door should be fixed to the coffin and that all those attending his funeral should call in at his local pub for a drink at his expense on the way to the cemetery. "You must call going to the cemetery", it was stated, "because I shall not be with you on the way back."

Being kind to 'our Gladys'

Funerals were only one aspect of local life and death with which I was brought into close contact through the *Batley Reporter*. The town's social activities also came under my scrutiny—particularly those centred on church and chapel. Every place of worship—and there were dozens of them—had these social offshoots and there was such a conglomeration of Women's Owns and Women's Bright Hours, Christian Endeavours, Men's Societies, Bible Classes, PSAs and PMEs (Pleasant Sunday Afternoons and Pleasant Monday Evenings) and scores of similar organizations under a variety of nomenclatures, that if they had all been reported fully there would have been too much wordage for a daily paper let alone a weekly. They were in fact reported very briefly—just the names of those taking part. "At the Zion Methodist Women's Own on Tuesday the speaker was Mr J Entwhistle, who gave a talk on 'My travels in Lapland.' Mrs W H Farrar presided and a vote of thanks was proposed by Mrs T Blackburn. Mrs A D Lumb was at the piano." If I had £1 for every report like that which I wrote I could buy a Rolls-Royce!

The job of collecting these snippets was known as "paragraphing" and it was organized by dividing the town into different districts which were allocated among the reporting staff. The rival paper, the *Batley News*, had half a dozen or more reporters engaged in paragraphing but on the *Batley Reporter* there were only three of us. I looked after Staincliffe, Hanging Heaton and other outer areas while Joe looked after Birstall and Soothill and Maurice central Batley. We had lists of calls which included every minister of religion in the area plus every pub and club and what were known as "general calls". The general calls were usually the gossip centres of the district such as the local grocer's or barber's shop where every morsel of news and tittle-tattle was disseminated almost as soon as it happened. Some of it was printable and quite a lot of it wasn't!

The most important events in most of the districts were the annual bazaars and sales of work and the other regular celebrations in the church calendar such as the harvest festival and the annual productions of the amateur dramatic and operatic societies. These productions, which one of us had to attend, were hazardous in the extreme, because although one was always told by the societies that they did not object to constructive criticism one very soon discovered that in fact they objected violently to the slightest suggestion of criticism of even the mildest variety.

A "review" had to consist of completely undiluted praise. This was very trying to young reporters anxious to flex their muscles as theatre critics but as anyone who has ever run a local paper knows it is an absolutely inviolable precept. Maurice and Joe ladled out paeans of praise with cynical detachment and their reports would usually begin "Another triumph was scored by the Gospel Hall Methodist amateur operatic society in their latest production of 'Rose Marie' which even exceeded last year's epoch-making production of 'The Vagabond King'."

Having visions of myself as a future James Agate I tried to present a more honest view but my efforts were usually in vain. Maurice and Joe would go through my report with a fine toothcomb and any suggestion of fallibility on the part of the producer or the cast was remorselessly excised.

I did once succeed in getting into print with the statement that one of the principals in "Belle of New York" was at times difficult to hear at the back of the hall, and this made me appreciate the need for caution far more than any of Maurice's or Joe's dire warnings. Two aggressive looking women came into the outer office within two hours of the paper appearing on the streets and asked if I was responsible for the attack on "our Gladys". I hastily pointed out that I had paid tribute to their Gladys's acting and vocal abilities. "Young man", said one of the women belligerently, "if you couldn't hear our Gladys at the back of the hall it's time you got your ears washed out. We have stopped your paper and we are taking the *Batley News* from now on."

Actually the *Batley News* let through more clangers than we did and once when the editor was away on holiday one of their staff got into print a review of a play which stated *inter alia* that the show was stolen by the prompter. On another occasion it was stated that the main character was played by someone whose performance was only marred by the fact that he repeatedly muffed his lines in the first act, had difficulty hearing the prompter in the second act and lost his moustache in the third act.

Dances, drink and the Co-op

Other local functions which it was my job to attend included the dances at the town hall, the campaigns of the Temperance Society and the monthly meeting of the Co-op. The annual dances ranged from the splendour of the mayor's ball where evening dress was *de rigueur* to the rag, tag and bobtail of the rugby league supporters' club.

The mayor's ball was the social highlight of the year and as the mayors and mayoresses of all the neighbouring towns were invited the clank of gold chains of office was almost as vibrant as the band. The event was the culmination of months of planning by the markets, baths and town hall committee and the corporation staff, and herculean efforts were made by the parks and cemeteries department to convert the austere town hall ballroom into a miniature Kew Gardens. Plants and flowers of all descriptions were arranged round the floor and there were banks of chrysanthemums at every entrance. The main set-piece of the display was usually a rock garden and fountain in the centre of the room. This was always very picturesque but hardly an ideal setting for the gay gordons or the military twostep and couples danced these numbers at their peril.

Supper was served in the council chamber for the VIPs and in the courtroom for the *hoi polloi* and as the catering was usually done by the Co-op it was substantial rather than genteel. The Co-op did not go in for cheese straws and canapes and chocolate eclairs; it went in for pork pies and ham sandwiches and plates of trifle. Whether it was a funeral or the mayor's ball did not make the slightest difference to the catering arrangements.

There was another unique feature of the supper arrangements in the council chamber and that was the serving of tea. This was brought in, in gargantuan brown tea pots, by two usually buxom waitresses. John Gregson, the actor, was very intrigued by this practice when he was invited to the Mayor's Ball during the filming of *Value for Money*. There were wine glasses on the table and when the waitress came round with a bottle of Graves and poured him out a quarter of a glass he presumed it was for tasting and quaffed the lot. The waitress regarded him in horror. "That was to drink t'toasts wi' " she explained. "There's tea coming if you're that thirsty."

The Temperance Society was a formidable force in Batley

in the nineteenth century and the town was noted for its rabid teetotalism which along with liberalism and non-conformity composed the three pillars on which the social life of Batley rested. The teetotallers had lost some of their fervour by the time that I came into contact with the Temperance Society but they were still a force to be reckoned with and under the dauntless leadership of their president, Mrs Herbert North, were still finding battles to fight.

It was said of Mrs North that she would throw you out of her house if you had a cork in your pocket but that was an exaggeration of her militancy. She was nevertheless a formidable advocate for her cause and served it with single-minded devotion to the end of her days. It would again be an exaggeration to say that Mrs North attributed all the evils of the world to drink—or intoxicating liquor as she always described it—but it would certainly be true to say that she invested it with wildly demoniac characteristics.

Listening to her denounce the brewers for the "vile trade" they carried on was like listening to Hitler denounce the Jews in pre-war Germany. Her eyes blazed with passion and her voice shook with emotion as she described in vivid detail the catalogue of human misery and degradation for which the brewers were responsible. As a young reporter I was spellbound by her oratory. Attending the temperance society meetings was the only thing in my life which has turned me to drink for relief. The *Batley News* man and I could not get out to the Wilton Arms quickly enough!

The Co-op meetings were sheer farce. The president was a dear little man called Joseph Richardson who had the peculiar ability of being able to address a meeting for ten or twenty minutes without anyone in the audience having the slightest idea what he was talking about. Certainly the two pressmen present had no glimmering of an idea of what he was talking about. I started taking a verbatim shorthand note of Joe's speeches at the Co-op meetings to see if they conveyed anything when one studied them carefully but they did not. The trouble was that he never finished a sentence. I found myself with pages and pages of verbiage and never a full stop. All one could do was to say that "Alderman Joe Richardson JP gave a detailed account of the activities of the society during the past month" —for it was a fair assumption that that was in fact what he was doing.

Why the Co-op found it necessary to hold a monthly meeting I never knew because, with one notable exception, hardly anyone attended it, and apart from Mr Richardson's verbal ramble nothing ever happened and nobody ever said anything of the remotest interest to anyone. The one exception was the meeting at which delegates for the Co-op congress were elected. This was held annually at Margate or some other seaside resort and as all expenses were paid by the society there was keen competition. Alderman Richardson opened the meeting with his usual aplomb and after the vote had been taken announced the names of the members of the society who would be accompanying him. But he invariably got them muddled up and a list had to be made later.

Town council debate

The event of highest importance in the diary of the *Batley Reporter* was the monthly meeting of the town council. This towered like Everest over every other happening in the town and was extensively reported. Maurice and Joe went into training for the meeting several days beforehand by going laboriously through the committee minutes and selecting those items which were likely to cause questions and debate. They took me along with them to the meeting to cover the very trivial items and to take an additional shorthand note of the main speeches just in case neither of them could transcribe his own shorthand when they got back to the office.

The meetings were conducted with some ceremony and after the councillors and aldermen had assembled—the aldermen in their robes of office—the mayor would march into the council chamber in full regalia, which consisted of a scarlet gown, a tricorn hat and, of course, the mayoral chain. He was accompanied by the town clerk in his wig and gown and the mace-bearer carrying the mace which he placed solemnly on a table in front of the mayor. Altogether it looked rather like a scene from the "Pirates of Penzance".

Most of the meetings produced no more lively topics than projected increases in rates or the re-siting of bus stops or planned extensions of the sewage works. Occasionally there was something in the committee minutes which really set the council alight. Such an item was a minute of the general purposes committee recommending that "a room in the town hall should be placed at the disposal of the Batley Conservative club in order that the club's registration under the licensing act could be transferred to the town hall on the occasion of a dance to be organized by the Conservative Association".

It looked innocent enough to the outsider but to anyone who knew Batley and the ardent teetotal principles of a sizeable and vocal minority of its people it was a time bomb which would explode as soon as the council met. Alderman Ben Richardson, the son of the Co-op president, took the pin out as soon as the minutes of the general purposes committee came up for the council's approval. To say he was appalled by the proposal to let drink be served at the town hall would be an understatement. He denounced it passionately as one of the most iniquitous and scandalous proposals ever to be put before the council in the town's history.

It epitomized the current degeneracy which was rocking the traditions of civilized life to their very foundations. It might be considered tolerable by some to have intoxicating liquor served at a dance if it was to be held at a club or public house although he was not of that persuasion himself. As he saw it drinking and dancing should on no account and in no circumstances whatever be brought together. But for the general purposes committee to approve the serving of drinks at a dance in the *town hall* could only be described as a sacrilege of the most outrageous kind. The town hall was a civic centre which evoked the civic pride of the townspeople. Was that civic pride held in such low esteem by the general purposes committee that it should be fouled in this disgusting manner?

He went on for a quarter of an hour or more talking about the decline of moral fibre in the contemporary world and when he at last sat down Alderman George Hunt rose menacingly to his feet. He was a large, formidable figure, one of the manufacturing fraternity, and he was known to like a drop of intoxicating liquor at any time—and more than a drop on occasions. "Of all the poppycock talked by that pusillanimous pussyfoot, Alderman Richardson, this takes the biscuit" he began.

Before he could continue, however, Alderman Richardson

leapt to his feet to ask the mayor whether Alderman Hunt, a member of the Conservative Association, was in order in speaking in the debate at all—a point which raised some barracking from the drinkers in the council who were rallying to their leader's call. The mayor, his tricorn hat slipping further over his left eye, listened to the chorus of barrackers apprehensively and said he did not know of anything in standing orders to prevent Alderman Hunt from speaking but he would ask the town clerk. The town clerk nodded his approval of the mayor's ruling and Alderman Richardson reluctantly sat down.

"We have heard a lot about morals from Alderman Richardson" Alderman Hunt continued. "Does he think he and his gang of teetotal fanatics are the only moral people in this town? Does he consider the rest of us to be drink-sodden scoundrels? The inference is there and I hope the council will take note of it."

He continued his speech to roars of hear! hear! "I have been disgusted all my life by the way people have been hounded down in Batley if they happen to like the odd whisky and soda", he went on. "If these people would really talk temperance instead of peddling prohibition, if they abandoned some of their narrow and vicious ideas, they would get far more people to support them. When all is said and done the town hall does not belong to the teetotallers. It belongs to the ratepayers and should cater for them all." He spoke for a quarter of an hour also and sat down to thunderous applause.

Excitement was intense as some of the other teetotallers now jumped in. Alderman Hunt, they declared, was talking absolute balderdash. As custodians of the ratepayers it was the council's duty to protect the town hall from the ravages of drunken mobs at dances. They should rid themselves of their prejudices and consider what would be worthy of the town they served and loved.

And so it went on for the next hour and a half, until the vote was eventually taken and the teetotallers were easily defeated.

Meanwhile the press perspiringly filled page after page in their notebooks so that this great debate could be read verbatim by the citizens in whose interests both of the contending parties claimed to be acting. The headline at the weekend ran "Drinking at town hall dances—Alderman Richardson objects on moral grounds—Alderman Hunt disgusted by narrowmindedness"—and the report occupied almost a full page!

Old fashioned journalists

One came into contact through the *Batley Reporter* with people in all walks of Batley life. The two people I saw most of were Maurice and Joe, who besides being my superiors were my guides, philosophers and friends. I grew very fond of them both during the three years I worked with them and kept in close contact with them for years afterwards until their deaths. Both were journalists in the old tradition with tremendous loyalty to their paper and an abiding interest in their work which made them almost oblivious to the very long hours they put in. They were in the office by 9 15 in the morning and frequently did not get home until eleven or twelve o'clock at night, depending on the pressure of evening engagements. And if they got a free weekend once in four they were very fortunate. Today's journalists would not stand such hours for a fortnight. They would be out on strike and to hell with loyalty to the paper.

Maurice was a large, somewhat ungainly fellow with white, dough-like features which suggested (rightly) that his health was not good. Joe was slighter in build but much more robust in countenance and constitution. He had a permanent look of harassment on his rubicund and rather grizzled face and liked to play the martyr whenever possible. "No, I'll take it, Maurice", he would say with reference to some unpopular evening engagement—a church vestry meeting or a lecture on travel in Patagonia at the public library. "I promised May [his wife] that I'd take her to the pictures but it can't be helped."

"Now Joe," Maurice would say firmly, "do you want to cover this or don't you—because if you don't I'll go myself?" "No, I've said I'll do it and that's that. It's no good being a journalist if you want any private life. . . ."

They had worked together for many years on opposite sides of a large table in a very poky little office and both used very ancient double keyboard Barlock typewriters. The deafening clatter when they were both in action made a road drill seem like a lullaby. I sat at a small table adjoining and made my contribution to the bedlam on an ancient Remington on which roughly half the letters did not work.

Maurice and Joe had two crosses to bear—the head office of the *Reporter* at Dewsbury and the opposition paper down the road—the *Batley News*. The head office was occasionally represented by the editor, a genial white-haired Welshman called Oswald E Jones, but usually by the assistant editor, Jim Sheard, a product of the heavy woollen district if ever there was one. Jim was in his fifties—about the same age as Maurice and Joe—and had sharp, hawk-like features and an aggressive manner of which tact was not a noticeable constituent. He rang the Batley office with great frequency to complain about the quantity of copy which was being sent down and his rasping voice was so high in volume that Maurice and Joe would often put the telephone down on the desk and listen to the onslaught from a comfortable distance. "I told you a column at the outside on this damned chamber of commerce meeting but there must be the best part of a bloody page here. Where can I put it? Just you tell me—where can I put it?" All three of us were often on the point of telling him!

Jim was the Beau Brummel of local journalists and was always smartly turned out in a check suit, bow tie and worsted cloth cap worn at a rakish angle. He smoked cigars incessantly and exuded an air of prosperity which offended Maurice and Joe because of their more straitened circumstances. He did not smoke his cigars on his salary from the *Reporter*—who had earned their reputation of being skinflint employers—but through the proceeds of his lineage connection, the buttress of many a provincial journalist at this time.

Jim acted as Dewsbury correspondent for all the daily and evening papers in Yorkshire and also for the national papers in Fleet Street and as Dewsbury was a good town for news stories, being a county borough, it was a remunerative business. What Maurice and Joe, who shared the much smaller lineage business in Batley, objected to was what they considered to be the unscrupulous manner in which Jim used the reporting staff at Dewsbury to serve his lineage ends. He would "milk" their copy day in day out and pay them the smallest possible pittance in return. "Sheer exploitation" Joe would grumble. "It's time old Jones (the editor) woke up to what's going on." Neither Joe nor Maurice could complain about Jim's lineage malpractices, however, as they would be badly hit themselves if such activities were prohibited!

The other cross which Maurice and Joe had to bear, the opposition paper, presented itself every Friday morning at about the same time as the *Reporter* was published. They would open it with apprehension and, if it was a bad week, turn over the pages with mounting depression as exclusive after exclusive came to light. It was unavoidable that the *News* should have exclusives because they were the primary paper in Batley and had a reporting staff of up to ten in number, all engaged in ferreting out local news.

But even if there were nothing more than a wedding or a death (and there rarely was) Maurice and Joe took it as a body blow and were inconsolable for the rest of the day. If it was something really serious like an eightieth birthday or a golden wedding they were ready for suicide on the spot. They had not even the heart to walk along the street to the Co-op cafe for lunch and glumly ate sandwiches in the office. Now and again, of course, the *Reporter* would have a scoop and this was an occasion for modest rejoicing. They would stride off to the Co-op with spring in their step.

Former cabinet minister

Maurice and Joe were, of course, as well known in Batley as anyone and people engaged in different spheres of local life were constantly popping into the office to deliver notes of speeches they had made and wished to have reported or to provide information for publication of the activities of the organizations or societies with which they were connected.

Prominent among these visitors was one of Batley's most famous sons, Sir Ben Turner, former Labour member of parliament for the Batley and Morley division and a cabinet minister in the first Labour Government led by Ramsay Macdonald. Sir Ben, at this time aged over seventy and a small, venerable figure with a flowing white beard, called in every Friday for a free copy of the paper and often spent half the afternoon gossiping about his days in the House of Commons and what Ramsay had said to him after cabinet meetings.

Sir Ben began his working life as a half-timer in a local mill at the age of ten. He worked one week from 6 am until 12 30 pm and went to school from 2 pm until 4 30 pm, and the following week went to school from 9 am until 12 noon and worked from 1 30 until 6 pm. He would recall how the early shift meant getting up at 5 am, walking two miles to the mill and not having a bite to eat until 7 30 am when he breakfasted on bread and dripping.

Although a working man his father was well versed in politics and encouraged young Ben to read *Reynolds News*, *Bradlaugh's National Reformer* and other socialist literature. He also took him to political meetings to hear famous left-wing speakers such as Charles Bradlaugh and Annie Besant and before he was twenty-one he was writing Labour news for the *Factory Times* and speaking at meetings as a representative of the Weavers' union. He married at twenty-one but did not have a honeymoon because his total savings amounted to £4 7s 6d and were required for furnishings. In any case he might have lost his job by taking time off for an unimportant thing like getting married.

His hardest days came soon after the birth of his two children when he lost his job due to a textile depression and was out of work for a considerable time. He recalled how the family lived on porridge—porridge warm and porridge cold, porridge with milk and porridge with treacle, porridge for breakfast, porridge for dinner and porridge for tea. He kept up his union work, however, and was eventually appointed secretary of the Leeds and District branch of the Weavers' Union at a wage of 5s a week, which he supplemented by his contributions to the *Factory Times*. He joined the Leeds Socialist Party and the Trades' Council and was elected as a delegate to the Trades Union Congress.

Sir Ben would often reminisce about his union activities and the thanklessness of the task of trying to increase the union membership and strength. He was regarded as a trouble maker by the employers and was not even popular with the mill workers, who were not union minded and regarded union leaders as work-shy parasites. His dream was one union for all textile workers for he believed that only by centralizing their power could the mill workers hope to stand up to the united strength of the employers. But despite the bad conditions in the mills—where some men were working from 6 am to 9 pm from Monday to Thursday and from 6 am on Friday right through till 1 pm on Saturday for wages of 30s a week—it was a heartbreaking job.

Sir Ben played a prominent part in the development of the Labour party and was a founder member of the Independent Labour party in 1893, attending the famous meeting at Bradford presided over by Keir Hardie. He was almost alone in carrying the Labour torch in Batley and won a seat on the town council as the first Labour candidate in the same year. He became Batley's first Labour mayor in 1914 and always chuckled when he recalled the complaint that he had made the town hall "common".

Whether Sir Ben made the town hall common or whether the town hall made Sir Ben fastidious is debatable but it was always said (I know not with what authority) that when Sir Ben was MP he would board the London train at Batley station wearing a cloth cap and travel third class as far as Wakefield, where he took down his case from the rack, replaced his cloth cap with a Homburg and travelled the remainder of the journey first class. He always had a twinkle in his eye and I would not put it past him.

Local squire

Another fairly regular caller was Major J P Critchley JP, of Batley Hall, the twentieth century equivalent of the old village squire. Known as Percy he ran a small farm in Upper Batley and was among other things chairman of the bench. He was a genial, red-faced man with a thick neck and did not talk so much as splutter. After he had delivered a judicial verdict the clerk of the magistrates, a somewhat unctuous little man, had always to translate it to the defendant, who could not have understood less of what the chairman was saying to him had he been speaking in Chinese.

In earlier days Percy's father, Walter, was an even greater

character than Percy. He was commanding officer of the local territorial battalion and the story was told of how he once marched a detachment of soldiers along Batley's main street, Commercial Street, and intended them to turn right down Wilton Street, commonly known as Co-op Street because that emporium was situated in it. But Walter got mixed up in making his commands and instead of shouting "right turn" shouted "left turn", whereupon the detachment turned left and began to march up Hanover Street. Walter got them back on to Commercial Street with some difficulty but still could not get them to go down Wilton Street and after trying several "left turns" and "right turns" without the desired effect shouted "right turn—I mean down Co-op Street", a command which will remain unique in the annals of the British army.

Walter, as a son of the soil, was also a very staunch supporter of Batley's annual agricultural show which was held annually at Mount Pleasant cricket and football field and served to remind the town of its rural past. One year Walter exhibited a prize pig and had it on show with a card at the front of the cage stating "This pig was bred by Mr Walter Critchley of Batley Hall." A millworker gazed at the pig reflectively for some moments and then commented aloud "Aye, and by God it's like him an' all."

One of Walter's failings was an inclination to fall very fast asleep without warning, not only on the bench but at meetings of one kind and another. Knowing him his neighbours were usually on watch for this and as soon as his first snore resounded through the chamber they quickly, and if necessarily violently, nudged him awake.

When on one occasion a new bank manager visited him at Batley Hall he was unfortunately not forewarned about this inclination and when Walter duly fell fast asleep during a discussion on the national economy or something the bank manager, a shy and retiring man anxious to make a good impression on the squire, was nonplussed. He tried raising his voice but to no effect and after waiting for ten minutes in a predicament of indecision he summoned up the courage to try and arouse the snoring squire by a gentle nudging. This was completely ineffective and the bank manager returned to his chair to reconsider the impasse.

He could not very well leave without his host being aware of it. He would awaken to find him gone without explanation and would consider it a grave discourtesy. On the other hand he could not very well prod him any harder than he had done lest he push him off his chair, on which he was now rather precariously balanced. The dilemma was apparently resolved after three-quarters of an hour by the entry of the squire's wife with afternoon tea. He responded subconsciously to his wife's clarion call of "Wake up Walter". He opened his eyes, saw the bank manager before him and said quite calmly "Now as I was saying Mr Blakeley, the main question is . . . ".

The municipal pianos

It was once put to me that Batley did not go in much for culture because it did not pay very well. Whatever the reason there has always been a dearth of cultural as distinct from social activities. There is not a bookshop in the whole town and if one wants to read—and one suspects that few do—one is dependent on the public library, or the free library as it is referred to in the Batley vernacular.

As with culture so with art and music. A small art gallery attached to the public library was set up by the curator of the Batley park museum but when the philistines got to know that some of the paintings were quite valuable there were immediate demands that they should be sold and thereby enable a reduction to be made in the rates.

The attitude to music can best be summed up by the story of Batley's two municipal pianos, which I reported in the *Yorkshire Post* in the 1950s. It all started with the announcement that a well-known jazz pianist had refused to appear in Batley ever again because he had been refused permission to play the grand piano in the town hall and compelled to use the upright, which he described as "an appalling instrument".

I followed up this announcement by interviewing the jazz pianist who told me "It does not even look like a piano and as for playing . . . well it's like a car engine with a big end gone. The last time I played the thing it was hopelessly out of tune and several hammers were missing. In fact I had to take the front off to get it to work at all. It may be all right for a canteen or a photographer's studio but for a town hall it's an absolute disgrace. I understand it was presented to the town by a shoddy manufacturer about thirty years ago and it could not have been much use when he had it. Perhaps that was why he gave it away."

He said he had been so incensed by the condition of the piano that he had written a strong letter to the town clerk. But he received a letter back saying that the matter had been discussed by the town council and they did not propose to take any action.

"Why won't they let you use the grand piano?" I asked him.

"God knows" he replied. "They seem to think we play with our feet."

Determined to get to the bottom of the matter I next interviewed the chairman of the market, baths and town hall committee who, I discovered, was in charge of the town's two municipal pianos. He turned out to be a former postman currently employed by a firm of weighing machine manufacturers. He readily admitted that he knew nothing about pianos at all but was satisfied, nevertheless, that there was little if anything wrong with the upright municipal piano. The jazz pianist who had complained did not know what he was talking about.

"He says you have banned him from playing the grand piano because you think he plays with his feet" I said. "What in fact is the reason?"

"I have never said jazz pianists play with their feet" he replied indignantly. "But we have been led to believe that they thump it a bit and even the upright has needed repairs after they have used it. Some people don't look after things as they should do, you know. We have the same trouble with the new back brushes we have put in at the public baths."

I put to him that the upright piano was hopelessly out of tune. He shook his head. "Nonsense", he replied. "We have it tuned by contract regularly once a year. And when it breaks down we always have it repaired straight away."

He shook his head more in sorrow than in anger. "The whole trouble is that they see the grand piano and aspire to play it" he said.

I asked him why they should not play the grand. Was it simply for decoration?

No, he replied, it was not for decoration but after due consideration the markets, baths and town hall committee had come to the conclusion that it was such a valuable instrument that it should be reserved for the annual celebrity concert, and had passed a resolution accordingly.

"The point is," he explained, "that the pianist we have for the annual celebrity concert must have a really first class instrument. Not being musical myself I don't know much about it but it's summat to do with pitch. A concert pitch is different from other pitches and the grand piano is kept in just the right pitch. If this here jazz pianist starts thumping it then it would very soon lose its pitch."

He was unable to tell me any more about the grand piano but suggested I go down to the town hall and ask the town hall caretaker about it. He was in direct charge of the two municipal pianos and might even let me see them.

This he did. They were both covered in dust sheets in the main hall and the grand was securely locked. "That's so that no one can fiddle about with it" the caretaker explained.

I asked him if it would do irreparable harm to the instrument to be used by a jazz pianist but he said that was a question he was not competent to answer. All he could say was that both the grand and the upright were first class German instruments and were kept in first class condition. It was not true that one had been given to the town by a shoddy manufacturer. They had both been bought reconditioned in the early part of the last war. He could not reveal how old they were or how much had been paid for them. It was not true to say they had been bought cheap as a job lot.

I left him with one question still to answer—would the grand piano be at risk if played by a jazz pianist? I decided to ask one of Batley's foremost musical authorities, Mr Fred S Gladwin, the conductor of the Batley male voice choir and organizer of the annual celebrity concert.

"There have been complaints about the condition of one of the town hall pianos" I said to him.

"I'm not surprised" he replied. "I've been complaining myself for years. Because of the condition of the piano we have decided never to ask a solo pianist to play at our celebrity concerts again."

"But surely the grand piano can be used for the celebrity concerts?" I said.

"Well," replied Mr Gladwin, "that's the one I'm talking about."

"But surely it's the upright that's faulty?" I said.

"They're both ready for the scrapyard in my opinion" he replied. "The grand is in an appalling state. A leg actually fell off when my wife last played it and it has never had to be moved since. On another occasion part of the lid came off. The town hall people patched it up with a large metal hinge but the solo pianist could hear it clanking and it ruined his performance. On another occasion the lid stuck fast and the pianist could not move it. The caretaker had to come on the stage and attend to it. And this was during a celebrity concert. But he could not do anything with it so he had to take the lid away and we finished the concert without it. It was these two incidents which prompted us never to invite a solo pianist to play again."

"And what about its pitch" I asked him weakly.

"Well," he replied, "it may be all right for amateurs but it's not really fair to ask professionals to play it. I'm afraid the trouble is that the markets, baths and town hall committee or whatever they call it are not musically minded. I have heard it said that the grand was chosen by a butcher. He may have been able to vamp it a bit but he was certainly no expert. He said he had chosen it because it would look nice in anyone's drawing room."

Mr Gladwin shook his head. "I've told them they could get quite a good one for a few hundred pounds but they won't hear of it" he said.

It could only have happened in Batley!

Value for Money

I have referred on several occasions to the novel of mine, *Value for Money*, which was published in 1953, filmed in 1955 and subsequently read on the radio and dramatized on television by the BBC. I do not refer to it again to try and push the sales—it has long been out of print—but because it played a small part in the story of Batley.

The book was based in the fictitious town of Barfield but the resemblance to Batley was much more than coincidental! I wrote the book primarily to characterize Batley and the attitudes of its inhabitants—in particular those of the rag and shoddy men who had long intrigued me by their absorbing interest in money and above all in getting value for it. So I built a story round a purely fictitious rag merchant called Chayley Broadbent who is left £50 000 by his father and celebrates by rashly spending a few pounds on a coach trip to London to see the rugby league cup final at Wembley. While in the West End after the match he gets involved with a gold-digging chorus girl, Ruthine West, who, when she learns of his money, sets out to relieve him of it and comes to Barfield as his uninvited guest.

Chayley had this unusual name because, when the vicar at his christening asked what he should name the child, his father replied in broad Yorkshire "Tha mun call him Chayley". And the vicar, being a south countryman and not knowing that Charlie was pronounced like that in Yorkshire, duly christened him Chayley. Chayley incorporated most of the characteristics of the Batley rag and shoddy men and the book opens appropriately with him arguing with the undertaker about the likely cost of his father's funeral.

Although the book proved to be very successful it also proved embarrassing. As soon as the first edition was published I was threatened with an action for libel by Mr John H Greenwood of Dark Lane, Batley, of whom I had never heard, and as a result had to publish disclaimers in *The Times* and other newspapers to the effect that a John Greenwood I had referred to had no connection with the said Mr John H Greenwood. Copies of the book had to be called in by the publishers and a printed slip inserted reading: "It has been brought to the author's attention that the reference to John Greenwood on Page 205 might be construed as referring to Mr John H Greenwood of Dark Lane, Batley, who although not also a university graduate has been a commission rag buyer for the past fifty years. No such reference was intended and the author sincerely apologizes to him for any inconvenience which may have been caused to him."

I had picked the name John Greenwood out of the telephone directory because there were so many of them and the object of the reference was to illustrate the fact that academic qualifications were of little practical use in the rag and shoddy trade and not nearly of as much value as native shrewdness and business acumen. The offending passage, spoken by Chayley, read "... but we are not without nobs in the trade you know even if some of their fathers could not read or write. There's one or two who've been to Eton in the town and quite a few to other posh schools. We've even got one ragger who's an Oxford MA—although you wouldn't think so to see him at the rag sales. If the auctioneer wants to get rid of a bad lot he always palms it off on John Greenwood. Buy owt, he will, the fooil."

Subsequently quite a lot of other people told me they had recognized characters in the book. They would come up to me in the street in Batley and say "I read your book. Got it out of t'library" (they always added that). "I recognized so-and-so—it were just like him." And as no one seemed to be in the least convinced by my protestations that none of my characters was "real"—which was the gospel truth—I began to think that instead of making me a bit of cash *Value for Money* was more likely to cost me a fortune in libel damages.

Consequently when the Rank Organisation made an offer for the film rights I was not at first very enthusiastic. But the filming, the first to be made in VistaVision, a new colour process, was a great experience and caused quite a stir in Batley when the producer, director, cameramen and some twenty-five actors and technicians arrived on location in the town. John Gregson, who took the part of Chayley, came up for about a fortnight but Diana Dors, who co-starred as Ruthine, was represented by her stand-in. Susan Steven, Derek Farr, Charles Lloyd Peck, Frank Peppingell, Jill Adams, Ferdie Mayne, Charles Victor and James Gregson were among others taking part.

Batley gave them an enthusiastic welcome and, as I have already said earlier, the Mayor invited most of the cast to his annual ball—an event which in its way was quite as funny as anything in the film. Some of Batley's inhabitants considered the film people quite mad and for evidence pointed to the fact that they had ordered the fire brigade out at 7 o'clock every morning to hose down the market place in order to make the cobbles shine! As for the film crew they were a little taken aback by the rag men's sense of humour. When the director approached one warehouse to obtain permission to take some interior shots the owner was standing at the door, idly watching the proceedings. The following conversation ensued:

Director: "Good morning sir. I wonder if you would have any objection to our taking some camera shots inside your rag warehouse?"

Rag merchant: "D'you mean you want to buy t'place?"

Director: "Well hardly that sir. It won't take more than half an hour."

Rag Merchant: "Come on! You've got plenty of brass. Make me a bid for it. I'll sell it you cheap. Trade's rotten as usual."

The bulk of the film was done at Pinewood Studios and I went there on a number of occasions, once expressly to write an article for the *Yorkshire Post*. "I had the uncanny experience yesterday", I wrote, "of going to Pinewood Studios and apparently walking into the council chamber and Mayor's parlour in Batley town hall. They appeared to be Batley's council chamber and Mayor's parlour complete to the smallest detail—until I observed that the coat of arms was different, that the name Batley had been replaced by Barfield and that the portraits of past mayors and aldermen adorning the walls were purely fictitious."

These two large rooms had been built in plywood to actual size from drawings and pictures taken in Batley and the resemblance was quite remarkable. Not that the reproductions of Batley ended at the town hall. Chayley Broadbent's warehouse had also been built most realistically in the studio and was complete with real bales of rags and artificial cobwebs laid by a special machine. The interior of the Co-op cafe and of an old Batley terrace house had also been constructed and perhaps the most striking of the lot was the reproduction of a corner of Batley cemetery with its monstrous tombstones which the director, Ken Annakin, had said made it seem like a scene from a lurid nightmare. No less convincing were some of the outdoor scenes of the Batley area which appeared as paintings on canvas backcloths.

The elaborate set building struck one at first as a colossal waste of time and money because the shooting which took place in all of them was very limited and occupied no more than a few minutes of screen time. And as soon as the shooting was completed the marvellous council chamber and Mayor's parlour and all the other creations were smashed up. But you soon realized that it was only by means of this tremendous attention to detail that the impression of complete authenticity was obtained.

The shooting itself was unexciting. It was a slow, laborious business and one day of watching it was enough for anybody. It was fascinating at first at 9 o'clock in the morning to see John Gregson and Susan Steven walking along the canal bank at Barfield—but it was not quite so compelling when they were still walking along the same stretch of canal bank at 6 o'clock that night, and had spoken perhaps half a dozen sentences all day.

"I've been thinking, Ethel," says Chayley, as they lean against a wall with the murky waters gurgling below them and the rag warehouses rising gloomily in the background, "haven't you ever thought that we might as well get wed and have done with it?" " . . . You really want to marry me Chayley?" says Ethel (his Barfield girl friend who has been waiting years for this moment). "Is this a proposal?"

It was a proposal (or as near to one as anybody ever got in Barfield) but a mighty slow one. It took a whole day to get the two minutes' screen time exactly to the director's satisfaction.

Of course before the cameras actually started clicking at all a good deal of preparation was necessary. First the shot had to be lined up with the actors taking their places on the set and chalk marks made on the carpet to indicate their exact positions. A rehearsal followed with the director telling the actors exactly what he wanted them to do and the actors then departed to be made up and the stand-ins took their places while bevies of lights were fixed above them and all round them and tests made of all descriptions. Then and only then did the shooting begin.

Acting in a film looks easy enough because there are no lines of any length to learn and mistakes can always be easily rectified by another "take". Appearances, however, are deceptive. Actors have to act in blood so cold that it must almost be freezing. A smile or a tear has to be turned on and off to order with the only "audience reaction" coming from the director, who is searching for the slightest flaw.

But although it was all grimly serious while the shooting lasted the atmosphere changed immediately it was completed.

The director beamed happily at everyone and said "That was fine". The actors sat down and sighed with relief. The tea was served and the cigarettes came out and later everyone trooped up to the theatre to see the "rushes" on the screen—the scenes which had been shot the previous day.

I was employed by the Rank Organisation as an "adviser" for a short period while the film was being made in the studio and before the move to Batley on location and it was quite the cushiest job I have ever had. Any advice I had to offer was completely ignored and when I did not bother offering any nobody asked me for any! But it gave me a glimpse of the film-makers' world which was diverting to say the least. Film-makers, I found, were people of sudden enthusiasms who indulged in frequent changes of course. And they had an obsession for conferences. I attended some of these conferences and the idea seemed to be that what was definitely decided at the last conference should be scrapped completely at the next. At one conference, for instance, it was decided to have a brass band contest in the film. I pointed out that this was not in the book and so far as I could see had nothing to do with the plot but although they listened to me politely they were not in the least impressed by my views and got to work with great enthusiasm on the brass band contest, going to the extent of hiring several brass bands for the purpose.

When I next went down to Pinewood a week or so later I asked them how the brass band contest was going and they looked at me blankly and said "Which brass band contest?" They had forgotten all about it and were now working on another idea which featured the opening of a creche! I pointed out that in the book it was the opening of a new sewage works and that a lot of people in Batley would probably not know what a creche was, but a creche it had to be, along with a swimming bath which Ruthine (Diana Dors) was to open by putting on a bikini and swimming a length.

I also tried hard to dissuade them from having a wedding reception in Chayley's rag warehouse, which was an even more unlikely event in Barfield than a curvaceous actress in a bikini opening a corporation swimming bath. But they continued to bash on regardlessly and the finished product was not nearly so disastrous as I expected it to be. Indeed they actually preserved quite a lot of the book and made quite a funny film, and the general reaction was very favourable.

The premiere was at the Odeon in the Haymarket (then called the Gaumont) and most of the cast were present, including Diana Dors in a dress so revealing that some of the guests from Batley were positively shocked. The town was well represented, not least by the local Member of Parliament Dr A D D (Bill) Broughton. I and the script writer, R F Delderfield, and a lot of others went on to a party at the producer's home afterwards and a good time was had by all.

Diana Dors was, of course, just right for the part of the gold-digging Ruthine and played it excellently. She was popular both on the set and off it—particularly on the set in one scene in an hotel bedroom in which she was fleetingly seen in the nude. Nudes were quite exciting in those far off days and there seemed to be many more technicians in the studio than usual that morning!

Diana told me that three factors were responsible for her success as a film actress, which had enabled her to turn down a Rank contract for £70,000 at the age of 24. The three factors were, she said, a 23 inch waist, 35 inch hips and a 35 inch bust. She had started her stage career with a song and dance act at the age of eight and at nine had won a school essay prize on what she wanted to be when she grew up. She wrote that she wanted to be a film star with a swimming pool and a cream telephone. She had got them both before *Value for Money* was made, along with a penthouse near Maidenhead containing a private cinema and three bathrooms!

John Gregson was also popular on the set and off it and a more modest, genial and down-to-earth actor it would be difficult to meet. I got on very friendly terms with him while the film was being made and was very distressed to read of his death in his early fifties a year or two ago. He was not entirely new to the mysteries of rags and shoddy, being the next best thing to a Yorkshireman—that is to say a Lancastrian.

The film travelled all round the world and for years after the premiere I got letters from former Batelians saying how delighted they had been to see Batley on the screen in Australia, New Zealand, the Fiji Islands and goodness knows where else.

The film is still dished out on television occasionally and whenever this happens I am invariably asked by someone in Batley whether I get any royalties from it. When I tell them I don't they look at me critically as if to say "You weren't very bright then were you? Fancy not putting TV repeats in your contract!"

Part two—The Yorkshire Post

Gentlemen's club

The *Yorkshire Post* is sometimes described as Yorkshire's national newspaper and a very fine newspaper it is. But during my ten years on the staff no one could accuse it of being objective about Yorkshire. Its devotion to the county was boundless.

It is, of course, quite fitting that Yorkshire's premier newspaper should show a pride in the county. Every Yorkshireman is proud of his county. Miss Lettice Cooper, the distinguished Yorkshire novelist, has written that there is a feeling in Yorkshire that Yorkshire is a club and that one is very lucky to be a member. I feel, however, that sometimes this pride is carried to excess and becomes parochialism. Just as there are some Londoners who think that civilization ends at Potters Bar so there are some Yorkshiremen who think the light of the world goes out at Doncaster.

All Yorkshire newspapers tend to pander to this parochialism by giving excessive attention to Yorkshire affairs, and some of them have an astonishing ability to drag Yorkshire into their columns in the most flagrantly irrelevant manner. A man has only to climb Everest or row a boat across the Atlantic and while the rest of the national press applauds his amazing feat the papers in Yorkshire will point exuberantly to the fact that his mother-in-law lives in Halifax.

The *Yorkshire Post* in my time, I am afraid, was not entirely innocent of this charge of parochialism and I think there was some justification for a southerner winning a magazine competition with a parody of the *Yorkshire Post*'s style. The contestants had to describe the manner in which well-known newspapers would report the breaking of the monsoon in Calcutta and some of the entries were very effective. Thus the

Financial Times was parodied like this: "Rice, tea and cotton shares were dull yesterday following the breaking of the monsoon in Calcutta. Bright spot was the drowning of 500 people in the floods causing Morticians Ltd to harden two points to 58¾ at the close." And the *News of the World* was parodied like this: "Startling allegations regarding the effect of the breaking of the monsoon on a thirty-four-year-old Indian tailor were made in court in Calcutta yesterday when Ahmed Singh, no fixed address, appeared accused of improper conduct in a public place." The winning entry parodied the *Yorkshire Post* like this: "Among the first Englishmen to be drenched in the monsoon which broke in Calcutta yesterday was Mr Keith Ramsbottom, younger son of Mr and Mrs John William Ramsbottom of Millside Cottages, Dewsbury."

In view of this boundless pride in the county it does not surprise me that when I look back through my *Yorkshire Post* cuttings books at the one and a half million or so words I wrote for that paper as a reporter and feature writer in the ten years immediately after the Second World War I find that approximately one and a quarter million of those words were devoted to Yorkshire and Yorkshiremen.

For a number of years I had a roving commission and wrote a feature two or three times a week under the heading "Such is Life". But I never roved much outside Yorkshire. And if I did Yorkshire interests were never far away. When I went to the south of France for the paper it was to get the impressions of a party of Yorkshire tourists in a Wallace Arnold coach. When I went to visit the British Army in Germany and Austria the only regiments I saw were the West Yorkshires and the Duke of Wellingtons. When I met the Queen she had to come to Pudsey to enable me to do so. And I interviewed Winston Churchill only because he came to Huddersfield town hall to speak in support of Lady Violet Bonham Carter during a by-election.

Indeed the only story I can remember which had no Yorkshire connections whatever was a visit to the United Nations Assembly in Paris to hear an important speech by the Russian Foreign Minister, Mr Vishinsky. I went to some trouble to phone a report of the speech through to Leeds and was disappointed to find on my return that it had only gone into the first edition—which went to London and the more distant parts of the country. When I complained to the chief sub-editor he replied to the effect that they had had to leave it out to accommodate a story from Brighouse. "Now if Vishinsky had been speaking in Brighouse," he added acidly, "we'd have used a column and a half in all editions".

I am sure the *Yorkshire Post* today bears little comparison with the *Yorkshire Post* I was first introduced to nearly thirty years ago. I am writing these words on the day the forty thousandth edition of the *Yorkshire Post* was printed and in a special souvenir supplement to mark the occasion the present editor, John Edwards, writes that the changes which have taken place since he took over the editorship in 1969 have been the most dramatic in the paper's history. "Previous editors mentioned in this supplement from 1754 onwards were running a paper produced by methods that Caxton would have little difficulty in recognizing. If Caxton came back and we were able to give him a tour of the *Yorkshire Post* building today there are still some processes that he would recognize—but there is more that would leave him breathless with disbelief."

Mr Edwards was referring to the printing revolution in which the *Yorkshire Post* has been one of the leaders. But the tremendous explosion of technology which has converted newspaper production from hot metal to photo composition and from linotype machines to computers, is not, I dare venture, the only revolution which has occurred since I first walked through the archway in Albion Street, Leeds, where the *Yorkshire Post* had its headquarters until it moved into its present streamlined complex in Wellington Street in 1970.

The *Yorkshire Post* as I first knew it had every appearance of a gentlemen's club. The reporters' room in particular could have been easily mistaken for a reading room in Pall Mall. A dozen or more venerable gentlemen, some with white hair and one or two with sticks, sat around in well-padded armchairs reading newspapers and idly discussing topics of the day. No one turned up before 10 15 in the morning and at 11 o'clock practically everyone went out for coffee at Fuller's cafe round the corner, returning to their newspapers about noon and continuing their *conversazione* until lunch at one. There were a few signs of quiet activity at the telephone in the afternoon but it was not until about 4 30 pm that anything really happened. Then the news editor's personal assistant would come out of the news editor's office and advise the chief reporter (just in case he had forgotten or gone off to sleep) that the news editor would like to see the news list as soon as it was available and in good time for the editorial conference at 6 pm.

This was the signal for the chief reporter to spring into action and he did so by passing on this information to the deputy chief reporter who then went into conference with the news editor's secretary—a man needless to say. All this was done without in any way disturbing the cloistered calm of the reporters' room and half an hour later, by a process which always remained a complete mystery to me, the chief reporter was handed the news list and briefed on its contents.

These contents were a complete mystery to me too because in theory they consisted of the stories and articles on which the reporters had been working all day. But as it was perfectly clear that none of them had done anything more energetic than make a few telephone calls—and as scarcely anyone had touched a typewriter—this was clearly not the case. I sometimes wondered if what the deputy chief reporter dictated to the news editor's secretary was a list of what was on at the pictures in Leeds, varied occasionally by what was on at the pictures in Bradford, but I suppose it must have contained something more to the point than that.

Not that the chief reporter or, in his turn, the news editor, seemed to be particularly interested in what was on the news list. The chief reporter merely nodded sagely when his deputy ran through it and then went to deliver it personally to the news editor, whose office was adjoining. The news editor it appeared seemed to take no more interest in it than the chief reporter and on some occasions would absentmindedly set off down to the editorial conference without it, returning hastily a few minutes later to collect it. He had obviously not read it and as he would have no time to do so before the conference started he would seek a quick briefing from the chief reporter, who would call in the deputy chief reporter and the three of them would walk along the corridor and down the stairs to the editor's room carrying on a peripatetic preliminary conference of their own.

The provision of the news list was not the only item in the chief reporter's arduous daily routine. His second most important function was to mark the diary and to this he dedicated himself with a real pride of craftsmanship. What he had to do was to mark people's initials against the events which were taking place in the Leeds area that day, and also to enter the initials of those members of the staff who would be required to be on late duty until 10 o'clock in the evening the following day. It seemed to me to be a simple enough job and when the chief reporter was away the deputy chief reporter did it in about fifteen minutes. But the chief reporter himself seemed to spend hours and hours on it. Whenever you went to speak to him, whether it was 11 o'clock in the morning or 3 o'clock in the afternoon, he would be juggling with different sets of initials, either deleting them from the diary or reinstating them. At frequent intervals he would go into conference with the deputy chief reporter and any other senior member of the reporting staff who happened to be available and they would discuss the acute problem presented by the fact that it was JW's day off tomorrow and who could possibly cover the Crown court? There was only WS, and WS had arranged to play golf at Sandmoor with the news editor.

"Well why not mark RG for the Crown Court and NB for the women's luncheon club?" his consultant would suggest.

"Mark RG for the Crown Court?" the chief reporter would say in horror. "RG is not capable of doing the Crown Court. He's only been here five years. We must have an experienced man to do the Crown Court."

The reporters' room was not the only geriatric leisure centre at the *Yorkshire Post*, as I found when I got "off the diary" and became a feature writer. I was allocated a desk in an office along the corridor near the sub-editors' room and told I would share it with Bremner.

"Who is Bremner?" I asked, never having heard of him and wondering why—I had been on the staff some time by now.

"Oh," said the news editor, "he's a sort of special writer. But he won't worry you. He doesn't spend much time in the office."

That was an understatement if ever there was one. I made the acquaintance of Bremner next morning. There was a shuffling noise in the corridor about 11 am and a sharp rapping on the door of the office. I opened it to find Bremner standing before me leaning heavily on two sticks, with one of which he had been rapping on the door. He was a rather distinguished looking, bearded man of about sixty and was obviously very incapacitated.

"Give me a hand, old boy", he said cheerily. "Not so good on my pins."

Taking his coat off and helping him into his chair was a rather prolonged and difficult process but eventually he got settled and asked me to pass him *The Times* from his overcoat pocket.

"Thank you old man" he said, opening it at the crossword page. "Now we'll see how long it takes me today. I did it yesterday in thirty-five minutes."

I tried to converse with him but it turned out that he was almost stone deaf and he could not hear a word I said. He had a hearing aid but it evidently wasn't working that morning.

He did the crossword in just over half an hour whereupon he tried to rise from his chair but could not do so and had to summon my assistance. I helped him to his feet and into his overcoat, handed him his two sticks, opened the door and propelled him into the corridor. I was quite prepared to take him to the lift, but he brushed my assistance aside.

"Perfectly all right now, old man," he said. "Thanks very much. See you tomorrow. Cheerio."

This performance went on practically every morning for many months in an absolutely identical manner except that some mornings he did *The Times* crossword more quickly than others. I never got to know him very well because his hearing aid was almost permanently out of commission and without it conversation was impossible. He was obviously a very erudite man and perhaps at some stage in his career he had done some writing. But I never saw him do any while he shared an office with me. Eventually he started coming in less regularly and then almost imperceptibly faded out altogether and I never saw him again. I have often wondered what happened to him.

His successor in what I now called my office was a very large, bucolic, ungainly man with rubicund features and a square jaw who rejoiced in the name of Richard Joy. He came from York every day—he was an old boy of St Peters—and had been on the reporting staff for some time. He informed me that he had just been appointed agricultural correspondent.

"I didn't know you were a farming expert," I said.

"I'm not", he replied. "But I'm told I look like one and I

have a bit of land up at Hebden so they've given me the job. I expect I can learn something about agriculture fairly easily."

He had obviously a long way to go because later that morning he looked up from a Ministry of Agriculture document he was studying with a furrowed brow and asked me if I knew what on earth an Aberdeen Angus was. I replied that I believed it was a brand of cow and he roared with laughter, thinking I was joking.

But although the method of his selection was somewhat eccentric he was a hard worker and turned out to be a very good agricultural correspondent and as, with the addition of a rakish hat and a rural stick, there was no agricultural correspondent in the country who looked more like an agricultural correspondent than he did, he proved to be an excellent ambassador for the paper wherever he went. He kept the job until his untimely death some few years later.

Joe Illingworth and other household names

I actually joined the *Yorkshire Post* as a sub-editor, a title which does not designate the editor's right-hand man as some people unversed in newspaper practice believe. There were fifteen or so sub-editors on the *Yorkshire Post* and their job was to prepare for the printers the "copy" which came to them from the staff reporters and correspondents—chiefly the correspondents! That is to say they had to correct any factual, grammatical or other errors, polish up the style of the prose, prune it of superfluities, make it snappy and easily readable, put a heading on it in a size of type designated by the chief sub-editor and watch its progress through the printing processes until it came back to them in the form of a galley proof. It was in the subs' room that most of the work was done on the *Yorkshire Post* and perhaps for that reason the sub-editors' view of the reporters was that they were useless parasites. Even when they did exert themselves enough to write anything their copy, they said, had to be virtually re-written before it was fit to go into the paper.

This was certainly true of some of the reporters as I very soon discovered. There was one, based at Bradford, who became my despair, and I discovered that it was only because he had broken everyone else's heart in the subs' room that his copy was coming to me. He had the reputation of being a very good shorthand writer and this he may well have been. But he had no idea of space and no idea of grammar. He never wrote less than a column on anything and there was never a full stop on the first two or three pages. As the chief sub-editor would usually mark the copy "two sticks"—which was the equivalent of about a quarter of a column—subbing it down to size was a perplexing task and if there was more than one story from him in your basket when you sat down at your desk at 6 pm the night was ruined.

The chief sub-editor, John Buxton, was one of the nicest men who ever breathed but he was bullied a bit by his deputy, a more forceful character called Joe Turner, who combined sub-editing by night on the *Yorkshire Post* with his practice as a barrister by day on the northern circuit.

Buxton was a very capable chief sub, so far as putting the paper together was concerned, but was too reticent and self-effacing to be an effective departmental head. He loathed asserting himself about anything and although he would invariably agree one hundred per cent with anybody who pointed out any defects about the organization he would never attempt to do anything about them. The result was that many of the staff nursed trivial grouses about one thing or another and vented them at Powolny's bar during the evening break.

People joined the staff and left it with great frequency and although I made a number of good friends in people like Bill Taylor, the commercial sub-editor, who later moved to the *Guardian* and became night editor, and Michael Hardy, who subsequently occupied a similar post at *The Times*, I did not find the atmosphere very congenial and soon decided that the subs' room was not for me. Consequently when I heard that one of the few young reporters, Arthur Brittenden, (later to become editor of the *Daily Mail*) was wanting to swop places with a young sub-editor on medical grounds I put my name forward as a volunteer and was duly selected, there being no other volunteers!

I concluded when I got into the reporters' room that the geriatric atmosphere had driven Brittenden to distraction but whether this was the case I never discovered.

One of my last jobs in the subs' room was to deal with the

copy of the paper's chief feature writer, Joe Illingworth, who was telephoning graphic accounts every night of the floods in Selby, which were by far the worst the area had ever experienced and were capturing the headlines in the national papers.

Joe Illingworth had been a household name in Yorkshire for a good many years through his writing in the *Leeds Mercury* and after that paper's merger with the *Yorkshire Post* on the outbreak of the Second World War in 1939 he proceeded to establish a considerable reputation for himself as a war correspondent.

There was a distinctive Yorkshire flavour about his writing which appealed to me very strongly and he combined a brilliant descriptive talent with a keen ear for Yorkshire dialogue and a sparkling sense of humour. When I started writing special articles myself Joe Illingworth was unknowingly my tutor, and later became my friend. He was a modest, diffident man who spent his early years in journalism in Bradford and had all the Yorkshire characteristics of that city. He was reliable, dependable, and without a trace of flamboyance or affectation or what J B Priestley would call la-di-da. Joe was as down to earth as Bradford wool exchange and as solid as Bradford town hall. We had many a game of golf together on the various Leeds courses and his generous praise for my early work was a tremendous encouragement to me. I was saddened to read of his death quite recently.

I succeeded him as chief feature writer in Leeds when he became London editor and one of the assignments on which I look back with particular pride was sharing with him the coverage of the present Queen's coronation in 1953. We both wrote descriptive pieces—he on the scene in the Abbey and I on the events in the streets—and a letter appeared in the *Yorkshire Post* the following day from a Miss M Johnson of Mowbray Square, Harrogate, which read "Sir, Congratulations on the magnificent June 3rd issue of the dear old *Yorkshire Post* with its superb photographs and delightful articles by those two brilliant journalists Joe Illingworth and Derrick Boothroyd. There is no paper in the world like the *Yorkshire Post*—so dignified and attractive. I have known it all my life of nearly sixty-eight years." To be linked in print like this with Joe Illingworth was a distinction indeed for I shall always believe he was one of the very best writers the *Yorkshire Post* has ever had—and it has had quite a number.

There were, of course, a number of writers on the *Yorkshire Post* in those days who were household names in Yorkshire but most of them were sports writers—J M Kilburn on cricket, Ian Guild on golf, the Duke (alias John Wyatt) on racing, Richard Ulyatt on soccer and Alfie Drewry on Rugby League. Joyce Mather had a big following as a women's writer, W L Oliver was well known in the art world and Ernest Bradbury was just beginning to build up the big reputation he now holds as music critic.

Although cricket was my first love in the sporting field I knew Kilburn less well than any of the others. His handsome, graven image-like face was a very familiar fixture in the press boxes at Headingley, Park Avenue or Bramall Lane and I had a very high regard for the quality of his writing. It had a literary distinction unrivalled by any cricket journalist I had read, except, of course, for Neville Cardus who had a gift which Kilburn in my opinion lacked—a keen sense of humour. He was always pleasant enough when I met him but he always struck me as detached and rather unapproachable and I was never able to establish any relationship with him.

Of course, it may have been my fault because he had every reason for regarding me as an interloper in his territory. In my feature writing days I was always expected to do an article about the big occasions in the cricket world in Yorkshire—such as test matches at Headingley and Roses matches at Bramall Lane—and often my brief was to write humorous human stories about men in the crowd rummaging in gargantuan picnic baskets and tussling with large pork pies or making uninformed comments on the game to their neighbours and even barracking any batsman who did not score quick runs.

To a cricket purist like Kilburn this sort of thing must have represented journalism in its basest form and I can well understand why he was never a contributor to my fan mail! Cricket to him was not an entertainment for the masses; it was an esoteric art for the sensitive few, and I don't think he included me in that category. He probably thought I didn't know the difference between a late cut and a leg glance, and wondered why the *Yorkshire Post* tolerated such hooliganism in print.

Although Kilburn was a fine writer on cricket—he has written a number of excellent books—he was not a great news reporter and had not on his own admission had any journalistic training whatever. He also strongly deprecated the modern vogue of writing about the personalities and off the field controversies of cricket rather than about the performance of the players and the strategy and tactics on the field. He did not have a keen news sense—and even if he had done, would have been reluctant to use it on what he considered to be trivial issues. I know he was often the despair of the sports editor who would get the usual column of impeccable prose from the match he was reporting but not a word about the story hitting the headlines in the evening papers concerning a leading player having a fight with a spectator outside the dressing room or a committee meeting being held behind closed doors to consider sacking the Yorkshire captain! Kilburn would sometimes be pursued by telephone to give his version of the incident but if he condescended to do so it was usually short and to the point!

Ian Guild had to my mind the pleasantest job on the paper—for whereas cricket only lasted through the summer, golf went on all the year round. He, too, was a very able writer and had a very warm, breezy personality which made him a popular figure wherever he went. John Wyatt, who was sports editor as well as racing correspondent (until replaced in the latter position by his son, Jack), was a dour, hard working, kindly man whom I would have liked to have known better. I knew his son well because he was a contemporary of mine and, together with Alfie Drewry, played cricket with me in the *Yorkshire Post* team. I also knew Dick Ulyatt and have no doubt he made a very able successor to John Wyatt when the latter unfortunately died fairly young.

In the sports team there was also Eric Stanger writing on association football. Eric was in the beginning in the reporters' room and in that capacity once came out with a comment on sub-editors which every reporter in the world will echo. Stanger, now also alas dead, was a thick-set man with black, curly hair, a square jaw and a very aggressive manner, and when he got annoyed the sparks flew. He came bounding into the reporters' room late one night very annoyed indeed, with a galley proof in his hand of a news story to the writing of which he had devoted the whole evening, and of which he was justifiably proud. It had been hacked by the sub-editors, as is the sub-editors' wont, and he came in almost dithering with rage. "Look at this", he cried, throwing his masterpiece on the reporters' room table. "Just look at it! Those bastards would sub Shakespeare!"

Joyce Mather, at that time the sole woman on the editorial staff and therefore women's editor, women's fashion writer and woman reporter all rolled into one, was a brilliant journalist in every sense. She had only one failing and that is common to every woman reporter I have ever come across—she was a rotten speller! I don't know why it is that women journalists cannot spell but they very rarely can. Joyce, however, could do everything else very well indeed. She had been for years on the *Leeds Mercury* and married the chief sub-editor, a man called Schofield who died tragically at an early age and left her a young widow. She was an attractive woman and why she never married again I don't know. Perhaps it was because of her own health which was not of the best. She suffered from recurring asthma and died in middle age.

Some women journalists can write effectively only on feminine topics. Joyce could write on feminine topics as well as anyone but in addition she was a first class reporter on any subject and could leave many of the men standing. She specialized on the Yorkshire social scene and had an encyclopaedic knowledge of the Yorkshire aristocracy and the county families which was of immense value to the *Yorkshire Post*.

She was an automatic choice for reporting the fashionable race meetings and other big social occasions and would come back from Doncaster, York, Thirsk or Wetherby with a notebook stuffed with information about the dukes and the duchesses, the earls and the countesses and the lords and the ladies she had encountered. She would describe in vivid detail not only what the ladies were wearing but which of their children they had with them, which schools they were at or which young men they were expected to be getting engaged to. It was always beautifully written and highly entertaining and, unlike many gossip writers, she always succeeded in remaining on the best of terms with the eminent people she wrote about. There have been women writers on the *Yorkshire Post* who went a good deal further up the journalistic ladder than Joyce Mather—such as Jean Rook who is currently reputed to be the highest paid woman in Fleet Street, to mention only one—but I don't think there have been any who could compare with her as a writer on the Yorkshire scene. She was a very cheerful and friendly person and had the affection of all who worked with her.

I have mentioned Jean Rook as one of the *Yorkshire Post* people in my time who got to the top of the journalistic tree but there were a number of others. Derek Marks, for a number of years editor of the *Daily Express*, came into the reporters' room on his return from a job in Africa and exhibited the hearty good fellowship and generosity of spirit which made him very popular in Fleet Street. He was not considered to be any great shakes as a journalist in Leeds but his remarkable talent for getting to know things from people without them being aware they had told him had no scope in Leeds as it had later in the House of Commons when he became political correspondent of the *Express*. Marks was a big, blundering fellow with a bucolic air about him which made one think of the Sussex downs. He had rare qualities of courage which were praised by many leading politicians at a memorial service held for him in London after his losing battle with cancer which ended at the early age of fifty.

Another budding national newspaper editor I have already referred to was Arthur Brittenden, editor for some years of the *Daily Mail*. Brittenden was a Leeds man but gave little indication of it either in his dress or his manner. He wore bow ties, spoke more like a BBC announcer than a dyed-in-the-wool Yorkshireman and had just a little bit of la-di-da. But in spite of these deficiencies—and in Leeds they were indeed deficiencies—he was always very affable and engaging and unknowingly did me a great service by enabling me to escape from the sub-editors' room. Like me, Brittenden was by instinct a reporter rather than a sub-editor. He had, indeed, a very highly developed news sense and also like me was one of the people Joe Illingworth took under his wing and gave the benefit of his experience. Brittenden did not stay long at Leeds and when he left to go to the *News Chronicle* he celebrated his departure in a typically flamboyant manner by throwing what was probably the biggest and wildest party ever seen in Hyde Park—Hyde Park, Leeds, that is! He and I always intended to meet again while we were both working in London—he in Fleet Street and I in the City—but somehow we never got round to it.

Another *Yorkshire Post* colleague and friend who has gone far is Ian Trethowan, who was political correspondent (or lobby correspondent as they were then known) of the *Yorkshire Post* in the early fifties. Ian, who is now managing director of BBC Television, was always based in London but I came to know him very well because we worked closely together covering the political party conferences and other big political events—Ian covering the serious business of the occasion and I producing the light relief.

In a way my contact with him in politics might be compared to my contact with Kilburn in cricket, but Ian was no political purist and much appreciated my descriptive sketches of the conferences.

No doubt through expert use of his natural charm in the right quarters Ian had a remarkable ability for unearthing cabinet or party secrets and it was a constant source of amusement to me at Scarborough and Blackpool conferences to learn that a secret session of the party leaders was to be held to discuss some controversial topic. The meeting would be held in the afternoon behind sealed doors and at dinner that night Ian would give me an account of the proceedings which could not have been more detailed if he had been hiding under the table. "Of course I shall have to be careful what I say in the *Yorkshire Post* tomorrow but I think I can give a broad outline of what went on without revealing my contacts" he said. He never revealed his contacts—even to me.

There were other budding celebrities in the *Yorkshire Post* offices in those days, as I am reminded practically every night when I see Peter Woods reading the BBC television news. He was at our York office but we saw him fairly regularly in Leeds. Another budding celebrity was attached to the *Evening Post*, Keith Waterhouse, who has achieved fame both as an author and as a playwright (Billy Liar and other works), and as a *Daily Mirror* columnist.

Although the two papers shared offices in Albion Street they were quite separate from one another and were poles apart in character and personality. The *Yorkshire Post* establishment regarded the *Evening Post* as a brash and rather vulgar publication staffed by journalists who might be quite able but were definitely not out of the top drawer. The *Evening Post* establishment regarded the *Yorkshire Post* as an antique white elephant staffed by stuffed-shirted old men and kept going by *Evening Post* profits.

It was certainly true that the *Evening Post* made the profits and the *Yorkshire Post* made the losses, but it was also true that the *Evening Post* did some very brash things—things which were so out of character with the *Yorkshire Post* set-up that it seemed inconceivable that the two papers had the same owners and the same board of management.

Perhaps the oddest thing that was ever done on the *Evening Post* was the appointment of Barry Horniblow as editor in the 1950s. Recently editor of the *Daily Mail* and one of Fleet Street's whizziest kids, Barry Horniblow hit the quiet labyrinth of offices in Albion Street like an atomic bomb. He employed Fleet Street hire and fire tactics as ruthlessly as they had ever been employed at the *Daily Express* or the *Daily Mirror* and created a state of pandemonium which left Albion Street breathless. Something like forty journalists were fired in his first twelve months and the whole paper was turned upside down and inside out and every other way it was possible to turn it. The directors got rid of him in the end with what was reputed to be a large golden handshake but not before he had made an imperishable reputation for himself and stirred up the *Evening Post* in a way which will never be forgotten. He was succeeded by one of the few *Evening Post* men who had survived the holocaust, the mild and amiable Alan Woodward who restored sanity to the office very quickly.

The *Evening Post* had some very talented writers in those days and I particularly remember Con Gordon whose sketches on the police courts in Leeds were quite brilliant. Others who made reputations for themselves in various sections of the paper were John Bolton, Edgar Craven, Ewart Clay (who succeeded Woodward as editor), Eric Hillas, Alfred Taylor and Ronald Wilkinson. All would probably have reached the top in Fleet Street if they had not chosen to stay in Leeds. And who could say they were wrong in that choice?

The *Yorkshire Post* staff, as I have indicated, took life at a much more leisurely pace than the *Evening Post* and what would have happened if a Barry Horniblow had been let loose in the *Yorkshire Post* is a nightmarish speculation. Frank Snape, the news editor, and Graham Walton, the chief reporter, would certainly have jumped straight out of the nearest window in despair, and Walter Stone and Henry Swale would no doubt have followed them. They were all past the stage of learning new tricks and, in any case, saw nothing wrong with the old ones. They may not have set the Thames on fire, or even the Leeds and Liverpool Canal, but they were delightful fellows to work with.

Frank Snape as news editor was my immediate boss for most of the time I worked at the *Yorkshire Post* and a kinder, more considerate boss it would have been hard to find. One always felt, however, that his main interests were at Sandmoor golf club and his Masonic lodge and he had a host of friends in Leeds who mourned his early death. Snape was popular with all the reporters because of his easygoing ways and had a reputation for signing expenses without even looking at them—a quality of tremendous appeal to all newspapermen! Once for a bet, a reporter who shall be nameless put down on his expenses the item "to taxi up office stairs, 7s 6d." Snape passed it but it was queried in the accounts department—or possibly caught by the eagle eye of the general manager, the inimitable Ernest Osborn. Osborn, in whom most executive power was vested in those days, was very diminutive in stature—I wouldn't think he was any more than four feet eight inches tall—but very shrewd in management.

Graham Walton was also an old dear, although obviously more interested in his cottage at East Keswick than in anything that happened in Leeds. How Walton and the other two senior men, Walter Stone and Henry Swale, came to be reporters in the first place I shall never know. They were completely at odds with the popular conception of reporters and with their sober and dignified bearing, quiet charm and old world courtesy, would have been more appropriately located on the aldermanic benches of some rural county council. They believed newspapers existed to report the facts—and only the facts—on matters of public concern. They had no time for the embroideries of modern journalism—the so-called human stories. They regarded them as chaff for the tabloids and looked upon scoops and all concessions to sensationalism as slightly obscene.

Of the younger reporters Ted Crossley was the most senior and had the title of night news editor, which meant that he was monarch of all he surveyed in Albion Street after 6 o'clock at night. Ted had been an officer in the Royal Marines during the war and was an odd combination of military efficiency and rigid disciplinarianism on the one hand and easy going journalistic tolerance on the other. He believed in journalists doing precisely what their editors instructed them to do, on the principle of theirs not to reason why, theirs but to do or die. "I know it's bloody lunatic", he would bellow as one argued with him (as reporters do) on the merits of a certain line of enquiry. "I agree with you one hundred per cent that it's bloody lunatic. But the editor has asked for it so we will bloody well have to get it . . . but let's go and have a pint at Whitelock's to start with."

Ted was a competent reporter and a very sound administrator but it was a surprise to many when he was appointed editor of the *Yorkshire Post* in succession to Kenneth Young in 1965.

Perhaps it was a case of the board being afraid of appointing another editor from Fleet Street as the *Evening Post* had done so disastrously with Horniblow and the *Yorkshire Post* had done none too successfully with Young—who had held the post for less than four years after succeeding Sir Linton Andrews.

Young was highly talented in literary and dramatic criticism and came to Leeds from the *Daily Mail* and the *Daily Telegraph* with impeccable credentials. He was no Horniblow but apparently he was not too happy at the *Yorkshire Post* and left to join Beaverbrook Newspapers as political and literary adviser. He has distinguished himself as an author, particularly as a biographer, and has a number of successes to his name, including an impressive volume on A J Balfour.

Soon after he was appointed editor he invited me to have lunch with him at the Leeds Club to discuss the possibility of contributing some articles (I had left the staff some years previously). He gave me an excellent lunch, much urbane and literary conversation and so many brandies that when we parted company at about 3 30 pm it was not until I got rather groggily to the bottom of Albion Street that I realized the subject of writing some articles had never been discussed. I rang him later and did a few pieces but I don't think my style of writing was quite literary enough for him. But I shall long remember that lunch!

Ted Crossley was a very different character, completely lacking Young's urbanity and social graces, and I imagine one of the hardest jobs he ever had to do during his editorship was to preside at the *Yorkshire Post* literary lunches which Young had initiated. He must have been quite out of his depth. But Ted was the sort of chap one felt instinctive affection for and there was widespread sorrow when he collapsed and died on a visit to London only four years after his appointment, his successor being the present editor, John Edwards.

Other seniors in the reporting room were Norman Bugge, Ernest Stott, Bob Greenwood and Fred Knowlson, the latter two, alas, also having died comparatively young. Bugge, a tall, dark and handsome bachelor whom the office girls raved over, combined general reporting with the jobs of motoring correspondent and lawn tennis correspondent which he wrote under the name of Norman Harnett. But his chief distinction to me was not his undoubted ability as a writer but as a cricketer. He was the opening bat for the *Yorkshire Post* first eleven and scored a graceful fifty practically every time he went in.

His opening partner in the *Yorkshire Post* first eleven, Ernest Stott, was the late night reporter and he was much better qualified as a batsman than as a writer. He was small and tubby with short legs and rolled rather than walked. He had a wonderful sense of humour in his conversation and was a born raconteur but by a strange quirk of fate was unable to be in the least funny on paper. His grim nightly task was to patrol the police stations, fire stations, ambulance headquarters, hospitals, and other emergency centres of Leeds from about 10 pm until about 2 am and collect news stories of the night's happenings.

And weird and macabre some of them were. He would keep us entertained for hours with uproariously funny descriptions of his activities and the drop-outs with whom he came into contact. If only he could have written of them as he talked of them he would have been the best writer on the paper. I chuckle still as I recall his story of the man who was taken to the infirmary in a fire engine suffering from being inextricably stuck in a lavatory seat.

In addition to his late night patrols he acted as the paper's air correspondent and was equally funny about his experiences in this sphere, although the funniest thing of all in his adventures as air correspondent was when he was lowered by a rope from a helicopter at Yeadon airport during some air gala. As he drifted down his braces burst with the strain and his trousers hit the ground some two or three minutes before he did.

The chief character in the sub-editors' room was undoubtedly George Stoney, a cultured Bradfordian who combined tremendous speed and efficiency as a splash sub—that is to say he handled among others the main story on the front page—with a very extensive knowledge of literature and an even more extensive repertoire of droll stories.

When a big news story breaks very late at night—a Reuter message to the effect that a war has broken out in the Middle East or a Press Association message to say the Government has been defeated in the House of Commons—it is panic stations for the sub-editors, and particularly for the splash sub. The story comes in to him in dribs and drabs from the teleprinters in the wire room and he has to sort it all out, get it into the correct sequence, write a gripping introduction, fit in all the late additions in the right order, make the finished text run smoothly in grammatical English, put striking headlines on it with the right number of letters to fit the selected type and see that it runs to the required length. Stoney did this night after night with unruffled calm, assisted by other senior subs such as the equally imperturbable Henry Heaton and Arthur Gownes and directed by perhaps the even more imperturbable chief-sub, John Buxton. Imperturbability in a crisis is an essential quality of a good sub-editor for the crises come with great frequency. Most journalists will agree that it is the sub-editors who make any paper and this was certainly true of the *Yorkshire Post*.

Not that the leader writers and feature writers, whom I have not yet mentioned, were unimportant. The great discipline about writing for a daily newspaper is the clock. Time waits for no man—and least of all for leader writers. It is never easy to write a crisp, strongly worded leader on some complicated and possibly highly specialized technical subject but it is a good deal easier when you have an hour or two in hand to research the subject in the library, get all the clippings out and prepare your words of wisdom in the quiet of the early evening. It is an entirely different matter turning out a similar leader working against the clock, with the edition going irrevocably to press say in three-quarters of an hour. The *Yorkshire Post* was well served with people for both eventualities.

The leader writing team was led by W L (Bill) Oliver, chief

assistant editor and included at various times Cyril Dunn, Bill Johnston, H M Raleigh, "Trapper" Yates and Andrew Weir. They were housed like moles in a room at the bottom of the staircase leading from the subs' room to the editor's room and had a separate isolated existence from all those on the top corridor. To the newcomers to the subs' and reporters' rooms the leader writers were as mysterious as the Mafia, if not perhaps as menacing. They beavered away all night in their cubby hole producing the comment and literary content of the paper and only came out into the light at the editorial conference each evening.

Oliver, who in addition to writing cogent leaders wrote (and still writes) authoritatively on art and books, was undoubtedly the most cultivated man on the whole editorial staff. He was also undoubtedly the nicest person on the whole paper. With his lean frame and his ascetic, rather cadaverous appearance he looked more like an Oxford don than a journalist and he would probably have been more at home in the reflective academic world than in the madly spinning journalistic orbit. If any one man could be said to carry the *Yorkshire Post* it was Bill Oliver. He was the editor's right-hand man all the time I was on the paper and a more loyal, able, conscientious and hard-working assistant no editor ever had. If there had been any justice in the world he would have succeeded Andrews as editor when he finally retired and it was understood that he long nursed that ambition. Perhaps he was considered to be not a forceful enough personality to be editor; perhaps he was just too nice; he did not get the job. He gave me much encouragement in my early years and the dozens of notes I got from him, scribbled late at night in between turning out vigorous leaders against the clock, congratulating me on the article I had written for that morning's paper, are still among my souvenirs.

I did not get to know Cyril Dunn very well because he left to join the *Observer* and become one of that distinguished paper's leading writers. He wrote leaders and also deputized for H M Raleigh who was in charge of the Northerner Two column, entitled then as now "This World of Ours". Raleigh was a stiff, rather pompous man with a most laborious sense of humour who, I believe, had been a professional army officer and he passed you in the corridor rather as though you were a bad smell. "This World of Ours" had none of the wit and whimsicality which it acquired later under the illustrious pen of the present incumbent of the Northerner Two position, Andy Weir, and most of us regarded it as a dead loss. One of its most tedious characters was Raleigh's dog, which had a name I can't remember—it may have been Nipper—and which made laborious entries into the column practically every day. Cyril Dunn must have been as sick of that damned dog as everyone else and on one of the nights when Raleigh was off duty and Dunn was deputizing for him, he wrote a heart-rending note describing the dog's death in a car accident. Raleigh never forgave him and left the staff not very long afterwards—presumably to inflict his dog on other readers.

No account of the *Yorkshire Post* personalities during this post-war period would be complete without reference to the photographer royal of Albion Street, Charlie Bowry. The photographic staff were the only people on the editorial side who served both the *Yorkshire Post* and the *Evening Post* and as they got around Yorkshire more than any other members of the staff they were in one sense the paper's leading ambassadors.

Charlie Bowry worked from Albion Street for thirty years and was probably the best-known newspaper figure in the north of England. Not everyone knew him by name—for photographers did not have by-lines in those days—but countless thousands knew him by sight. With his round, red face, his portly frame and his infinite if sometimes exasperating capacity for taking pains he was a character indeed. Some said he was the original of J B Priestley's newspaper photographer in *When We Are Married* but Charlie would only have been in his youth when that inimitable play was written.

He would turn up at a function—usually at the last minute—looking more like a country squire than a photographer and he would insist on holding up and if necessary reorganizing the whole proceedings whilst he meticulously set up his equipment, punctiliously paced out his distance and got exactly the picture he wanted. But if his approach caused exasperation his craftsmanship evoked keen admiration and among his many letters of appreciation was one from Buckingham Palace.

It is not every famous personality who jumps for joy at the sight of a press photographer and Charlie infuriated Sir Thomas Beecham on one occasion at a concert at Leeds town hall. He crept down the centre aisle like a hired assassin and took a picture of the orchestra while it was playing pianissimo. Unfortunately his flash bulb exploded violently and showered the unsuspecting conductor with glass. Sir Thomas almost tore his hair but Charlie succeeded in soothing him down by sheer force of character and whenever Sir Thomas posed for photographs in Leeds subsequently he always asked after him.

Sir Malcolm Campbell was another of his famous admirers. One day at Coniston where Sir Malcolm was making an attempt on the speedboat record Charlie was one of the scores of photographers waiting to snap him. Sir Malcolm posed patiently for twenty minutes. When they had all finished he prepared to get into the boat. At that point Charlie stepped forward. "Now all these photographers have finished with you, Sir Malcolm, I would like to take a proper picture of you—and I would like you over here . . ." On later visits to Coniston Sir Malcolm would always say he could not consider starting until Charlie had finished with him.

He spared no effort to get a picture and in the winter often struggled through six-foot snowdrifts on Standedge Moors to get an exclusive shot of a line of snowbound vehicles—for one of which he won a prize of a hundred guineas. His zeal landed him in all sorts of trouble. Once in a military display at Catterick he stayed crouching in the path of the march past just a second too long and got hopelessly mixed up with the band. There were bugles to the right of him, drums to the left of him and trombones all over him. The General taking the salute was not at all amused.

I went out with Charlie Bowry on many a story and it was always an entertainment. My last memory of him is returning with him late one night to the *Yorkshire Post* office in the rather broken down old Ford car he possessed. Albion Street at that time of night was populated by the professional ladies of Leeds (this was long before the ban on soliciting) and as we drew up outside the archway entrance one of them knocked at the car window and invited Charlie to sample her wares. "Nay lass, I'm afraid I'm too old for you," he said. "I'm like this old Ford—I need starting by hand and even then I can't keep my bloody engine going." He died not very long afterwards aged 67.

W L Andrews

From the photographer royal I have only to go to the king himself—Sir Linton Andrews or WLA as he was known to his staff and the legions of readers of his personal column "It Seems To Me". William Linton Andrews was a Hull man and came to the *Yorkshire Post* via Fleet Street and the *Leeds Mercury*, of which he became editor in 1923. He succeeded Arthur Mann as editor of the *Yorkshire Post* on the amalgamation with the *Leeds Mercury* in November 1939. He stayed as editor until his retirement in 1960, when, in recognition of his services to the paper, he was given the title of Editor Emeritus. He was for many years a prominent figure in the journalistic world and was chairman of the Press Council from 1955 to 1959.

I owe much to Andrews because it was he who printed my first article in the *Yorkshire Post*, he who picked me out as a descriptive writer and he who gave me the opportunity to make a name for myself on the paper and write hundreds of articles for it under my own name.

The first article of mine he printed was early in the war when Bert Boshell, the dispatch manager of the *Yorkshire Post* and a family friend, showed him a letter I had written home whilst serving in the Merchant Navy. I was in the Persian Gulf at the time and described a visit to the reputed site of the Garden of Eden at the junction of the Tigris and Euphrates rivers. It appeared as a leader page article in the *Yorkshire Post* under the heading "Paradise Lost—a pilgrimage of disillusion to the Garden of Eden" and had my name in large capital letters. I wrote several other articles from distant parts of the world for both the *Yorkshire Post* and the *Evening Post* under such colourful headings as "Film or crocodile as cinema choice" and "Fifteen hundred goats sacrificed to the Goddess Kali" and they no doubt helped to get me a job on the paper after the war.

But as I have said I started on the *Yorkshire Post* as a sub-editor and did not make any impact whatever until I changed places with Arthur Brittenden and went into the reporters' room. Andrews must have observed some descriptive talent in my work—although it seemed pretty mundane to me—and called me down to his room one night. "You wrote quite an amusing piece on the Batley by-election this morning," he said. "I see there's what they call an all-star wrestling match at

Leeds town hall tonight. Why not go along and do a light piece on it?"

I stared at him in bewilderment. I could not have been more surprised if he had asked me to try my hand at pornography.

"An all-star wrestling match, Mr Andrews?" I said doubtfully.

"Yes, why not? We could do with a bit of light relief in the paper."

So to Leeds town hall I went, returning to the office two hours later and writing my light story. "A thousand people howled with derision and a woman shouted 'Go home to your mother' at Leeds town hall last night as the eighteen-stone giant Anaconda, billed as the Swedish Scissors King, hopped round the ring in apparent agony, gripping his ears between his fingers and grimacing fiercely at the referee. He was opposing Hooker Rawlings of Dewsbury in an all-star wrestling contest and he alleged by his fluent gestures that Rawlings had pulled his ears. And ear pulling, like gouging, scratching, biting and hair plucking, is not allowed in all-star wrestling, described to me as a refined version of the old all-in style.

"You may twist the limbs of your opponent until he screams and bites the mat and you may throw him about the ring until the boards threaten to cave in. You may even kick him in the teeth provided it is a drop kick with the flat of the foot and not the toes.

"The referee, a brave man, was unimpressed by the giant's protests and ordered the fight to continue. The giant didn't like it and, whether by accident or design, the referee was soon pinned in a corner against the ropes and forced to make an ignominious escape through two pairs of legs. But Hooker Rawlings was the real object of the giant's wrath. He was made to suffer mightily for his auricular indiscretion. He was smashed to the ground until his bones shook and had his ankles twisted until they seemed to crack and, finally, in a sea of arms and legs, he had to submit. The giant marched proudly from the ring. 'Go home to my mother indeed' he seemed to murmur."

I went on to state that these all-star wrestling contests were held at Leeds town hall every fortnight and attracted crowds of supporters from all over the West Riding. "Most of them seem to come for entertainment and the woman next to me said she always preferred it to the Empire. 'You get such a variety of groans', she added. I asked her if she thought all-star wrestling a cruel sport. 'Well,' she replied, 'the object of boxing is to knock the other fellow out. The object of all-star wrestling is merely to pin him to the mat. It doesn't hurt half as much'."

I finished my story with the feeling that it would be quite good for the *Evening Post* but was hardly the *Yorkshire Post*'s cup of tea and took it into the sub-editors' room and put it discreetly in the chief sub-editor's tray. I went and had supper in the canteen and returned to the subs' room in search of a proof of my masterpiece a little later on. But I couldn't find one. The chief sub-editor was busy superintending the make-up of pages in the case room so I went over to his desk to see if by any chance the story had not yet been through his hands. It had. It was on his spike!

Furious I took it off the spike and went down to the editor's room. Andrews was busy reading masses of proofs and looked up distractedly.

"I went to the wrestling match at Leeds town hall" I said.

"Wrestling match? Which wrestling match?"

"The one you told me to do a light piece on. Here it is. I have just taken it off the chief sub's spike."

Andrews took it from me. "I quite forgot to warn him about this" he said, beginning to read the article. I waited for him to laugh but there was no sign—no indication whatever whether he liked the article or thought it was complete tripe. When he looked up at me without even a smile I concluded it must be tripe.

"Very good", he said. "Very funny. You must write some more like this."

He took up his pen and wrote a heading across the top of the page "Grins and groans at all-star wrestling".

"How do you spell your first name?" he asked.

I told him.

He wrote "By Derrick Boothroyd" on the copy and handed it back to me. "Give it to the chief sub, will you?" He paused. "But no. On reflection perhaps it would be better if I gave it him myself."

It appeared on the back page next morning and was my first by-line. My only regret about it was that I might have made things a little awkward for the chief sub, John Buxton, for whom I had the highest regard. I mentioned it to him later but he was not at all put out. "If I'd known the editor had asked for it I would have sent it out for setting" he explained. "We just thought you'd gone mad."

I often wondered why Andrews liked my light articles so much because he did not strike me—or indeed many people—as a man with a particularly keen sense of humour. He was rather large and ponderous in size and his manner could be described in the same words. He was, of course, an extremely able man and many more renowned judges than I have described him as a brilliant journalist—an opinion I would fully subscribe to. But he did not strike one as having a very agile mind and although he was a most prolific writer with an acute sense of observation, a mellow descriptive talent and an unfailingly keen news sense he was not a very stylish writer. He could be forceful but he tended at times to pontificate and had little of the light touch which he liked so much in my writing.

He was above all a very quick and fluent writer and long years of practice had enabled him to write with the very minimum of correction. He was one of the few journalists I have ever come across who could dictate a thoughtful leading article on a complicated subject with scarcely ever the need to correct a word. He would dictate articles to his secretary walking up and down the room and when she had typed them for him he would send them out as they were written. This is a tremendous accomplishment as any journalist who has written page after page on his typewriter and thrown them into the waste paper basket will tell you.

Although Andrews was respected by most of his staff it would not be true to say that he was loved. He was a shy, reticent, somewhat aloof man by nature and was not a born mixer although he may have appeared to contradict this by the eagerness he showed for public life and the great gratification he undoubtedly got from his knighthood. Journalists being journalists were quick to observe his liking for the limelight and there was speculation for years as to when he would become Sir Linton, just as there was similar speculation on when he would get his honorary degree at Leeds University. Leeds University was an institution he was very devoted to and all aspects of the University received very adequate coverage in the *Yorkshire Post.* The cynics said the prospect of an honorary degree was the only reason for this devotion but he had a genuine interest in the academic world and was always anxious to help and encourage young people.

Another of the organizations he patronized with great enthusiasm and much coverage in the *Yorkshire Post* was the Brontë Society. He always enjoyed mixing with the literary celebrities of Yorkshire, such as Phyllis Bentley and Lettice Cooper, and often spoke to gatherings of bookmen. He would sing the praises of Yorkshire authors on these occasions but his words were not always from the heart. I remember talking to him at the office late one night about the latest novel of one author on which he had written a most flowery review that morning. I said I intended to read the book. "I shouldn't bother if I were you", he said. "Just solid Yorkshire pudding." I was quite horrified!

Andrews did a lot of public speaking but although he had great charm and dignity on the platform, and was an excellent ambassador for the paper in any circle, he was not a very effective public speaker and sometimes became boring. The president of a Yorkshire Chamber of Commerce who was a friend of mine once asked me if I would use my influence to get Sir Linton as he then was to be the chief speaker at their centenary dinner. Knowing that they really wanted a man who could entertain them with a few humorous stories I said I didn't think he would be suitable at all but they were insistent and I asked him and he accepted. He spoke for about forty minutes and it was a very polished performance dealing with the industrial problems of the nation. I met the president later in the bar. "You were right", he observed.

As I have said Linton Andrews was somewhat aloof and some members of his staff said he was distant and unapproachable. He did not mix much with the staff and hardly knew some of them. A sub-editor called Evans, who subsequently went to the *Daily Telegraph*, told a very funny story about calling in to see Andrews one night on his way upstairs to the subs' room. He had been on the staff five years and wanted to discuss the question of a rise in salary. He had his hat and coat on and knocked at the editor's door.

"Come in", said Andrews.

Evans entered and Andrews looked up from his proofs.

"Good evening, Mr Andrews", said Evans.

"Good evening", replied Andrews. "Now don't tell me but I think we have met before somewhere . . . "

I remember another occasion when Andrews stopped me on the top corridor after speaking to a reporter at the door of the reporters' room.

"Who was that fellow, Derrick?", he asked me.

"It was . . . " I replied.

"Really" he said. "Has he just joined us?"

"Oh no" I said. "He's been here about five years."

Andrews loved the *Yorkshire Post* and in some ways it was more a home to him than his house at West Park, particularly after the death of his wife. They had no children and the office was his only absorbing interest. He was there literally morning, noon and night. And as he grew older he became increasingly reluctant to retire. Another celebrated Yorkshire journalist, Guy Schofield, who had edited both the London *Evening News* and the *Daily Mail*, was chosen to succeed him and joined the paper as deputy editor so that he could be groomed for the editorship. But time went on and Andrews gave no indication of relinquishing his office. Eventually Schofield became tired of waiting to step into his shoes and stepped out altogether. This, rumour had it, was much to Andrews' relief and it was a good few years later before he finally retired at the age of 75. And even then, in his new role of Editor Emeritus, he spent a good deal of time in Albion Street, retaining the services of his loyal and devoted secretary, Edith Weir, to whom he continued to dictate articles.

Edith Weir, known better to some *Yorkshire Post* men under her maiden name of Edith Fry, was a *Yorkshire Post* institution herself, if such a clumsy description can be applied to such a charming person. Edith became Andrews' secretary when he was editor of the *Leeds Mercury* as a girl in her teens and always recalled the first letter she ever wrote for him which was addressed to the editor of the *Daily Mail*, Carmelite House, Fleet Street, London. Edith in her inexperience addressed it to Carmer Lighthouse, Fleet Street, receiving from her new boss the amused comment "I'm afraid, Miss Fry, that there are no lighthouses in Fleet Street."

Edith, who was a capable writer herself and wrote any number of book reviews and other features for the *Yorkshire*

Post, was married to Alan Weir, a sub-editor on the *Yorkshire Evening News*, and after its closure, on the *Yorkshire Post*, and her brother-in-law, Andy Weir, was Northerner Two. Edith wanted to retire years before Andrews did but he would never let her and when her husband died tragically in middle age she agreed to stay on. She was a source of great companionship and comfort to him in his old age. He died in 1972 aged 86 and when his will was published for over £100 000 it was revealed that he had bequeathed the bulk of his estate to Edith in gratitude for her many years of loyal service. The large amount of his estate caused surprise because editors do not usually become such wealthy men. But he was a shrewd investor on the Stock Exchange and probably made as much money that way as he did from editing the *Yorkshire Post*.

Many tributes have been paid to Linton Andrews and, in view of their previous relationship, perhaps the most generous was that of Guy Schofield, now a director of United Newspapers who own the *Yorkshire Post*. He wrote "Of the many newspaper editors who have been my friends I would say some had more flair and some a more arresting pen but I cannot think of one who combined such a wide intuitive sense of the game with a more fluent way of playing it. He was a courageous editor. He made up his mind and that was that."

I wrote to him from London in 1966 to congratulate him on his eightieth birthday and he replied with a long, hand-written letter in which he wrote "Your memories of our working together delighted me. Like an old headmaster marking the progress of a former star pupil I have followed your career with the friendliest interest and when reading the *Stock Exchange Gazette* I saw you had been appointed its editorial director I felt this was an honour well deserved. The party on May 27th was thrilling. I never expected anything of the sort. Most of the stuff one writes seems to perish like snow in a flood. But thanks to kindly publicity in *The Times*, the *Yorkshire Post* and other papers for which I have worked, several hundreds of readers were prompted to write to me. I simply can't acknowledge the messages individually but I am trying with Edith Weir's indispensable help—she is still my secretary—to write to old colleagues who wrote of my Northcliffe and Albion Street days. . . . Next year I shall have a new experience. I have accepted an offer from Southern Illinois University to be a visiting professor and give a series of lectures. The pay is good and I shall enjoy getting out of the rut."

Leeds by day—and by night

I have long maintained that London is the only fully civilized city in England but as provincial cities go Leeds is not bad—or at least wasn't bad when I worked in it immediately after the war. It was a prosperous, bustling city with a wide spread of industry, a reasonable selection of restaurants, four theatres, numerous cinemas and hardly any one-way streets at all. You could drive a car about Leeds in comfort. You could go where you wanted to go and not only where the authorities want to send you. And this was under the regime of a noted chief constable called Barnett who had the reputation of being the motorist's enemy. Whenever I am misguided enough to take my car into the centre of Leeds these days—or as near the centre as one can get—I always have a desire to put a sticker in my back window saying "Come back Barnett. All is forgiven!"

Leeds in those days was a city I knew well and was very fond of. Its buildings were very Gothic and very black and its shops were, if not altogether Dickensian, certainly a little old fashioned. It was a cosy, friendly city which somehow made you feel at home. Today Leeds has been cleaned up and virtually rebuilt and has more in common with an American city than with the Leeds of the 1950s. It has a vigour and youth and brashness about it which I suppose are very desirable characteristics in the late 1970s but I'm not sure I like it quite as much as I used to.

As a journalist based in Leeds I saw a good deal of the city's life. I saw it at work and I saw it at play. I attended functions at the hotels—chiefly the Queens, the Metropole and what was then the Great Northern—I ate at the restaurants—usually Powolny's, Spinks or the White Horse—and I drifted round the pubs—usually Polly's bar in Bond Street or Whitelock's in Briggate. I went regularly to the theatres—the Grand, the Royal, the Empire and the City Varieties—and frequently to the cinemas. And I wrote about the city's big occasions—

degree day at the University, test matches at Headingley, cup ties at Elland Road, children's day at Roundhay Park, bank holidays at Temple Newsam and the feasts at Hunslet, Holbeck and Woodhouse Moor.

But of all my old haunts in Leeds it is perhaps appropriate that the one which takes indisputable precedence in my mind is the town hall. I spent hundreds of hours in Leeds town hall attending one or other of the tremendous galaxy of diverse functions which were and no doubt still are held in that great building. Where else could you see a high sheriff in black knee breeches and white satin blouse walking down a corridor on his way to an Assize Court followed by a workman in overalls carrying a plate of fish and chips? You saw it at Leeds town hall where fish and chips and justice were dispensed on broadly equal terms.

It was officially estimated that well over a thousand people passed along those corridors every day. Bewigged barristers breezed back and forward with sheaves of papers wrapped with pink ribbon. Efficient looking solicitors, in black coats and striped trousers, discussed defence strategy with their clients. Stolid policemen stood guard at practically every door. Droves of witnesses fidgeted on benches. Inscrutable jurors retired and returned led by picturesquely attired ushers carrying wands. Perspiring porters staggered round with stepladders. Casual cleaners bustled about with buckets. And always a hungry multitude queued down the steps leading to the civic restaurant in the basement—where about a thousand meals a day were served.

Not that the town hall activities were restricted to dispensing justice and fish and chips. They covered the whole gamut of human activities. The woman with a lost look about her was probably searching for a Civic Society whist drive in the crypt. The man with the double bass was no doubt seeking the rehearsal room for the symphony concert. The youth with the cauliflower ears was obviously coming to make arrangements for a wrestling match. Dinners, dances, meetings and exhibitions; gymnastic displays, snooker tournaments, flower shows and concerts. At one time or another the town hall housed them all and every room available for public use—including the Victoria Hall with its seating accommodation for two thousand—was booked at least a year ahead.

I spent a lot of time in the Assize Courts—of which there were four in various parts of the building. The Crown Court was the most popular with the public and the one where most drama was enacted.

With its heavy, brown Victorian furnishings and its grim, spiked dock—the same dock from which Charles Peace was sent to the scaffold in 1879—it had a macabre gloom about it which sent a shiver down even an onlooker's spine. The judge in his wig and scarlet robes sitting majestically beneath a deep, red canopy with his white gloves and his black cap by his side was an impressive, terrifying figure.

I saw a number of men sentenced to death in the Crown Court and it was always a fearful business. There would be a few moments of relaxation when the jury went out after a long trial to consider their verdict and the barristers, solicitors, pressmen and court officials would mingle in the corridors immediately outside the court and discuss not the case but the latest cricket score at Headingley or other news of the day. Some would slip out for a quick drink at the Victoria across the road.

But after about half an hour the jury's return had to be expected at any moment and no one strayed far from the court's precincts. Sometimes the jury would be out for only an hour—although that was rare in murder cases—but sometimes they would be out for three, four, five hours or even longer. The longer they were out the greater the dramatic build-up—and the greater the atmosphere of electric tension while the formalities were gone through—"Gentlemen of the jury, have you considered your verdict?"

One usually found oneself thinking of the poor devil in the dock rather than the victim, because the poor devil in the dock was a person like yourself. You had observed him closely for several days. You had seen him give evidence and probably go through the torture of cross-examination. You had heard all the circumstances of the case, often in ghastly and horrifying detail, and if you were pretty sure the prisoner was guilty you had been appalled and outraged that human beings could be capable of such dastardly deeds. Hanging was really too good for him.

But that was before the jury retired. Now his fate had been decided and as the judge put on his black cap and said in that fearful, solemn voice that he would be taken to a place of execution and hanged by the neck until dead you had an instinctive sympathy for him. He was going to pay for his crime by a week or two in the condemned cell and an early morning walk and it seemed grotesque and horrifying that a civilized society could exact such vengeance. It took more than another drink at the Victoria afterwards to clear one's mind of a sense of guilt.

The most dramatic moments I ever spent in the Crown Court were in a little publicized trial of a murder which had been committed in a residential area of Leeds not far from the University. The defendant, a young man of quite unviolent-looking appearance, based his defence upon a very strong alibi and the prosecuting counsel went to great lengths to puncture this alibi without success, until late in the trial he pressed a series of questions on the defendant relating to the time he said he had arrived home on the night of the murder. Writing from memory the examination went something like this:

Counsel: "You are quite sure it was 11 pm because you heard the church clock chime as you went up the road to your home? Is that correct?"

Defendant: "Yes."

Counsel: "You are quite sure you heard the church clock chime 11 pm—it could not have been any other clock? The town hall clock, for instance?"

Defendant: "No. I am quite sure it was the church clock."

Counsel: "Then it may surprise you to know that I am going to call witnesses who will prove beyond any shadow of doubt that on the night in question the church clock did not chime at all, because throughout the whole of that week it had been out of order and under repair."

The defendant's case collapsed and he went to the scaffold.

Of course, it was not every day that there was a murder trial. But the less sensational trials were often just as fascinating and one went through conflicting emotions as one watched the procession of human frailty and wickedness pass through the dock and saw some of the lesser criminals sentenced to terms of imprisonment for anything from housebreaking to fraud. Your savage disgust for the unrepentant young hooligan who had struck the old woman over the head with a cosh would be speedily transformed into deep compassion for the nervous little cashier who had succumbed to temptation after a lifetime of honest labour and embezzled money to provide luxuries for his sick wife.

By comparison the Civil Court was considered by some reporters to be arid and dull. It certainly lacked the theatrical atmosphere of the Crown Court for the simple reason that there was no one in the dock and the judge wore robes of a sombre black instead of the more dramatic scarlet. And the cases—usually concerning claims for damages by people injured in accidents—involved detailed examinations of photographs, plans and sketches and long medical dissertations on the nature and effect of the injuries received. A barrister would spend a quarter of an hour or more demonstrating with his fountain pen how the broken sections of a thigh bone had failed to join. But the judgements were always worth waiting to hear, being almost always brilliant object lessons in what some would call cold logic and others pure law.

Some reporters also found the Divorce Courts dull but here again I was absorbed, if for no other reason than that the only crime of the couples who came into it was their failure to be able to live together. Husband and wife would sit on the same bench in the well of the court, behind the barristers' table, and look everywhere but at each other. Apart from answering questions in the witness box they took little part in the proceedings. Their role in the tragedy had been played before they came to court. In court they were merely pawns in the legal game to be moved about by their counsel as required. They would sit there all day in one of three moods—apathy, sadness or violent indignation—while the whole melancholy history of their marriage was dissected, from the day they came out of church to the day of the final separation. All their secrets were revealed, all their intimacies laid bare. The demands of the law were unyielding.

The stories differed widely in detail but in essence were always the same—the love between two people had died. Sometimes it was clearly mostly the husband's fault and sometimes clearly mostly the wife's. But more often than not in defended cases you revised your assessment of blame as the hearing proceeded. As you listened to the wife's indignant story of how the husband went out on drinking bouts, or kept late hours, or made unreasonable sexual demands, or carried on with other women, or threw crockery about the kitchen or used foul language ("Will you tell his Lordship the exact names he called you?") you looked across at the mild little husband and said to yourself "What an appalling rotter you must be!" But when you heard his account of the domestic disturbances your reaction was somewhat different. As he told about his wife's constant nagging, and the ceaseless interference of her relatives, your sympathy was strongly aroused. You began to think you would also have begun to throw crockery round the kitchen in such circumstances. Your final verdict, very often, was that it was six of one and half a dozen of the other.

But perhaps the most saddening feature of these cases was the violent hate and bitterness that were sometimes displayed by husband and wife with only a few years of marriage behind them. It is said that love and hate are neighbouring emotions and the Divorce Courts in Leeds provided melancholy proof of it every day. And yet, as in the other courts and all good drama, the tragedy was leavened with occasional flashes of humour. The growing despair of a barrister as his loquacious client insisted on saying what she heard instead of what she saw or what she did. The mounting impatience of the judge as a barrister pursued a clearly unprofitable line of enquiry—and his final sedate and dignified explosion "Really, Mr . . . , I cannot see the value of asking the witness to list her husband's idiosyncrasies. To begin with she obviously doesn't know what the word means and in any case I am sure I should have great difficulty if you asked me to recite my own idiosyncrasies, and even more my wife's idiosyncrasies."

There was polite laughter from the barristers' table—in which censured counsel joined through grinding teeth—and a titter from the policeman over in the corner by the door, who one thought was fast asleep. Sometimes there was even a flickering smile from the husband or wife—but in the Divorce Court that was the nearest to enjoyment either of them was likely to get.

For real theatre in Leeds one went to the Grand or the Royal. At the Grand there were London previews and touring companies with star studded casts and at the Royal there was repertory. I saw a great many plays either from complimentary seats in the stalls or an even more privileged position in the wings, a fair number of revues and musical comedies, and at Christmas inevitably the pantomimes. I sometimes interviewed the stars at the Grand and always found the comedians the most miserable of people. George Formby, I remember in particular, almost had me in tears in his dressing room at the Grand telling me about the vast sums he paid in income tax.

The repertory players intrigued me more than the stars. What was it that attracted them to this gruelling profession which, according to a speaker at one Equity meeting I attended to discuss drastic measures to reduce the numbers of new entrants, provided only "unemployment, under-nourishment, disillusionment and heartbreak." I interviewed Mr Laurence Storm, producer for the Court Players, on this subject. "I get hundreds of enquiries every season", he told me. "If a young man or woman really wants to act there is nothing Equity or anyone else can do to stop them."

I spent the best part of a week at the Theatre Royal studying repertory life. It was a Tuesday morning when I put in my first appearance. The repertory company's week had just begun and with the opening night of the current play safely behind them they were hard at work on next week's production. The producer sat at a table near the curtain with the cast around him. Not very glamorous figures any of them. The actresses had the minimum of make up and were dressed for warmth and comfort—most of them in trousers. The company were reading the play from script and it went on very tediously for hours and hours. By the following morning, however, the players would have to know the whole of their parts in act one by heart—and their only time for study would be between 2 pm and 6 pm when the first evening performance of the current play began. By Friday morning they would have to know the whole play—and for the leading characters that would mean learning something like 400 speeches by heart.

"My only free time is between 2 pm and 3 pm" the leading lady told me. "And I spend that having my hair done and preparing my clothes for the evening performance."

For this most exacting of jobs the leading men and women in the better class repertory companies like the Court Players were being paid less than £15 a week—and out of this they had all their stage clothes to buy. The management provided only period costumes. "An actor does not keep as big a wardrobe as he used to but it has still to be fairly extensive" Mr Storm told me. "I remember the days when I had to wear twenty-six different lounge suits and twelve pairs of pyjamas in one season."

None of them could explain satisfactorily to me why they did it. "It's part of you", they all said. "You have either got it in you or you haven't." I was rather glad I hadn't—and yet they were all obviously very happy in their work.

Plays at the Grand and the Royal did not exhaust Leeds's theatrical potentialities. There were revues and sophisticated variety at the Empire in Briggate and revues and music hall turns at the City Varieties off the Headrow. The City Varieties with its risqué revues was the favourite rendezvous of journalists and because I once did them a write-up which Harry Joseph, the proprietor, considered good enough to exhibit in a glass case in the bar he bestowed on me the right of free entry to the theatre for the rest of my life! I was also given the privilege of wandering backstage whenever I felt like it and talking to the artistes in their dressing rooms. As some of the artistes were ravishing beauties like Phyllis Dixey this was a highly-valued privilege, although I was often disillusioned. I saw one stunning beauty who captivated me in the stalls by her nude posing act—it was, absurd as it now seems, strictly illegal in those days for a completely nude performer to move as much as a muscle on stage. I went round to interview the beauty in her dressing room and when I knocked at the door a bored voice shouted "Come in". I entered and found her sitting in a chair examining her feet—still with nothing on. But she shattered my reverie with a sentence. "Me bloody feet is killing me tonight" she said in the broadest Yorkshire.

As everyone now knows through the "Good Old Days" on television the City Varieties is the oldest music hall in the country and has been functioning for at least 150 years. Built originally as a supper and concert room by Charles Thornton there are few famous variety stars who have not trod its boards. Charlie Chaplin was there in the late nineties as one of the Lancashire Lads and Sir Harry Lauder played there at a salary of £6 10s a week—which was £5 more than George Formby (senior) received when he made his first appearance. Harry Weldon, Vesta Tilley, Wilkie Bard, Charles Coburn, Harry Tate, Eugene Stratton, Little Titch, Dan Leno, Vesta

Victoria, Hettie King, Ella Shields and Harry Champion are among those who played there in the days of gold sovereigns and hansom cabs.

The manager at the Varieties in the 1950s was a well-known theatrical character called 'Pip' Pawson who started out as a comic with a pierrot show on the sands at Redcar. He took a dim view of the modern fixation with female glamour and sighed for the good old days when there were gas jet footlights and the audience threw rotten eggs or oranges at any artiste who wasn't up to scratch. The management could be critical, too, in those days he told me, showing me an old book where comments on the week's performers were recorded.

Charles Coburn was top of the bill at one show for £30 a week and opposite his name was the verdict "poor". Another artiste, Beatrice Toy, received £12 and the comment "rotten". Several others received the ultimate in denigration—"never again". But even this was better than the comments on two other artistes. One was "paid off—inebriated" and the other was "too drunk to appear".

Harry Joseph was a friendly character and I had many a drink with him in the long bar off the dress circle—and with his son, Stanley, who succeeded him on his death. When I wrote the article about the City Varieties which was given the honour of display in the showcase in the bar I concluded it like this: "What, then, of the outlook for the music hall? Will the City Varieties still be drawing the crowds fifty years hence or will television have killed it? The present owner of the theatre, Mr Harry Joseph, is supremely optimistic. Far from killing the City Varieties he feels that television will give it a new lease of life." If ever there was a prophetic statement that was it!

One fascinating district of Leeds I discovered and explored while writing on theatrical topics was the theatrical digs-land of the city tucked away between Woodhouse Lane and Meanwood Road, Cobden Place, Lofthouse Place, Ella Street and St George's Terrace. This was where the population of theatreland departed after the curtain had fallen and the footlights gone out. It was not a glamorous area by any means and the landladies complained bitterly that it was shabby and neglected. The faded red brick terrace houses, with their iron palisades, their four or five stone steps, their brooding bay windows and their pocket-handkerchief gardens, had a musty gloom about them redolent of aspidistras and antimacassars. But, the older landladies hastened to tell you, it was not so when Charles Coburn and Vesta Tilley walked home up these cobbled streets. It was quite a fashionable residential area.

But if the area had fallen on hard times it had not lost its delightful Bohemian atmosphere. Where else in Leeds at half past eleven in the morning could you knock for five minutes at a front door and have it opened by a blonde vision in a dressing gown complaining that you have wakened her up? Blonde visions in dressing gowns abounded in this area until lunchtime, when the theatricals got dressed and went down into Leeds looking like models in a fashion parade.

An acquaintance of mine in theatre digs-land was seventy-nine-year-old Mrs Fanny Driver, a small, white-haired woman who had been "taking theatricals" at 23 St George's Terrace for over thirty years. "I've had all types here", she told me. "Albert Modley spent two pantomime seasons with me. He's a nice chap is Albert. His only complaint was that the dogs in the street woke him up. But I told him he should get up earlier. I mean, dogs have a right to bark at half past eleven in the morning, haven't they?"

Mrs Driver began catering for theatricals at Holbeck with some members of the Carl Rosa Opera Company. The very same week she got an urgent request from the stage manager at the old Queen's theatre. Could she possibly fit in a new artiste by the name of Miss Gracie Fields? "The top liners stay at hotels nowadays", she said. "It comes off their tax so I don't blame them. But a lot still prefer to stay in digs. I mean you can't drift around in dressing gowns in hotels all morning can you?"

Another landlady with a legion of stories about theatricals was Mrs Doris Atkinson. She and her mother before her had catered for theatricals for half a century. She specialized in catering for child performers. "I've got the Tiny Tappers in at the moment" she told me in her kitchen, turning to attend to a battalion of boiling pans. "Eight little girls and their matron. They're a grand lot and rehearse in my back garden. But, oh what a bother there is nowadays with children! First the education officer comes to inspect the rooms and arrange for them to go to school every day and then the health officer calls to see if I'm overcrowded. Why, when my old mother had Haley's Comets she never knew how many there were. She used to have to go up and count them when they were asleep in bed."

The landladies usually let the theatricals what were known as "chats"—in lay language bed-sitting rooms. Single girls and married couples usually preferred to buy their own food. They came and they went, always leaving their autographed photographs behind them to preserve old memories and embellish the interior decorations. And bustling Leeds half a mile away never knew anything about them at all!

Roundhay Park and Temple Newsam

Of the outdoor events in the Leeds calendar in those days the greatest was undoubtedly Children's Day. It was held every year in early July at Leeds's premier playground, Roundhay Park, and was regularly attended by crowds of over 100 000. With some justification it was claimed to be an event unique in the world. As Leeds's premier newspaper the *Yorkshire Post* had no option but to go to town on it, and it was invariably the subject of a long leader page article.

As the *Yorkshire Post*'s chief feature writer it was for more years than I care to remember the bane of my life and the prospect of writing a glowing description of the events, punctuated with entertaining "human stories" about the participants (how Jacqueline Smith had come from a measles sick bed to win the talent competition with a masterly recitation of "Sitting on the doorstep eating bread and jam") and a regular flow of humorous incidents ("I don't want to be claimed" protested Andrew Peterson after three hours in the lost children's tent, "I want to be taken home in a police car") filled me with mounting apprehension from the middle of June onwards.

Thousands of Leeds schoolchildren took part in the proceedings and the Queen of Children's Day, usually a fourteen-year-old girl dressed in a flowing white satin dress, was crowned by the Lord Mayor or Lady Mayoress of the city in a ceremony held in the centre of the vast arena near Waterloo lake. There were attendants and page boys in equally exotic attire and after the crowning ceremony the Queen and her retinue would be conveyed in procession round the arena led by no less a figure than the Chief Constable in his full regalia.

This was all very well when the sun was shining but unfortunately it did not always shine and I attended Children's Days held in pouring rain and got drenched with the rest of the multitude. But the one I remember most vividly was held in a gale of almost hurricane intensity. It blew off the Queen's crown and the Lord Mayor's topper and produced the unseemly sight of the attendants chasing them round the arena. It made the red carpeted dais out in the centre of the arena look like a raft in a storm-tossed sea, with the Lord Mayor and Lady Mayoress and other leading civic officials clinging precariously to its deck. It even blew out all the jets in the gas cookers in the marquees surrounding the arena and made it impossible to provide the shivering children with cups of tea. But there was the usual ocean of pop so I don't suppose they cared much about that. I heard one boy boast to another of all he had drunk. He listed half a dozen different varieties of pop and added as an afterthought "There wasn't any tea so I had two cups of orange juice and one glass of washing up water".

After the crowning ceremony the rest of the day was devoted to sports championships and they seemed to go on for ever. Emboldened by years of children's day reporting I slipped a protest into one article about the boredom of these events and the next year the committee, evidently deciding that the best way of silencing me was to let me into the club, sent me an impressive badge with "OFFICIAL" in big letters. Feeling much more important than usual I carefully pinned it to my buttonhole. Immediately a belligerent father appeared from nowhere and said to his wife "Here's one Alice'. He approached me menacingly. "Now then," he said, "wh'ere do we get a seat to watch our Margaret in the high jump?" I looked at the vast crowd and said tentatively that there appeared to be a bit of grass left unoccupied at the top of a promontory known in Roundhay Park as Hill 60. "Grass?" he repeated belligerently. "The grass is wet and my missus has rheumatics. What are you going to do about it?" I replied that I wasn't really an official at all and gave him my badge.

Rivalling Roundhay Park as a summer venue for the people

of Leeds was Temple Newsam, a fine Jacobean mansion acquired by Leeds corporation from Lord Halifax in 1923 and hailed at the time as the future Hampton Court of the north. It never fulfilled this promise but Leeds corporation were always anxious to promote it and one of their bright ideas was to install in the grounds the famous Henry Moore sculpture, Reclining Figure. Henry Moore was said to be delighted with the site his sculpture had been given but I speculated in the *Yorkshire Post* whether he would be equally delighted by the cultural reactions of those who flocked to see it. Two visitors' conversation I reported went something like this:

She: "There it is, Fred—that green thing over there. Crikey, what a monstrosity."

He: "It's . . . it's like an elephant. Or maybe half an elephant."

She: "But what's it supposed to be?"

He: "Nay, lass, I don't think anyone knows. It just reckons to be art."

She: (emphatically) "It's neither nowt nor summat, Fred. Nowt nor summat."

Hunslet Feast and a Headingley poltergeist

I got a lot of fun visiting the various fairs held annually in Leeds—or feasts as they were known. The main ones were Hunslet Feast on Hunslet Moor, Holbeck Feast on Holbeck Moor and Woodhouse Feast on Woodhouse Moor. Hunslet was my favourite. It had a real atmosphere about it—particularly after 10 o'clock at night when the pubs were, as they say in Hunslet, "looising".

The crowds rolled in from all directions and there were long queues for the big wheel and the waltzer and a desperate scramble for cars on the dodgems, while the men at the side stalls could not take people's money fast enough. "Come along now, come along now! Sixpence a time and the winner takes the pick of the stall. You can have a china doll or a teddy bear, a chiming clock or a canteen of cutlery. You can have a pair of blankets or an eiderdown or a china tea service or an electric iron. It's a fair, square, genuine game and someone must win every time." Someone but never you!

While the people of Hunslet played they ate—ate hungrily of every conceivable concoction—brandysnap, lollipops, peanuts, toffee apples, liquorice, candy floss and potato crisps. There were stalls selling bags of roast potatoes and others selling plates of peas and pies. There were cockles and mussels, hamburgers, shrimps, prawns, doughnuts and hot dogs. And everywhere there were fish and chips being eaten out of newspapers with the generously applied vinegar sharpening the night air with its tang.

When the pubs had finished "looising" the pace of things was stepped up. Girls in jeans and fancy hats jitterbugged in pairs to the raucous music of the hurdy-gurdies while their boy friends expended their energy on coconut shies or tipping the lady out of bed.

I usually finished my trip with a visit to one of the gypsy fortune tellers who would lead me into the inner recesses of her caravan past a large crystal bowl and a number of half-crowns and read my hand for nothing if I promised her a mention in my article. The original Gypsy Rose Lee told me I should live to be eighty but would not make much money. She also told me I should be going across the water and that a removal would be coming into my life.

"Well you're right there" I said, thankful to be able to confirm something. "We are in the throes of a removal now."

She was so delighted that her brown face positively gleamed. "Tell 'em that" she said. "Tell 'em I predicted you were going to remove."

"And live to be eighty?" I queried.

"Oh yes, probably well over eighty."

"But I won't make much money?"

Her face clouded. "Well . . . I didn't mean you wouldn't make any money. I meant you wouldn't make a lot of money. Not as much as you'd like to, I mean . . . but who does?"

There were many odd jobs which came my way in Leeds and none odder than the Headingley poltergeist. It started with a middle-aged couple, Mr and Mrs Haithwaite, who occupied a semi-detached house near the cricket ground in Ash Grove, Headingley, complaining about things going bump in the night—and indeed during the day as well.

"It's past a joke" Mrs Haithwaite told a squad of reporters

from the local and national papers. "We have been having the spirits for weeks."

"What sort of spirits are they?" asked one of the reporters solemnly.

"Well, I don't know . . . spirits are spirits, aren't they?"

"What exactly do these spirits do Mrs Haithwaite?"

"Do? They move things about. Today, for instance, a medicine bottle has fallen out of a cupboard on to the floor, an electric light bulb has dropped out of its socket, a plant pot has been smashed to pieces and the washbowl has come out of the bathroom to the top of the stairs. It's not good enough."

One reporter had the brilliant idea of contacting the Leeds Psychic Research Society and asked Mrs Haithwaite if she would give permission to their organizing a seance in order to exorcise the spirit. Yes, she said, she didn't mind what they did as long as the spirits were got rid of.

On the way back to Leeds another reporter—I seem to remember it was Stan Hicks, the irrepressible Leeds staff man of the *Daily Mail*—put forward another brilliant idea. "I see the great Fogel, the mind reader, is appearing at the City Varieties this week" he observed. "How about getting him in as well as the Leeds Psychic Research Society?"

Scenting publicity, the great Fogel was only too keen to investigate. So were the Leeds Psychic Research Society, as well as a member of the International Brotherhood of Magicians who had been discovered by another reporter in the city.

Late that night, after the great Fogel had finished his performance at the City Varieties, a party consisting of about a dozen reporters, half a dozen photographers, three or four members of the Leeds Psychic Research Society and the man from the Brotherhood of Magicians solemnly assembled in the attic of the Haithwaites' house and Fogel quickly took charge of the proceedings—an event which did not greatly please the Leeds Psychic Research Society whose delegation was headed by their chairman.

"Right," said Fogel, "I'm going to exorcise the spirit—but first I must be bound in this chair and this tambourine must be placed across my knees."

This all seemed a bit irrelevant but he produced ropes and a tambourine and everyone helped to tie him to the chair. While this was going on it was announced that a policeman had arrived and was on duty at the front door—possibly to arrest the spirit if it decided to make a hasty exit.

"Right," said Fogel, "will you now please form a circle round my chair and all hold hands?"

We did as we were told and Fogel gave the instruction to put the light out.

At this point, however, the photographers protested that they had not had an opportunity to take photographs of Mr Fogel in his chair and there was a five-minute halt in the proceedings while this rather important little matter was attended to. The photographers got down on their knees and there were a series of brilliant flashes and repeated cries of "Hold it". It was a most unlikely setting for a seance.

The room was then plunged into darkness and we stood in a sniggering circle waiting for something to happen. Eventually, of course, it did. There was a sudden crash and Fogel's tambourine flew across the room.

This greatly excited one of the members of the Leeds Psychic Research Society and he shouted "The poltergeist is with us—I will now proceed to question it."

He asked if the spirit was responsible for happenings in the house—saying that it should answer by giving one knock to indicate "yes" and two knocks to indicate "no". Two clear knocks were heard from the direction of Fogel's chair, and the members of the Psychic Research Society became so excited that they began to fire questions at the poltergeist thick and fast. "Give the spirit a chance" said Fogel. "Tell him to spell out his name."

The Psychic Research Society had a quick conference as to how this could be done and the outcome was that the poltergeist was asked to spell out his name by giving a knock when the appropriate letter of the alphabet was announced. The chairman of the society promptly proceeded to go through the alphabet and the first knock came with the letter "H". He started again and the second knock came at "O". Eventually the name HOUDINI was spelled out.

This was the signal for Fogel to ask for the lights to be put on. He was still sitting tightly bound in his chair and it was not clear how he had made the knocks although it was quite clear to everyone in the room except the members of the Psychic Research Society that he had been responsible for them.

He confirmed it after he had been untied. "Gentlemen," he said, "I have proved that the mysterious happenings in this house have been caused by a human agency."

How he had in fact proved anything was not clear to anybody. But at this the seance broke up and the press, the Psychic Research Society and Fogel all departed, Fogel assuring Mr and Mrs Haithwaite that they would probably not be troubled by the spirit any more. But the Leeds Psychic Research Society were far from satisfied by the night's proceedings and the chairman announced that they intended to make a further investigation of their own. "It doesn't add up" commented one of the members. "I can't see what on earth Houdini has got to do with it."

That was only one of the many questions that were left unanswered. But some months later one of the papers did a follow up to the story and alleged that the incidents in the house which had so disturbed Mr and Mrs Haithwaite were the work of a practical joker well known to them.

Dales characters

The dales have always been Yorkshire's chief pride and joy and no doubt always will be. Southerners who tend to think of Yorkshire as a large collection of dreary mill towns cannot be made to realize until they have seen them that the seven river valleys which run diagonally across the county and are remembered by the mnemonic SUNWADD—Swale, Ure, Nidd, Wharfe, Aire, Don and Derwent, possess some of the finest scenery in the whole of the United Kingdom.

As a roving reporter for the *Yorkshire Post* I spent a good deal of time in the dales and came to know most of them very well. And to know the Yorkshire dales is inevitably to love them. Swaledale, Uredale (or Wensleydale as it is always known), Nidderdale and Wharfedale were my favourite haunts because when one gets as far south as Airedale industry is protruding its ugly head. I went frequently to Richmond, Reeth, Gunnerside and Muker; Leyburn, West Witton, Aysgarth and Hawes; Knaresborough, Birstwith, Summerbridge, Pateley Bridge and Ramsgill; Otley, Ilkley, Bolton Abbey, Appletreewick,

Burnsall, Kettlewell and Buckden. The very names are music to the Yorkshire ear.

It is strange when you come to think of it that although the beauty of the county is dominated by the dales Yorkshire's premier inland resort, Harrogate, is not in a dale at all. It is on the fringe of Nidderdale but actually lies on a bleak plateau between the forest of Knaresborough and the Vale of York.

Harrogate like Ilkley, which would probably qualify as Yorkshire's number two inland resort, owes its fame to its spa waters. That, however, is where the comparison with Ilkley ends. For whereas Harrogate has done everything it can to develop itself as a resort Ilkley has done practically nothing. I wrote about this striking contrast in a *Yorkshire Post* leader page article in 1951 and what I said then is just as pertinent today. Ilkley was then spending £300 a year on publicity. Harrogate was spending just twenty-five times as much. Harrogate had a big publicity and entertainments organization with a number of paid officials. The promotion of Ilkley as a resort was handled among a host of other things by the clerk to the urban council. Harrogate spent large sums of money on street illuminations; Ilkley spent nothing because the pre-war illuminations had worn out and were considered too expensive to replace.

I expected to find at least the Ilkley tradesmen protesting against this lack of development but not a bit of it. Ilkley was quite happy as it was. "Enough people come here without us setting out to attract them," a Chamber of Trade official told me. "I don't think there's any interest in developing the place."

I had to search pretty hard before I could find anyone who did not take this attitude. Eventually an hotel proprietor conceded that Ilkley council needed a squib under them. "It could be made into a marvellous tourist centre but they are dead from the neck up" he declared, adding rather bitterly "If they put some ducks on the tarn they think they've done wonders."

Ilkley was very cost conscious. "Take the swimming pool" said the Chamber of Trade official. "Do you know it cost us a three halfpenny rate?" I said I didn't know but what about all the people it attracted to the town. "That's just the trouble", he added. "You can't move in the place at weekends."

I was hardly surprised to find that Harrogate regarded

Ilkley not as a competitor but as a bit of a joke. "Ilkley?", said an official. "You mean the place without a hat. Where exactly is it? I've lived in Harrogate for years and I've never been to Ilkley yet."

Most of my dales articles were written around dales personalities—of whom there was a plentiful supply. There was Robert Burrow of Hawes, for instance, one of the last surviving saddle and harness makers in Wensleydale. Then (in 1948) an old man of over seventy, he had never really reconciled himself to the internal cumbustion engine. "It's all cars today", he complained. "I remember the time when a hundred farmers used to come to this market on horseback every Tuesday—and I used to be up till midnight with work. Now they all come in cars and I go home at five o'clock."

He shook his head and put the harness he was stitching on the bench of his curious old workshop. "But they'll never do entirely without horses up here, you know", he said. "They can't do their shepherding in cars and they can't take lorries over fields. But things are not what they were in the dale. The lads nowadays think nowt of places like Hawes. Not that I can see much wrong with it. There are five pubs, a couple of clubs and Mr Sykes works the pictures twice a week in the market hall. What more could they want?"

Another character was Kit Jones of Leyburn whom I interviewed just before his eightieth birthday because he had written a book. Kit was as well known as the bellman in Wensleydale and had lived on Jubilee farm most of his life. Unlike most dalesmen, however, he had travelled a good deal in his young days and had had a variety of occupations—ranging from pageboy in an aristocratic household in London (£9 a year plus a suit of livery) to dishwasher in a Chicago hotel.

"I have called my book 'Ups and downs'," he told me in the lounge of his daughter's hotel in Leyburn, the Bolton Arms. "I reckon I've had as many as anybody in these parts, except for old Tommy Byker, who had one leg shorter than the other."

He produced a typescript of his book—prepared for him by the local schoolmaster—and had me glance through it while he gave a running commentary. "You'll see there's a lot about horses. I always loved horses—I've lost a lot of money on slow ones and won a lot on fast ones. And a lot about trainers—old Dobson Peacock, the uncrowned king of Middleham, and his two sons, Matthew and Harry—nicer men you couldn't meet. And have you got to the bit about the Guller, the horse with the big hooves . . . ? And that story about the two little sucking pigs . . . ? And all about that broadcast we made from the King's Arms in Redmire in 1940? I played my concertina at that and sang 'Selina'. Here, I'll show you . . . "

He produced his concertina from somewhere and sang 'Selina' for my benefit. Selina, it seemed, was a Redmire maiden whom a Redmire young man called Jeremiah Brown had jilted. Kit sang it with such gusto that his daughter came running in to see what had happened.

I hadn't time to finish reading his memoirs of Leyburn so he insisted I took the book away with me and returned it later. I was very struck by the last chapter. "I am a landowner in a small way", he had written. "Down in our little cemetery, right opposite our farm, I have bought a bit of ground seven feet by six of which someday I shall be owner occupier. I have put three rows of flowers round it and they all bloomed this year—a row of aconites, a row of snowdrops and a row of daffodils. So some day—but I shall not be able to hear him—someone will say 'Kit Jones is laid there'."

I have always intended to go to Kit's grave one day to see if the flowers are still blooming but like so many other things I have never got round to it.

One of the most amusing interviews I did in the dales was on a refuse tip in the Pateley Bridge area with a man called Mark Atkinson who was about to retire as chief rodent officer to the Ripon and Pateley Bridge Rural Council. Mr Atkinson, an upright man with an Edwardian stiff collar, piercing blue eyes and a ruddy complexion, talked to me about rat-catching with tremendous relish and enthusiasm, regaling me with the full details of the slaughter of over 400 which he had accomplished by "nobbling 'em" with a stick in one afternoon.

"It was on a farm near where I live in Markington", he told me. "They were threshing stacks and there were five or six of the little beggars running out at once—big 'uns too, some of 'em. I was nobbling 'em so fast I couldn't count 'em—but I counted 400 bodies when I'd finished and I had witnesses to prove it."

I asked him if "nobbling 'em" was not a bit primitive in this day and age and he hastened to explain that he also used stealth and cunning where appropriate. He spent his time at the favourite breeding grounds—refuse tips and sewage disposal works—and despatched the rats he encountered by one of several methods according to the local conditions. Poisoned food was his most popular weapon, with poison gas running a good second. Ferrets he very rarely used.

"Of course there's more in the art of poisoning rats than meets the eye", he observed with professional pride. "I wouldn't say rats are over intelligent but they certainly aren't fools. You've got to kid 'em. You've got to feed 'em for three days with unpoisoned food to build up their confidence and encourage them to bring their pals round. I call it pre-baiting. Then on the fourth day you put the poison in. A nice bit of zinc phosphate—and Bob's your uncle."

In hen runs an even greater degree of guile was required. For, as Mr Atkinson pointed out, "you can't go scattering poison around in hen runs without poisoning the blinkin' hens." So traps were employed—and decoys used to lure the rats to their destruction.

"They like hen runs does rats", Mr Atkinson observed, examining a rat hole in the refuse tip we were standing on, which was big enough to accommodate a rabbit. "Have you ever seen a rat walking off with an egg? They clasp it against their chest with their front legs and hop away with it on their back legs. It's the queerest sight you ever did see."

The achievement which gave Mr Atkinson most pride was when he was once called to an emergency job. A man wanted six live rats to help him train a terrier. And the chief sanitary inspector asked Mr Atkinson if he could supply them. "I had 'em at his office in a cage next morning" he told me. "It's a bit of a trade secret how I got 'em, I might tell you, but I could do it again if I had to."

Mr Atkinson had no strong views on the description of his job as that of rodent officer. "They can call me what they like", he said. "Rodent officer, rodent operative, pest destruction officer—they've all sorts of fancy titles nowadays. I don't mind. I call myself a rat-catcher—and I just go on catching rats."

Burnsall Sports furore

I soon learned that dalesmen take their sports activities very seriously. One of the principal events in the Wharfedale sporting calendar was and no doubt still is Burnsall Sports, which date back to Elizabethan times. Thousands of people turn up every year on "the first Saturday after the first Sunday after the 12th of August" to watch flat racing and other events on the banks of the river and the famous fell race which came into existence over a hundred years ago as a result of a wager in the village inn. A villager, Thomas Young, backed himself to run up to the top of Burnsall Fell and down again and did so one night after closing time. There are scores of entrants every year for this rigorous test of stamina and the race, like all other events, is run under strict Amateur Athletic Association rules.

I went to Burnsall Sports early in the 1950s without advance knowledge of their wholly serious intent and to the subsequent horror of the organizers and villagers wrote a light piece about them in which I said that as far as I could see the feature of the sports which received most attention was a simple little notice on the door of the gaily beflagged Red Lion inn reading *BAR OPEN ALL DAY*.

I reported that an official had told me about the origin of the sports in Elizabethan days and had added "But, of course, they're much more organized nowadays than they used to be". That, I wrote, may be true but at the same time they had lost none of the rustic simplicity which was their main charm. The runners in the 440 yards men's open flat handicap could, for instance, mistake the clay pigeon shooting in the neighbouring field for the starter's gun and tear 220 yards round the track before the starter could retrieve them.

The competitors in the seven-mile walk could get mixed up with the crowds and passing traffic and defy the efforts of the entire local police force to sort them out. The timekeeper could be missing when a race finished or the starter missing when a race was about to begin. And an urgent appeal for the loan of a pair of binoculars could be made over a loudspeaker on behalf of the committee when the fell race was half over and the runners who had been dots in the distance were now becoming recognizable figures. The appeal for the binoculars particularly intrigued me and I asked an official why they were needed at this late stage. "Oh" he replied casually, "we want to make sure which are runners. Last year we waited ages for one chap to come in before someone spotted it was a cow."

To make matters even worse I referred to the spectators as being as picturesque as the scenery—with moustachioed country gentlemen in rakish caps and bucolic farm workers in starched collars, not to mention the bandsmen from Hammonds' Sauce Works in scarlet tunics and caps.

The heading to the report was "Sport in the Dales—its lighter side", but there was certainly no lighter side in Burnsall when it duly appeared in the *Yorkshire Post* on the Monday morning. The colouring was distinctly black. Angry letters were written to the editor condemning this outrageous assault on a village institution and if I had ventured beyond Bolton Abbey I should probably have been strung up on a rope and suspended from Burnsall Bridge.

But passions cooled during the subsequent twelve months and when the following August came I received an invitation from the committee to come again to Burnsall Sports and redeem myself. I arrived with quaking heart and the first reactions to my presence were not very favourable. "Oh it's you is it", said an official. "The 'burgomaster' wants to see you."

The "burgomaster" was an honorary title bestowed on Mr Robert Smith who had been honorary secretary of the sports for over forty years. I ran him to earth at the base of a new 65 foot Maypole which had just been erected. To my relief he greeted me quite benevolently. "Mind you", he said severely, "we didn't like it. We don't mind a joke but you made it look as though the sports were run by a crowd of yokels. You can take it from me they are all under Amateur Athletic Association rules and are as well organized as any in England."

I said humbly that I had not intended to criticize the organization and the misunderstanding must be due to my ambiguous turn of phrase. My apology melted the last of his rancour and he went on to talk to me about Burnsall past and present. "You see we value tradition here because Burnsall is a very old village" he told me. "We have a full record of rectors from the thirteenth century—and evidence of the church long before that. And what's more it is a village that has changed very little in the centuries. In the last hundred years, for instance, we have had only four new houses built here—and we consider that's quite enough."

He paused and looked at the sports arena—where the perfect natural setting of fields and fells was enhanced by the sight and sound of red-coated bandsmen playing melodies from "The Maid of the Mountains". "Years ago", he said, with what seemed like a longing for things past, "a whole week was given up to feasting at this time of the year but now it's only one day. Of course village life was different then. There were a lot more characters in those days."

The notice outside the village pub—"BAR OPEN ALL DAY"—was still drawing more attention than the 220 yards open but when I wrote my report that weekend I studiously avoided it. The heading was "Burnsall Sports combine AAA rules with tradition" and I received an appreciative letter from the committee saying all was forgiven!

Rent day feast at Jervaulx

A colourful event in Wensleydale, impossible to imagine away from the countryside, was the half-yearly rent day feast for tenants of the Jervaulx estate. I attended one of these feasts when Mr W L Christie, the owner of the estate, was ninety-five-years-old and claimed to be the oldest landlord in the country. He was certainly one of the most highly respected and on this particular rent day a presentation was made to him by his tenants of a beautiful Hepplewhite table, a reading lamp and a leather album containing the tenants' names. There must be precious few landlords who can boast of that sort of presentation.

The feast was held in the Blue Lion Inn in East Witton and some thirty tenant farmers and their wives were present. They and their predecessors had been coming to the event ever since 1816. The rent paying was done first. The tenants sat and renewed acquaintance in the hall of the pub surrounded by brass warming pans, plate racks, pewter and antique furniture, and went in to pay their dues to the landlord one by one. They came out smiling broadly—as though they had been receiving money rather than paying it.

The feast was held in the parlour amid antique corner cupboards and grandfather clocks. Mr Christie sat at the head of the centuries-old, long oak table wearing a rose in the buttonhole of his grey tweed suit and talked about his horses at Middleham and current racing form in general. "What's wrong with him", I heard him ask about one horse from my position between two stout farmers down the table. "Are his joints stiff?"

There were great plates of roast beef and boiled potatoes and great plates of well-sherried trifle to follow, with equally great plates of jam tarts for those with any room left for them. Then, after the loyal toast had been drunk with pints of beer, four steaming jugs of punch appeared—a rum punch going one way round the table and a gin punch the other, according to tradition. The jugs and the glasses were all over a hundred years old and were the prized possessions of the landlady of the Blue Lion, Mrs Fletcher, also, of course, a tenant of Mr Christie's.

The speeches were short and to the point. The presentation was made by Mr Geoff Allison, the man with the longest farm tenancy present. "It is a pleasure", he said simply, "to live on an estate where the landlord, agent and tenants all live as a happy family." The Reverend A P Durrant, a former vicar of East Witton for eighteen years, spoke next, saying they all looked upon Mr Christie as the grand old gentleman of the dale. "Long may he be spared to us as the head and mainspring of this happy, united and friendly family gathering", he declared amid loud applause.

And then, standing as straight as a ramrod and looking not a day over seventy-five, Mr Christie replied—in a firm voice tinged with emotion. He thanked the tenants for their valuable presents—and the even more valuable thoughts behind them—and also referred to the happy relationship which had existed for so many years. He finished with these words: "I cannot imagine any more pleasant life for anybody who is fond of the country like we are than to live on an estate like this surrounded by tenants who are not only prosperous but have such friendly feelings toward their landlord. To my mind that is the ideal life for anybody."

Stalactites at Gaping Ghyll

Some of my dales trips were not so relaxing. A Whit Sunday pot-holing expedition to Gaping Ghyll, the biggest pot-hole in

Britain and the seventh biggest in the world, was one.

Gaping Ghyll is situated three miles from anywhere between Ingleborough and Pen-y-Ghent. To reach it you walk a mile or more down a farm track and a further two miles over the hills. It is extremely difficult to find and if a *Yorkshire Post* photographer and I had not met a pot-holer en route, complete with tremendous spiked boots and a gigantic rucksack, we should probably never have found it.

"Why do people go pot-holing?" I asked our guide as we heaved and struggled after him, an unlikely looking pair carrying attaché cases containing our sandwiches and some rudimentary pot-holing equipment. He turned so that he could see us round the edge of the 80 lb rucksack. "For adventure, I suppose", he replied. "We have a few cranks who go looking for fossils but most of us just go for fun. Of course we're always trying to find a passage to Clapham Cave—there are miles of passages you know." He turned and strode on. "Of course", continued the voice from somewhere in front of the rucksack, "most people think we're lunatics."

We reached our destination eventually and dressed up for the parts we were to play. But there was certainly no fear of our being mistaken for genuine pot-holers. Our equipment did not look right and even when we put on our helmets we decided we looked like a couple of commercial travellers very thinly disguised.

"You go down on that", said the secretary of the Bradford Pot-hole Club, whose guests for the day we were. He pointed to a flimsy little bosun's chair which dangled at the end of a rope below a gantry across a corner of the yawning chasm.

My photographer suggested I go first so that he could take my picture to accompany the article I should be writing. I suggested he should go first in order for me to describe his descent. Seeing our apprehension the secretary hastened to assure us it was perfectly safe. "This is the last word in pot-holing gear" he said. "We've never had an accident yet."

To our unbounded relief we did not break the record. I finally went first and was lowered down into the clammy darkness quite smoothly. The only trouble I encountered was a heavy shower of water from an underground stream. On arrival at the bottom a man with a light in his helmet sprang out to release me from my harness and I found myself in a vast hall of rock which, he proudly informed me, was 500 feet long by 110 feet high by 90 feet wide.

"Bradford town hall would easily fit in here", he said solemnly.

"Really?" I replied with equal solemnity. "But don't you think it would be a trifle inconvenient?"

But there is no scope for humour in pot-holing and without registering any reaction to this sally he produced a large skull for my inspection. "I've been down here seven hours and have just found this in one of the passages", he explained. "What do you think it is?"

My photographer (now arrived on the scene) and I examined it closely. "I suppose it could be a pterodactyl" I suggested, remembering he had been seven hours finding it in conditions of the greatest discomfort. "Or possibly a plesiosaurus. It might even be an iguanodon." My photographer who was not very happy about coming pot-holing in the first place, examined it critically. "It's a bloody sheep" he said grimly. He was unquestionably right.

When he had got his camera and flash bulbs ready our guide suggested an exploration of the east passage. "There are some lovely stalactites on there", he promised. "Not far. Just a hundred yards or so. And very easy going." I was dubious about it but my photographer suddenly became enthusiastic. It seemed he had never photographed stalactites before.

We climbed at least three vertical rock faces and we crawled for what seemed at least half a mile through thick mud and slime. We were never off our hands and knees and were almost flat on our stomachs some of the time. There was so little headroom at one point that the photographer had to take off his helmet to get through. In taking it off he ended the life of a stalactite which had been proceeding quite uneventfully for at least 300 years. My problem was the light on my helmet. It would only stay on when I shook my head. And when I shook my head the stalactites fairly danced around me.

We stumbled on and after sundry other minor mishaps we encountered some girls in a cave. My photographer decided they would make a better picture than the stalactites—it was too dark anyway for stalactites—and spent the next quarter of an hour posing them as he wanted them. By this time I was feeling cold and distinctly wet. "What do we do now?", I asked our guide.

"Well, unless you would like to look for a passage to Clapham Cave we go back."

So back we crawled. "I think it's much more interesting coming this way don't you?", our guide asked. My photographer made a movement with his camera and I thought for a terrible moment he was going to throw it at him.

The secretary was having tea in a tent when we eventually reached the surface, covered in mud and slime.

"Now", he said briskly, "have you enjoyed it?"

We replied that it had certainly been an experience we should not forget in a hurry—and we loved the stalactites.

"It grows on you, you know", he said. "The sport is getting more popular all the time. We get a lot of visitors, too."

He sipped his tea thoughtfully. "Of course everyone thinks we're idiots spending weekends doing this."

"Do they really?" I said. "Whatever for, I wonder."

Angling contest at Nether Poppleton

A less demanding Sunday engagement was the Ouse Angling Championship at Nether Poppleton, near York, one of the big events in the northern angling calendar. No fewer than 470 anglers took part—and, I need hardly add, took it terribly seriously. After drawing lots for position they lined both banks of the river at twenty-yard intervals with their maggots, worms, paste and multifarious other accoutrements spread around them. The angling line stretched for several miles.

They were far too intent on watching their floats to talk to a visiting journalist and I got into serious trouble by venturing to within ten yards of one angler who claimed I had cast a shadow over the water which would drive the fish away.

Fortunately not everyone angles in an angling championship and in a rustic pub up the road I was able to discuss the sport with the committee. They were the hardworking body who made all the arrangements and drew up the rules—such as barring trout because they were out of season and prohibiting the use of blood worms, hemp seed and squat because they happened to be popular with the fish and would make catching them too easy.

"I suppose the chief attraction of angling is that it is a quiet, contemplative activity", one member of the committee told me. "It's an escape from the pressures of everyday life."

But there was, I discovered, far more to angling than sitting and thinking about the universe. To start with you had to study the habits of fish with clinical thoroughness. You had to know, for instance, that when the current was swift they would make for the "quiet slack"—which meant that you had to fish in the sluggish pools beneath the willows. You must know, too, that if the river suddenly rose the fish would make for the banks where fresh food would have been washed in.

You had also to be expert in the art of deception for fish were not fools. If your bait looked in the least suspicious they would merely smile at it scornfully and pass on their way. The maggot which looked like a maggot would get you nowhere. It must be coloured pink, green, blue or yellow and look the living image of a caterpillar.

Having learned all I could about the sport I returned to the river to see how big the piles of caught fish were becoming. But although I walked the whole length of the contest there was not as much as a tiddler to be seen. Perhaps, I thought, they had stuffed them all in those great panniers they carried.

I returned to the pub for more refreshment only to learn that there had been dramatic happenings up river. A portion of the bank had collapsed and one angler had fallen in and had had to be rescued by another.

The contest lasted three and a half hours in all and I suppose I must have spent about three hours in the pub. When I went to see the weigh-in I was expecting great things but, alas, it was not to be. Only 190 of the 470 anglers had got anything to weigh and the winner—a Mr J Myson of Shipley—had a total catch of two fish—a bream weighing 4 lb 3½ oz and a roach weighing 1½ oz. It seemed an unjust reward for a hard day's work. "I don't think more than half of us had so much as a bite" one contestant told me disconsolately as he packed his tackle. "It's been the worst day I ever remember."

I rather fancied I had heard plenty of anglers say that before.

"It's the glorious uncertainty that gets you", said another contestant.

"What uncertainty?" I asked him with a very straight face.

Film stars at Malham

Dalesmen are nothing if not down to earth. I thought the picturesque village of Malham (population 142), famous for its tarn and its cove, would be intoxicated with excitement when it was announced that Bette Davis was coming over from Hollywood to make a film with her then husband, Garry Merrill. I went up there after hearing that a party including the director, producer and script writer had been to the village on a reconnaissance tour.

I spoke first to a retired villager called Gilbert Brown. "Excited?", he said dourly. "What is there to be excited about?"

"Well, it's not every day they make films in Malham is it?"

"No, and it's a damned good job too", he replied. "Film people waste a lot of time and money. They take thousands and thousands of pictures and never seem to use any of 'em. And they bring hundreds of assistants with 'em and only a handful ever do owt."

I gathered that Mr Brown had studied film making a year or two previously when shots had been taken in the village for a film starring Googie Withers and John McCallum called "A Boy, a Girl and a Bike."

"I watched 'em on it for weeks", he told me. "They got us villagers to stand on the bridge. We all put our Sunday clothes on for it. And what happened? I went specially to Skipton to see the film. There were three shots of Malham and they didn't last five minutes. And the picture of the people on the bridge wasn't damned well used at all."

He leaned heavily on his sticks and gazed over the hills in the direction of the tarn. "We don't want to see Bette Davis. We saw enough of Googie What's-her-name and John Who-d'you-call-him last time. What we want to see is Malham Cove and Gordale Scar—the finest scenery in England—you tell 'em that from me."

Rather dispirited I called at the local post office and met the village postmistress, shopkeeper and café proprietor Mrs Gwendoline Ingham. She was no more enthusiastic than Mr Brown.

"They've asked if they can use my shop for filming", she said. "I've told 'em they can—so long as they don't hold up some repairs we're doing. I had it out straight with the director this morning. He's an American. Quite a nice chap. Can't remember his name. They have such peculiar names, film directors, don't they?"

She served some customers before continuing the conversation. " 'Course, we're not big film fans around here" she explained rather unnecessarily. "The nearest cinema is in Skipton. But we do have a man comes with a portable outfit to Airton, two miles away, on Saturday nights."

She directed my attention to a notice on the wall announcing that Airton's next attraction would be "Lancashire Luck" plus an oriental mystery called "Hong Kong Nights". "That's more in our line than Bette Davis really", she said. "I can't say I go for Bette Davis."

She eyed the tins of condensed milk and processed peas in her shop window. "Still I suppose it'll be good for trade", she said cheerfully. "There'll be a lot of folk coming to gawp at her."

I met Bette Davis and her husband at an hotel in Settle later that day, together with about a score of other pressmen, and an equal number of photographers. She sat swinging her legs on a stool at the bar, helping herself to cigarettes from her husband's pocket, and answered the usual inane series of questions. Meanwhile the director, Irvine Rapper, was going into ecstasies about the Malham scenery. It was arresting. It was exciting. It was compelling. It had a cold, earthy quality. It was perfect for a film such as they were making, a film of tremendous mood.

I asked how they had been received in Malham. "They're really friendly", he replied, "really friendly." Friendly, he might have added, but not very enthusiastic. For it takes more than a film star to create excitement in places like Malham.

The smell at the Women's Institute

One of the most diverting stories I ever tackled in the dales was that of the smell at the Women's Institute headquarters in the village of Masham, near Ripon.

The trouble had started several months before I got on to it—and how I got on to it I can't remember. The Women's

Institute—boasting 100 members and forming the backbone of social life in the district—were holding one of their regular meetings in what was known as the WI in College Lane. No one seemed to remember exactly which meeting it was or what was the nature of the business. It might have been one of the musical evenings and social half hours or a debate followed by community singing. I met one member who said she thought it was the night Mrs Clutterbuck gave a talk on her flight to New Zealand.

At any rate, whichever night it was a peculiar smell was observed for the first time—a most offensive smell which clogged the nostrils and made members breathe through their mouths. A smell which, as one member put it, could only be described as a stink.

No one said anything about it at first, of course. It would not have been very ladylike. And a smell was not an easy subject to raise at a meeting of a Women's Institute. It needed handling with diplomacy and tact. Consequently the windows were merely opened and the proceedings hurried to their close.

Any hopes that the smell was temporary were, however, dashed at the next meeting. It was there again—and if anything stronger and more pervasive than before. Several members did not stay for supper and those who did consumed it with unusual speed.

It was about this time that the news leaked out that Harry Hill next door was keeping pigs—twenty-three of them to be precise in sties almost under the institute's kitchen window. And because Mr Hill was the local coal merchant and was well known and highly respected it created a most delicate situation. For in the country you had to live and let live—and pigs, after all, were pigs.

However, after a special committee meeting Mr Hill was finally approached. He received the complaint in the calm and courteous manner they would all have expected. "He was", the treasurer, Mrs Bradley, told me, "only too anxious to help. He promised to see what he could do."

His efforts were, however, quite unavailing—largely owing to the prevailing wind—and at the next meeting the smell was just as pronounced. The institute's dilemma was now complete. They had either to groan and bear it or call in the rural council. And calling in the rural council was not a step to be taken lightly in a convivial community like Masham—particularly when the complaint concerned a man so well-liked and highly respected as Harry Hill.

The members escaped from their dilemma temporarily by moving the venue of some of their meetings. The eiderdown-making demonstration was held in the Wesleyan chapel and the bulb competition in the village hall. They had to come back to the headquarters for the debate and community singing, however, and they found that instead of mellowing in their absence the smell was all the worse for being stale. It hung about the room so heavily that, to quote one member, there might have been a litter of pigs under the table. Even the stirring words of Blake's "Jerusalem" which adorned the wall over the fireplace failed to rouse the members to meet the challenge.

"It was a terrible smelly do", Mrs Lumbley, who held the position of hostess, told me, dilating her nostrils in horrible retrospection. "We had the windows wide open but a lot of people walked out before the end. Only twenty-nine stayed for supper and I had a whole lot of cakes and sandwiches left."

The smell, in short, was threatening the Women's Institute with total disaster and at last, reluctantly and not without a full debate, a decision to approach the rural council was made.

The course of events was now out of the institute's control. The wheels of bureaucracy had begun to grind. The medical officer and the sanitary inspector called to inspect the premises and the clerk of the council called to see Mr Hill. There was much talk of by-laws and nuisances and drainage and ventilation and some reference to Acts of Parliament.

But still the smell persisted and when Mr Thornton came to speak on antiques there were only about thirty members present to hear him—in spite of the exceptional interest of the subject.

Mr Hill was, of course, completely co-operative throughout and readily agreed to give an undertaking to the clerk of the council that he would dispatch the pigs to the bacon factory as soon as they reached the requisite weight of 140 lb. "We don't want to cause anyone any bother at all", his wife told me earnestly. "After all my husband has his business to consider—and it's coal not pigs. He's out delivering now."

I asked her how long it was likely to be before the happy day (for the Women's Institute) of the pigs' dispatch. "Well", she said speculatively, "we're feeding 'em up on fattening meal as fast as we can and it shouldn't be more than five or six weeks. Of course, we could send them a bit sooner if they went as pork but you don't get nearly as much money for pork and we don't want to lose on them, do we?"

She looked pensively toward the sties and then towards the Women's Institute room. "Mind you", she said, "I don't think the women will lose their smell when we do get rid of the pigs. It's my firm belief it's something else. There has been a peculiar smell in the place for twenty years to my knowledge."

I looked at her with a mixture of incredulity and horror. "You really mean to suggest", I said, "that it might not be the pigs after all?"

She shrugged her shoulders non-committally. "You had better ask some of the women what the sanitary inspector said", she replied mysteriously. "They've had half the floor up already."

And it was quite true. One of the Women's Institute officials reluctantly confirmed it. The sanitary inspector had told them the ventilation was poor and that there were other defects which needed attention. Which just went to show what happened when you approached the rural council.

"But the sanitary inspector can say what he likes", said my informant. "We still say it's the pigs."

Alongside my article on the smell in my cuttings book is a handwritten note signed W.L.A. reading "What a beautifully written article! You have made the smell delicious—at least to read about!"

Holiday stories from Scarborough

It was August bank holiday weekend 1950 and Frank Snape, the *Yorkshire Post* news editor, was planning some features for the bank holiday Monday paper. "Why not pop over to Scarborough and do a holiday story?", he suggested to me. I wasn't too keen because I planned to pop over to Old Trafford and watch the Roses match.

"What sort of a holiday story?" I asked.

"Oh, anything you like", he said in his usual expansive but

not very helpful manner. "You know, something light. What people are doing and so on."

"They'll be eating and sleeping mostly", I said.

"That's it!", said Snape. "Write about them eating and sleeping."

So with this slender brief I made my first visit to Scarborough to do a holiday story. "If happiness can be measured in terms of eating and sleeping", I telephoned from the Grand Hotel, Scarborough, on Sunday night, "this is undoubtedly the happiest bank holiday since the war. I was with the holiday crowds in Scarborough yesterday and I am with them again today, and the amount of eating and sleeping going on has to be seen to be believed. Soon after lunch yesterday I walked along the foreshore from the Spa to the Lighthouse Pier and saw only three people with their jaws at rest. And two of these were drinking from bottles. I was so fascinated by this universal mastication that I made a list of what I saw people consuming. To give that list in full is unfortunately impossible because of the newsprint restrictions." (Newspapers in those days were sometimes no bigger than four pages.) "I can merely say that it included apples, oranges, pears, grapes, nuts, plums, prawns, oysters, winkles, mussels, shrimps, potato crisps, candy floss and waffles. Plus, of course, ice cream in all its shapes and sizes—from the homely cornet to strawberry glories and cherry delights.... Almost the only people awake on Scarborough sands at 3 o'clock yesterday afternoon were a hundred or so delighted children watching a Punch and Judy show, a man in plus fours arguing with his small son about how to build a castle and a perspiring stout man in yellow braces who had just heard the lunch-time score at Old Trafford. 'Yorkshire 74 for 5', he kept repeating to himself mechanically. His bank holiday was ruined. Those who were not sprawled out in deckchairs on the sand were slumbering in shelters on the Esplanade, on benches in Peasholm Park, on the grass on Oliver's Mount, in cars round the Marine Drive. There was one small and ancient vehicle with a Leeds registration number parked beneath Castle Hill with seven in, and luggage. And all their mouths were wide open and had expressions of beatific contentment..."

The article was printed on the back page of the *Yorkshire Post* on Monday with the heading "The eaters and sleepers by the shore" and Frank Snape was delighted with it. He rang me up at Scarborough and told me to stay on and do another holiday story for the next day's paper. From then on he saw to it that I was shipped off to Scarborough to do holiday stories every Easter, Whitsuntide and August bank holiday for the next few years. They were easy enough to write the first time, the second time and even the third time but when it got to the fifteenth time it was a little more difficult to strike an entirely novel note.

I was, however, greatly assisted by a number of representatives of Scarborough corporation—notably the town clerk, Eric Horsfall Turner, and the press officer, Colin Crofts. These two men spearheaded Scarborough's drive during the 1950s to promote itself as the queen of watering places and attract the new type of British holidaymakers who had come into existence during the post-war years as a result of holidays with pay and other social improvements.

Before the war Scarborough had been a select resort for the upper and middle classes for over 200 years. It had followed the lines of development of the inland spas such as Harrogate but toward the end of the seventeenth century acquired for itself a new attraction not available in Harrogate. A Scarborough doctor with the name of Wittie became an ardent advocate of the health benefits of bathing in sea water as a variant from drinking spa waters and, despite the prevailing prejudice against baths of any sort, a new fashion was soon established. By 1732 the bathing season at Scarborough was a great event and was described in a letter written in that year as follows: "It is the custom for not only the gentlemen but the ladies also to bathe in the sea. The gentlemen go out in boats and jump in naked directly. The ladies have the conveniency of gowns and guides."

In the nineteenth century Scarborough's development as a seaside resort continued apace and large numbers of hotels were built—including the big four, the Crown, Grand, Pavilion and Royal. Lots of boarding houses and apartments were also provided for the less well-to-do but the resort concentrated on preserving its selectness and few concessions were made to the tastes of the masses. A rash of inferior restaurants and amusement arcades lined the foreshore fairly early in the present century but these amenities were essentially for the day trippers. The Esplanade, the Spa, the Peasholm Park area and most other parts of Scarborough remained the fortress of the middle classes. Evening dress was *de rigueur* on the Spa after sundown and entertainment was confined to an orchestra and one or two pierrot shows.

Eric Horsfall Turner and the progressive members of the town council and other local organizations such as the hoteliers' association realized after the Second World War that Scarborough had to change radically if it was to retain, let alone expand, its holiday trade, and they set out quite systematically to convert Scarborough into a modern family resort.

They had no intention of turning it into a Blackpool or a circus town as many of their local critics maintained. They were all in favour of novel ideas and enterprise and did all they could to attract them—but only if they came into the category of what was considered appropriate for a family resort. Amusement arcades were tolerated but they were strictly confined to the foreshore. The more dubious attractions of Blackpool's Golden Mile, such as hurdy-gurdies, flea circuses, freak shows and strip tease performances, were barred completely.

There is no question that it was due to this policy, and to the very effective manner in which it was implemented, that Scarborough is the successful seaside resort it is today. Watching this policy take shape as I did in the 1950s was not only an absorbing experience but an unfailing source of good copy, and if I wrote one article about events in Scarborough I must have written a hundred.

Space ships and mechanical elephants

My first meeting with the town clerk and the press officer was on a tunny fishing expedition as a guest of Mr Joe Tansey, a wealthy Skegness businessman, who came to Scarborough every summer for the sole purpose of catching tunny—the huge fish found in the North Sea for many years which had brought into existence the British Tunny Club in Scarborough in the 1930s. Tansey hired a herring boat for five or six weeks and went out fishing for tunny as often as he could. It was an exciting sport because the actual fishing was done from a small dinghy rather than the herring boat and to land a tunny often involved being towed by the giant fish round the ocean for several hours.

I had come over to write a descriptive article on a tunny fishing expedition and Colin Crofts was on a similar mission for the old *Leader* magazine, a contemporary of *Picture Post*. Eric Horsfall Turner was an enthusiastic angler for fish of any description and had recently added tunny to his list. The four of us met in the cocktail bar of the Grand Hotel for pre-lunch drinks and expected to set out in search of tunny at about 2 30 pm. Our host, however, had other ideas and the pre-lunch drinks developed into a three-hour session in which lunch played no part at all. We staggered down to the harbour at about four o'clock and retired to our bunks on the herring boat for the rest of the day. The sea was very rough and I waited for Crofts to be seasick and he waited for me to be seasick. It transpired that we had both been in the Merchant Navy.

The trip was a failure. Despite the most extensive search we never saw a tunny of any description. The only fish we did see were half a dozen herrings thrown to us by another herring boat we encountered and which we cooked in oil for breakfast—the tastiest breakfast, incidentally, that I ever remember. There were some positive results from the excursion, however. Crofts was subsequently appointed press officer to Scarborough corporation and I was invited to cover the latest of Scarborough's publicity stunts, the purchase for £4 100 of Britain's last full-rigged ship to sail under the red ensign, the *Hispaniola*.

The *Hispaniola* arrived at her anchorage in Scarborough after a 700-mile voyage from Appledore in Devon and thousands of holidaymakers turned out to see her. The event was stage managed to attract as much publicity as possible and a party of pressmen and officials, including the Mayor and Mayoress of Scarborough, went out in a flag-bedecked launch to greet her. But unfortunately things did not go quite as smoothly as planned. Before the launch had reached her anchorage the *Hispaniola* found it necessary for some obscure reason to weigh anchor and move out to sea, with the result that for half an hour or more the VIP launch was vainly chasing the *Hispaniola* in the direction of Germany. We eventually caught up with her three miles out to sea but it was impossible to board her as planned and all we could do was escort her into harbour, where she was to be converted into a floating aquarium.

The *Hispaniola* was followed by many other outrageous novelties. There was the famous life-sized mechanical elephant weighing 18 cwts with 9 000 parts and a Rolls-Royce engine fitted in its stomach, which gave enthusiastic children and sheepish adults rides on its back on the Spa at five miles an hour. It waggled both its tail and its trunk and according to its owner, Mr Frank Stuart, was far more remarkable than a live elephant because it could carry eight adults whereas a real one could only carry six. And Mr Stuart should have known for, amazing to relate, I discovered him to be a Fellow of the Royal Zoological Society.

"Mechanical elephants may not be exactly in the old Spa tradition", I wrote, "but it should be noted that this little frolic takes place at a discreet distance from the white-painted bandstand and the hanging baskets of geraniums where the orchestra is playing 'Maid of the Mountains' just as decorously as ever."

Perhaps the most controversial "attraction" in Scarborough was the £6 000 space ship, 60 feet long by 18 feet wide and weighing 10½ tons. This was fitted with two electric motors which made the floor vibrate and the illusion of space travel was given by a back projection film. This was launched with great publicity after being christened *Anastasia* by actress Frances Day and a Mr John Wilder of the Interplanetary Society—no scientific touch was neglected by Scarborough corporation.

"The first people to travel to the moon in Scarborough's new space ship will be the members of the town council" the handouts proclaimed. They did not add that many people in Scarborough were saying that they hoped they would stay there. It was not so much the space ship itself which excited anger as the situation of it at the foot of the St Nicholas gardens overlooking the south bay. This location was bitterly attacked by the Ratepayers' Association and other local bodies because, it was claimed, it ruined the view.

"I am appalled", wrote one ratepayer, "that Scarborough should be defaced by this tawdry and hideous so-called attraction. It is no more like a space ship than a dead whale."

To which the council replied that if the space ship was to make money it could hardly be tucked away in a back street. They emphasized once again that if Scarborough was to maintain the striking reputation it had now achieved for itself as a progressive and enterprising resort the public must be continually provided with novel forms of entertainment.

Together with the mayor and mayoress, the ever-charming Mr and Mrs J W Hardcastle, the live-wire chairman of the entertainments committee, councillor Ken Tringham, the town clerk and other VIPs some sixty of us were taken on the "maiden flight" of the space ship by a pilot called Dan Dare wearing a red space suit and jack boots and a wonderful pressurized helmet as big as a kitchen sink. He warned us that we should not be able to see out of the portholes because of the tremendous speed and directed our attention to a screen in front of us on which the tele-view cameras would record our progress. There, he explained, we should see Scarborough recede into the distance, the earth spin on its axis behind us and the moon take shape in front of us. It was a wonderfully realistic performance and I was not too surprised to learn that Dan Dare in real life was Mr George Hopkins of Leeds who for seventeen years had been stage manager of Kirby's Flying Ballet, a popular pantomime attraction.

The space ship was the apotheosis of Scarborough's search for novelty and a season or two later I was reporting complaints that the council were pursuing a more restrictive policy towards novel forms of entertainment. "The council has never forgotten the furore there was over the space ship" I was told. "Now the pendulum seems to have swung right over. They won't even have bathing beauty competitions. A national Sunday newspaper wanted to organize one on the beach this season but the council would have nothing to do with it. Their current outlook seems to be that Scarborough should recapture the spirit of its golden age—when the Londsboroughs and the Sitwells were in their hey-day and the main attraction was the Spa parade. What they seem to forget is that the prosperity of Scarborough today depends not on the people who stroll on the Spa but on those who queue for the dodgems."

This truly remarkable comment was elicited by the corporation's determined stand against a so-called jungle exhibition staged in a converted basement on the foreshore by two young men who described themselves as herbetologists. It included three pythons, a boa constrictor, a mongoose and a fruit bat. Scarborough town council may not have been quite sure what a herbetologist was but it sensed danger and resolved at a meeting that if the exhibition was not closed forthwith an enforcement order would be made under the Town and Country Planning Act. To this the herbetologists replied by giving notice of appeal to the Minister of Housing and Local Government and pending his ruling the exhibition remained open.

"I can't see why they want to stop us earning an honest living", one of the herbetologists told me as he showed me an 18-foot Indian python eat six chickens at a meal.

The Spa moves with the times

But if Scarborough corporation entertainments were beginning to lose their revolutionary sparkle there was no sign of it on the Spa, where the decision to drop the entrance fee to sixpence and to put on an ice show was described as "a measure of the social revolution of our time". "The Spa Company are bowing to the inevitable", the manager, Mr Dennis Lovell, told me.

In view of the hallowed place the Spa held in Scarborough's affections this was probably the greatest blow of all to the traditionalists although they seemed to take it quite calmly—so calmly that one of them was prompted to write to the *Scarborough Evening News* deploring it. "Is it", he asked, "because words fail us, or is it just the modern attitude of couldn't care less?"

It was the late Victorian and Edwardian era that was the golden age of the Spa. That was when Lord Londsborough had a house in the Crescent and took his guests down to the Spa every evening. In 1871 they included the Prince of Wales and Princess Alexandra and a special dramatic entertainment was put on for them by Mr J L Poole, including a programme of music by Meyer Lutz.

There was and probably still is a painting hanging in the town hall of the splendid scene on the Spa that night, with the Prince of Wales leaning carelessly against a lamp post. All the best people of Scarborough are grouped round him in top hats and frock coats and dresses sweeping the ground. Not that all these people were actually there. It is said that many of them paid the artist a commission to include their faces on the picture.

The glory of the Spa goes back much further than 1871, however. Its history began in 1620 when a Mistress Farrow chanced to walk along the shore one day and discovered some fresh water springs which were turning the pebbles russet. She tasted them and thought they might have medicinal properties. "The waters were afterwards", say the history books, "in great reputation with the citizens of York and the gentry of the county and at length they were so generally recommended that persons of quality came from a great distance to drink them."

The first Spa House was erected on the site about 1700—the same site on which a china shop stands today. The Spa House was little more than a wooden hut but under the management of its eccentric governor, Dicky Dickinson, it soon became a fashionable lounge for those ladies and gentlemen of quality who were able to spend three months of the year at Scarborough curing themselves from the indulgences of the other nine.

The eighteenth-century attraction of the waters was supplemented in the nineteenth century by the attraction of the parade to the accompaniment of music, the orchestra going round with the hat. By mid-century there were other attractions. "The Spa", wrote a contemporary author, "is the delight of young ladies, the hope of widows, the hunting ground of adventurers and the joy of the two-and-sixpence-an-hour horseman."

The Spa's golden age ended in that fateful August of 1914. The waters continued to be dispensed after the First World War but they were now quite an incidental attraction. The accent was on music and under the conductorship of the famous Alick Maclean the orchestra built up for itself a national reputation. Since the end of the Second World War, with the taps of its wells gone rusty and the famous waters available no longer, the Spa had been reluctantly and laboriously making up its mind to enter the brave new world of jeans and fancy hats, candy floss and pineapple glories.

I finished a nostalgic article about the Spa with an imaginary meeting near the bandstand with a ghostly figure in a top hat and frock coat and mutton chop whiskers. "Tell me", he said sorrowfully, "is it true that some of the ladies nowadays wear fancy hats bearing the inscription 'kiss me quick'?" I admitted, reluctantly, that it was. "But not on the Spa so far" I added quickly. "It hasn't come to that yet." At which he heaved a sigh of relief and disappeared!

Scarborough in the 1950s was stimulating to say the least. The corporation spared neither effort nor expense in stage managing its new attractions and securing for them the maximum publicity and, chiefly due to the efforts of Colin Crofts and Eric Horsfall Turner, Scarborough became a mecca for itinerant journalists from practically every newspaper and magazine in the country. They were dined and wined at the leading hotels and at the numerous cocktail parties at the town hall and the resulting reports and articles in their journals secured for Scarborough more column inches of publicity than any other resort in the country. There were critics on the council and off it who said it was all a gigantic waste of money but if the same amount of publicity had been purchased in the advertising columns the cost would have been a hundred times greater. And what a lot of fun would have been missed!

How much on the ball Scarborough was in the publicity field is perhaps best illustrated by the story of Bridlington's wind shields. Bridlington stole a march on Scarborough by hiring out these stretches of canvas which were staked down in the sand to protect one from the north east wind. Scarborough adopted them the following year. But Scarborough called them "suntraps!"

Changelessness of politics

Although as a feature writer I covered practically anything that was going, politics were my speciality and throughout the 1950s I was closely involved with all aspects of politics in Yorkshire. I covered three general elections—in 1950, 1951 and 1955—and innumerable by-elections. I also always attended the party conferences when they were held in the north—that is to say at either Blackpool or Scarborough—and kept in pretty close touch with events in the fifty-six parliamentary divisions into which Yorkshire was divided at that time. It was an exciting period politically with both the main parties holding office in turn and many of the political giants of the twentieth century occupying the political stage. The Labour party was dominated by Clement Attlee, Stafford Cripps, Herbert Morrison, Hugh Dalton, Emanuel Shinwell, Hugh Gaitskell, Aneurin Bevan and Jennie Lee and the Conservative party by Winston Churchill, Anthony Eden, R A Butler and Harold Macmillan. I met all the political stars at election meetings or in the bars and lounges of the Grand Hotel at Scarborough and the Imperial Hotel at Blackpool and got to know some of them quite well.

My entry into Yorkshire politics was via a celebrated by-election in the Batley and Morley constituency in 1949. It was caused by the death of a very popular MP, Hubert Beaumont, who was a deputy speaker of the House of Commons, and the contest was taken very seriously by both Transport House and Conservative Central Office because it constituted a crucial test for the Labour government elected in 1945. There had been a fall in the Labour majority from 19 000 to only 3 000 at a by-election in Edmonton a few months previously and Batley and Morley was looked upon to provide the answer to the vital question—was Labour on the way out or was Edmonton merely a flash in the pan? It was a straight fight between the two parties and the candidates were a Huddersfield solicitor, Max Ramsden, and a Batley general practitioner, A D D (Bill) Broughton. It quickly developed into a very lively campaign which hit the national headlines almost every morning as the two parties' big guns came up from London to try and sway the electorate.

Looking through my cuttings books makes me realize how little politics has changed in nearly thirty years. Max Ramsden's campaign was based on four central themes—all of which would be equally relevant in 1976. The first was a call for a drastic reduction in government expenditure. "Let's get back to the good old days of Liberal finance, of retrenchment and of reform", he declared. "They were good years. They didn't squander public money in those days as it is being squandered today."

His second theme was that something must be done about the

crushing burden of taxation—"which is destroying initiative in all ranks of society and also damaging production". Thirdly, every man and woman must be brought back into production—"and that includes the hordes of administrative officials who sit filling in forms from morning to night". And, fourthly, restrictive practices whether by employer or employee must be abandoned. "These are the sort of practical measures which must be taken if we are to deal with the economic crisis", Mr Ramsden declared. Twenty-seven years and about a dozen governments later the message remains precisely the same!

The Socialist battle cry was a little different. They were all the time looking back instead of forward to the bad old days of "Tory misrule". At every election meeting the Socialist speakers dangled the grim spectre of unemployment before the electorate. Mr Jack Jones MP (not the present leader of the Transport and General Workers' Union) trotted out a sad little tale of how he bought an engagement ring with his gratuity from the First World War only to have to pawn it the following Christmas Eve. And Miss Jennie Lee made the blood run cold with her chilling story of "the Thursday night knock"—the knock of starving neighbours at her mother's door in the Rhondda. But perhaps the Socialists' best contribution to political realism was the pamphlet they distributed picturing "a group of bonny babies brought up in Socialist Britain". It transpired that they had got the wrong picture—one of the babies turned out to be the Duke of Kent taken in 1936! The Socialists distributed these with another pamphlet appropriately entitled "Let's have the truth".

As everyone in Batley and Morley realized the result of the by-election was a foregone conclusion—"they would vote Labour here if they put a donkey up"—and Dr Broughton was duly elected with a majority of 7 686 compared with 11 592 at the general election. He proceeded to represent the division for the next twenty-seven years—to date.

The 101 other by-elections I covered during the subsequent years were almost equally predictable—one of the many nonsensical features of the British electoral system. There was always some simulated excitement and speculation but I honestly can't remember a single one where the result was in very much doubt. The build-up of passion and partisanship was really all a political game—played in grim earnest by the two main political parties and any outsiders who cared to enter. The chief victims were the candidates, poor devils, who were called upon to perform all sorts of absurd contortions in the very questionable cause of parliamentary democracy. The most futile circus tricks were performed at the morning press conferences which were held by the leading candidates, trying hard to stir up some interest in the slumbering electorate. We pressmen would go round from one conference to the other and the candidates, spurred on by those eager beavers, the constituency party agents, would hold forth with great eloquence on "the main issues of this important by-election which the whole country is watching". But the plain fact was that there were really no issues except those which they invented—and as for the progress of the campaign the country could not care less. All they were remotely interested in was the result.

The Conservative press campaigns were often directed with just the right degree of blatant cynicism by a fascinating character from the Yorkshire headquarters, David Scott-Atkinson. His long, languid figure would be reclining with its feet on the desk when one walked into the by-election battle headquarters and in his arms would be his Pekingese dog, known throughout the Yorkshire political area as Amber, the Tory bitch. "Bloody hell, you again!", he would greet me. "I've just worked myself to bloody death filling you with bloody crap on the by-election at . . . Aren't you ever satisfied? What do you want to know this time—by the way I can confirm that the Socialist candidate is knocking off the Conservative candidate's wife in the Liberal committee rooms but there is no truth whatever in the story that the Conservative candidate told the Labour candidate it would be perfectly all right if the gentleman apologized."

Scott-Atkinson and his assistants—usually a bevy of glamorous girls—would together fabricate some of the issues on which the election was to be fought by the Conservatives and the candidate would then be produced. And whether the majority was 10 000 in his favour or 20 000 against him he would always express himself as "soberly confident" of victory. What is more the Socialist candidate would use exactly the same words. Never "very" confident or "pretty" confident or "fairly" confident. Always "soberly confident". It is the first law of by-elections that all the candidates must be "soberly confident".

Scott-Atkinson's opposite number in the Labour party was the Yorkshire agent, John Anson, and he took things just as seriously as Scott-Atkinson took them cynically. Like most Labour election officials Anson had no semblance of a sense of humour and regarded all pressmen as lackeys of the capitalist press lords. It was impossible to convince him that even representatives of Conservative newspapers such as the *Yorkshire Post* were not "ordered" what to write. This pathological suspicion of the press is no doubt as strong today as it was then, and is in my experience one of the main reasons why the Tories usually get a better press in elections than the Socialists. I would add that in all my political writing for the *Yorkshire Post* I was never, ever, told what to write by anyone.

The general elections were more fun than the by-elections because on these occasions there was obviously more point in the contests and political passions were more genuinely roused. As well as attending meetings I spent my time accompanying the candidates on their canvassing rounds and I set the scene in an article on the 1950 campaign in the central division of Leeds, where the Conservative candidate was Mr William Barford: "The loudspeaker van drew up in a long cobbled street of shabby back-to-back houses with worn yellow steps and window sills and cracked, paintless doors. The gas works loomed up over the housetops and there was a brewery at the corner.

"The loudspeaker shattered the morning stillness. 'This is William Barford your Conservative candidate saying good morning and hoping that on February 23rd you are going to vote for a government that believes housing, the cost of living and freedom are the great issues of this election.' Nothing happened for some moments. Then three or four dogs started barking and the inevitable crowd of children came racing round the corner. They gathered round the van and peered inside it curiously as though it were a mobile zoo. They all wanted leaflets. One small boy with a pair of roller skates under his arm wanted to know if Mr Barford was Mr Churchill. They were all very interested. They seemed to be the only people who were.

"But no! Doors were opening and housewives were

appearing. The local grocer was peeping through his shop window. A woman in a dust cap opened a bedroom window and leaned so far out that I feared for her safety. The candidate got out and we went down the street, knocking at every door. The dogs and children followed in a bedraggled procession. One little boy cried bitterly because his mother had got a leaflet and he had not. Some housewives were interested; some weren't. Some flew upstairs to do their hair; others appeared in curlers. Some agreed with everything that was said to them, obviously worried that the potatoes might be burning. Some said vaguely 'Yes that's right. I shall have to see what I can do.' Others said 'Well I shall have to ask my husband.' One was the quintessence of brevity. 'Not today, thank you', she declared and shut the door in Mr Barford's face. He said it made him feel like a fishmonger.

"A woman in a one up and one down invited us in to inspect the great patch of damp across her ceiling. She would vote Conservative because the Socialists had done nothing about it. Another woman said she was going to vote Conservative because her neighbour spent her family allowance on bingo. One said she was voting Socialist because she was not interested in politics. Mr Barford might have converted her if it had not been for a brown mongrel called Tex. Tex strolled up and down during the discussion and someone—certainly not Mr Barford—said 'Get that dog out of the way'. 'That dog!' said the woman aghast. 'How d'you mean that dog? That's my dog. That's Tex. Good dog Tex.' Conservative hopes drooped."

Among the miners

I always contrived in general elections to spend some of my time in the South Yorkshire mining area because it was there that the electioneering really got warmed up. In constituencies such as Barnsley, Normanton, Hemsworth, Penistone and the Dearne Valley the Socialists always had huge majorities and everyone realized that the Conservative candidates didn't stand an earthly chance of being elected. The miners took their politics very seriously, however, and what is more had a certain admiration for anyone fighting against overwhelming odds.

One candidate in the 1950 election they admired very greatly was the Conservative contender in the Dearne Valley, where the Socialists had the biggest majority in the country—over 35 000. She was a sculptress and author, Mrs A L G Dower, and when I arrived at the Darfield church school I thought I had got to the wrong meeting. Surely a crowd of three or four hundred could not be waiting to hear the Conservative candidate in such an area!

"Is this Mrs Dower's meeting?", I asked a miner at the door. "Aye, that's right. She'll be here in a minute. Wonderful woman, Mrs Dower." She came striding up the gangway in a duffle coat as soon as I had found a seat—a tall, handsome woman with a presence about her suggesting energy, drive and no monkey business. There were cries of "She's here" and loud applause. "She seems very popular", I said to a woman in a shawl beside me. "Oh aye, she is love", was the reply. "Everybody likes her round here. If only she was Labour she'd walk in. It is a pity!"

Mrs Dower spoke for twenty minutes without a murmur of interruption and answered a volley of questions for over half an hour—and after the official meeting she adjourned to the Cross Keys hotel and had another unofficial meeting in the tap room. "Mrs Dower", said an elderly miner clutching a pint of bitter in one hand and a battered pipe in the other, "if yon' bloody Conservatives don't give you a safe seat next election it's a damned disgrace."

Another woman fighting a hopeless battle against a 26 000 majority in Hemsworth was pretty Miss Jean Asquith who had made a name for herself as a prominent Young Conservative. The miners had a soft spot for her, too. "She's a good lass", they told me. Miss Asquith never made much impression on the majority at Hemsworth but she evidently made an impression on the Conservative candidate in the neighbouring constituency of Doncaster and eventually became his wife. He was a future Chancellor of the Exchequer, Anthony Barber.

But perhaps the most entertaining day's canvassing I ever had in South Yorkshire was with Denton Hinchcliffe, Conservative candidate for the widely scattered Penistone division—Socialist majority 18 000. I joined him in Dodworth Bottom, a black sprawl of nineteenth-century miners' cottages. He was setting up his loudspeaker van and was warned by his companions, who had done a reconnaissance, that the natives were hostile. "Hah", said Mr Hinchcliffe, the light of battle in his eyes, "we will go and have a word with them shall we?" I followed him rather reluctantly round the corner trying to look as neutral as possible. We were met by a solid phalanx of housewives with mops, dusters, one or two dogs and several babies. "Gerrawaywiyer", they greeted us in chorus. "You're wasting your time round here."

"So you're satisfied with the cost of living?", asked Mr Hinchcliffe. There were one or two sniggers. "Gerrawaywiyer", repeated their most militant spokeswoman with a baby in her arms. "We know what will happen if you lot get in. Unemployment like it was before." She went into a long description of the hardships in Dodworth Bottom between the wars and Mr Hinchcliffe had to interrupt her to point out that her baby was doing its best to slice out its tonsils with the knife it was sucking.

Deciding we were not making much progress in Dodworth Bottom we moved on to Hoyland Common. They were more good humoured here but just as adamant. "The Tories want a pool of unemployment like they had in 1930" declared an articulate old miner with a stick. "Do you know who was in office in 1930?" demanded Mr Hinchcliffe. "Yes, Winston Churchill" was the reply. "Well he wasn't! There was a Labour government in office in 1930." The man with the stick shook his head. "All lies" he replied. "Gerrawaywiyer!"

"Of course it's not all as bad as this", said Mr Hinchcliffe, as we walked back to the loudspeaker car. "You have seen only the black spots. I shall get 16 000 votes in this division." He did—but it was 18 000 fewer than his opponent.

Of course, it is not only during by-elections and general elections that the politicians are at work in the local constituencies. Indeed some of the hardest and least rewarding work is the grinding tedium of trying to arouse some political enthusiasm in the electorate when everyone has better things to do. I wrote a "Such is Life" sketch about an evening's political action in Stanningley, near Leeds, entitled "Politics and the man with the euphonium". It featured the agent of one of the Leeds constituencies, Mr Thickbroom, and the prospective Conservative candidate, Mr Kirwin. I found them testing their loudspeaker one summer evening on a waste piece of ground in front of the cemetery. I observed that it was going to be difficult to attract much attention. "We'll rouse 'em" said Mr Thickbroom eyeing a large pile of gramophone records. "We got an audience of fifty on Armley Moor the other night."

He began with selections by the regimental band of the Grenadier Guards and followed with Land of Hope and Glory, the Drum Major and Glorious Devon. But to no avail. It was not until the opening bars of the William Tell Overture had shattered the Stanningley stillness that the first potential members of the audience arrived—a woman snivelling lugubriously into her handkerchief and two boys in jerseys sucking lollipops.

"The main thing is for the electors to see us in action", Mr Kirwin told me, running through his notes. "You have got to work a division up—and it means putting in a lot more time and effort than people realize."

He broke off to speak to a policeman who had just arrived on a bicyle. He informed us solemnly that he did not think there would be any trouble—Stanningley was usually pretty quiet until the pubs closed—but that he would be standing by just in case. Duly comforted by this assurance the agent switched off Pomp and Circumstance and opened the "meeting".

"Now ladies and gentlemen", he began in a voice which was amplified by the loudspeakers so much that it almost made the gravestones in the cemetery tremble, "I want to call your attention this evening to a meeting called by the West Leeds Conservative Association to give residents in this area a chance of hearing from our candidate the policy of the Conservative party."

He gazed at the snivelling woman and the two small boys who had now been joined by a dog and a man with a pipe and went on with sudden inspiration "There may not be many of you present yet but I feel sure we have an unseen audience who can hear what we are saying." This was a flash of genius. It raised the meeting on to a higher plane altogether. It seemed utterly futile no longer. The visible audience may be almost non-existent but the invisible audience could well fill the Albert Hall!

Mr Kirwin, a Leeds schoolmaster, spoke eloquently for

about half an hour, comparing the achievements of the Conservatives with the muddle and mismanagement of the Socialists. I was not, however, able to follow him as closely as he deserved because of an apparition approaching us slowly up the road. It was a man carrying, unmistakably, a euphonium and why he was bringing it to a Conservative meeting in Stanningley goodness knew.

After he had been standing with the visible audience of three (plus dog) for five minutes or so my curiosity overcame me and I asked him why he was carrying a euphonium. But he was evidently a little deaf and did not grasp the purport of my question. "Yes", he said gravely "it's a very fine instrument. It's worth £100 today and I bought it for £27 10s fourteen years ago." To which I replied, with one eye on Mr Kirwin, that here was another flagrant example of Socialist mismanagement and muddle. Just think of it! Euphoniums costing nearly four times as much as they did fourteen years ago!

Aneurin Bevan and Winston Churchill

I always used to say that I came away from the annual Labour party conference an ardent Conservative and from the annual Conservative party conference an ardent Socialist. This was unduly cynical but there is something rather demoralizing about party conferences to those who are not zealots—and they include a good many Members of Parliament, not to mention cabinet ministers. Party conferences undoubtedly serve a useful purpose—to keep the enthusiasm of party workers in the constituencies as near boiling point as possible and to give them the illusion that they are active participants in policy making—but they do not in my experience contribute very much to what might be called the intellectualism of politics. They provide an arena in which the party fanatics can besport themselves but they do nothing to strengthen one's faith in the democratic process.

The Labour party conference was always the most entertaining because it was not so well stage managed as the Conservative conference. The Socialists liked to call each other "brother" but they rarely manifested much brotherly love. Indeed some conferences I attended made one seriously wonder whether they disliked the Conservatives as much as they appeared to dislike each other!

The leading rebel in the Socialist camp in the 1950s was, of course, Aneurin Bevan, one of the finest orators I have ever heard. I didn't care for him as a man because class bitterness seemed to have corroded his soul and clouded his judgement but he was always much pleasanter to talk to over a pint of beer than he was on the public platform.

Bevan always addressed a public meeting in support of the leftist Labour magazine, *Tribune*, immediately before the party conference opened and his speech sometimes stole the conference thunder. Speaking with a slight lisp and a great feeling for words he would usually begin with a fierce attack on the capitalist press and proceed to lambaste the Tory party and all it stood for. If he had stopped there all would have been well but he usually went on to lambaste his own colleagues and the policies of his own party. He had a wonderful sense of humour and could reduce an audience to roaring laughter quite effortlessly. But even his sense of humour was malicious and he had a habit of spoiling the effect of a speech by a few careless asides.

I always remember one *Tribune* meeting at which Bevan made a most brilliant hour-long speech which repeatedly drew cheers and applause and would have brought the house down if he had not ruined it by a misguided and totally irrelevant attack upon, of all things, the Church. He was talking about the imposition of health service charges by a Conservative government. "If the churches of Great Britain had the essence of Christianity in them", he declared passionately, "they would have condemned the Conservative government for introducing them. It was an immoral act. The churches are fond of quoting from the Bible and using the parables but they are passing by the sick as much as ever the Pharisees did."

The audience was stunned and there were indignant cries of protest—a thing unheard of at a *Tribune* meeting. Bevan seemed to realize that he had gone too far and tried to cover up by saying there were, of course, some good churchmen who had condemned the churches. But the damage was done and the fine feat of oratory ended on a most discordant note.

Mr Attlee, the Labour leader, was always conspicuous by

his inconspicuousness. He would sit on the platform with his head down over the table and when he was not doodling he appeared (deceptively no doubt) to have dropped off to sleep. He was a man of few words but of firm principle and was respected by the party to a degree never reached by Harold Wilson.

Herbert Morrison was another rather colourless platform character, all glasses and quiff. He was the chief butt of the Bevanites who, with typical fraternal feelings, cheered themselves hoarse when they succeeded in driving him off the National Executive after over thirty years' service.

The conference histrionics were provided by such people as Emanuel Shinwell, Arthur Deakin (general secretary of the Transport and General Workers' Union), Sir William Lawther (president of the Miners' Union), Bessie Braddock, Ian Mikardo and the three leading ladies of the party, Jennie Lee, Edith Summerskill and Barbara Castle. Arthur Deakin, the bulldog of Socialist orthodoxy, hated left wingers almost as much as Nye Bevan hated Tories and although his vituperations were not nearly as polished and articulate as Nye's no one could stir up controversy more effectively.

Deakin was as blunt in manner as he was in appearance. I remember one conference at which, as the "fraternal delegate from the TUC", he lashed the Bevanites unmercifully. He was frequently interrupted by shouts, boos and jeers and at one stage a crowd of left wingers began to sing the Red Flag. It was one of the rowdiest demonstrations ever seen at a Labour party conference. Will Lawther was his vocal ally in lashing the left and he used to love to tell the leftists to "shut your gobs".

Compared with this the Conservative conferences were very mild beer. They tended to be dominated by grand-mannered women in flowered hats who never seemed happier than when they were calling for the return of flogging and defending capital punishment. But the Conservatives knew much better than the Socialists how to put on a show and the address by the party leader, which always brought the Conservative conference to a stirring conclusion, was political theatre at its best.

This was particularly the case when the leader was Sir Winston Churchill. There was an atmosphere about a Churchill meeting which I have never seen at any other political meeting in my life. The hall—the Spa Royal Hall at Scarborough or the Winter Gardens ballroom at Blackpool—was packed to capacity long before the meeting was due to begin and the mass of expectant people were entertained by rousing martial music on the organ. With perfect stage management the VIPs of the party would then make their individual entrances on to the platform to enthusiastic roars of applause. Lord Woolton, the party chairman, would be one of the first to enter, looking as genial and avuncular as only he could look—he was not called "Uncle Fred" for nothing. He would be followed by such people as Sir Walter Monckton, Lord Alexander, Peter Thorneycroft, Rab Butler, Harold Macmillan and, last but not least, the broadly smiling, handsome figure of Sir Anthony Eden.

Finally the great man himself would appear to a torrent of cheering—a rotund, almost Dickensian figure in a formal black coat and striped trousers, a spotted bow tie and an old-fashioned watch chain stretching across his ample waistcoat. In his chairman's remarks at the last Churchill meeting I attended Sir Anthony Eden described him as "the greatest man upon this earth" and as Sir Winston gave his hour-long address this was the thought which constantly recurred. The meeting was, one felt, far more than a Conservative party rally. It was an historic experience in many people's lives. "Yes," one felt some of the audience would be boasting to their grandchildren in forty or fifty years' time, "I once heard Winston Churchill speak."

Although by this time undoubtedly failing, Sir Winston was still remarkably alert and on this occasion showed in several quick asides that his brain was still very nimble. He made a slip, for instance, in saying that a Conservative government had restored national sovereignty instead of solvency. He corrected it at once and added "It's quite a natural mistake because the two really go together". And he showed in other asides that his puckish sense of humour was still keen. He paused during his speech at one point to have a drink from a glass on the table in front of him—and amused everybody by quaffing half a tumblerful. "It's only water", he chuckled. "I'm only drinking it to show you I can!"

There were also stirring emotional phrases rolled out with effortless eloquence. He declared that "in the vast tumultuous world which towers up around us under the shadow of the nuclear age no single country can control its destiny alone". And there was this vivid passage, delivered with mounting emotion in a call for an end to feelings of hatred against the Germans: "Let the dictators whose wickedness wrought these terrible deeds carry their awful records into history. Let Hitler (and here Sir Winston's face was suddenly contorted) take his shame to hell. Let the peoples of the world extend the hand of friendship and forgiveness to each other and walk forward together through the mysteries of life in freedom, justice and peace."

Churchill usually stayed at the Grand in Scarborough and Bill Larbolestier, the manager and a personal friend of mine, told me once of the difficulties in catering for him. He put the kitchen staff in disarray one morning by ordering champagne and oysters for breakfast. He also horrified the police during one of his trips to a Scarborough conference as Prime Minister. He was met at the station on arrival from London and he and Lady Churchill were put in the Corporation Rolls with the Mayor and Mayoress, the very popular Joe and Ida Hardcastle. A police car led the mayoral car and a police car followed it. The cavalcade did not get very far down Westborough, however, before the great crowd of well-wishers brought it to a halt. Whereupon Sir Winston turned to the Mayor and said "Let's walk the rest of the way Mr Mayor. It isn't far to the Grand Hotel is it?"

To the Mayor's consternation and the horror of the police Churchill got out of the car and set off to walk to the Grand Hotel. He was almost immediately swallowed up in the crowd, as were the Mayor and Mayoress and Lady Churchill and the four of them had to push and shove their way along Huntriss Row without any police protection whatever. Along with a crowd of other pressmen I was at the doors of the Grand Hotel when the Mayor and Mayoress and Lady Churchill succeeded in getting through but there was no sign of Sir Winston. Meanwhile the chief of police was going mad and Lady Churchill was not in the least amused. "It's too bad, Winston", she told the reprobate when he finally arrived, grinning broadly and making the "V" sign to the surging crowd around him.

It was one of the most exciting nights the resort had ever had.

Royal tours

After Joe Illingworth went to London royal tours in the north of England came into my province and I covered several as a Buckingham Palace accredited correspondent. This entitled me to travel in one of the small cavalcade of cars which followed the royal car wherever it went and to a place in the entourage which accompanied the royal party round the factories and housing estates which were on the programme of inspection. My tours were always with the Queen and the Duke of Edinburgh and the most notable was their West Riding tour in 1954. It began in Barnsley and the first day took in Wombwell, Rotherham and the surrounding mining areas before finishing up in Sheffield. The following day included Bradford and the heavy woollen district.

The mining areas gave a right royal welcome to the Queen and the Duke. Their route was lined with people all the way and the customary drabness of the South Yorkshire towns and villages was effectively concealed by flags and bunting. Sheffield greeted them with a royal salute of twenty-one guns fired by the 27th (Sheffield) Field Regiment Royal Artillery and the programme included the usual mass displays by countless thousands of schoolchildren on local football fields, and inevitably a visit to a steel works where a huge red hot boiler was specially flattened for them by a thundering 7 000 ton press. They were then whisked off to the University where the Queen incorporated the jubilee session amid the usual academic antics by Chancellor, Vice-Chancellor and staff in their full regalia.

The second day, in Bradford and the heavy woollen district, was just as hectic with more mass displays by schoolchildren on football fields and visits this time to wool textile mills. There was also a visit to a corporation housing estate where the Queen took afternoon tea with one of the tenants.

I suppose it is inevitable that there should be a dreary formality and uniformity about royal tours but it is not until you have accompanied the Queen on one of these that you realize what hard and tedious work they are and what a strain and a fatigue they must be. As one journalist put it on the West Riding tour: "It would kill me in six weeks, and I haven't even to wave." The wearisome repetitiveness of stepping in and out of cars, shaking hands and making polite conversation with pompous local officials, simulating interest in endless factories and trying to show enthusiasm for boring displays of juvenile gymnastics are enough to daunt the stoutest heart. But as everyone knows who has seen the Queen in action on these types of engagements she does her job supremely well. People from all walks of life always reported afterwards that they found her easy to talk to, and seemed surprised that they should have done. Perhaps the best tribute during the West Riding tour came from a workman at J Cawthra & Co's Perseverance Mills at Bradford where the Queen was shown some of the mysteries of textile manufacture. "She seemed to be so interested", said the workman, "you'd think she'd never looked round a factory before."

I watched the Queen at close quarters at many social functions of one sort and another but she never seemed to enjoy herself quite so much as she did at race meetings. I covered several royal St Legers at Doncaster and several royal Grand Nationals at Aintree and her reactions were always the same. It was probably not only her great interest in racing which made her so relaxed and happy but the fact that among racegoers she could be more herself. She was able to walk through the crowds to the parade ring more casually than she could walk in crowds anywhere else. People watched her, of course, but in an unobtrusive sort of way. "She has not come here to be gawped at" the racegoers seemed to say to themselves. "She has come, like us, because she's interested in racing, so don't let's spoil her afternoon by paying her too much obvious attention."

Leger Day at Doncaster

Leger Day was always a big day at Doncaster whether the Queen was there or not and I used to enjoy mingling with the crowds on Town Moor just as much as mingling with the mighty in the paddock. There was always an atmosphere about the Moor—a friendly, strident, rumbustious atmosphere which made the paddock seem dreary by comparison. There were, of course, far better facilities for entertainment on the Moor than in the paddock, where all you could do other than watch the racing was walk in and out of the champagne bar and consume alcohol and smoked salmon sandwiches. On the Moor there were all sorts of diversions. You could eat jellied eels out of teacups under red striped umbrellas and Southend cockles out of saucers under blue striped umbrellas. You could eat plates of hot peas with mint sauce and hot American hamburgers with fried onions. And in air reeking of vinegar you could eat fried fish and chips in your fingers at quaint little mobile stalls which poured smoke so prolifically out of their tall metal chimneys that you expected them to take off like helicopters at any moment.

Not that eating was the only diversion. There were dodgem cars and roundabouts and a variety of other activities not remotely connected with racing. I remember joining one such crowd who were watching a man smash up boulders with a hammer. Another crowd were watching a man tattooed with butterflies across his shoulders swallowing an iron chain a yard and a half long. This was a process as agonizing for the crowd as for the man himself—so much so that before he had time to haul the chain up again from his inside and take the hat round his audience had dispersed. "Don't appreciate nuffink", he muttered bitterly in cockney tones as I added my contribution to the three pennies and one halfpenny in the hat. "Here's me swallowing a chain all day long and they take it as free entertainment. I tell you, mister, the Leger's not what it was. I mean, would you swallow a chain of that size for threepence halfpenny?"

Odd sporting contests and Lady Docker

Race meetings such as the St Leger were not by any means the only big sporting events I attended in Yorkshire. I never missed a test match at Headingley and in the days when people used to queue all night outside the ground to be sure of getting in to watch the Australians I wrote about crowd scenes until I had said everything that could possibly be said about them. I also watched tennis at Scarborough in the company of such celebrities as Fred Perry and Dan Maskell and also attended some of the big soccer matches at Elland Road—although

Leeds United were not in those days the great team they were to become. But some of the other sporting occasions I wrote about were less traditional.

There was, for instance, the world Nipsy championship at Ryhill where sixty-two-year-old Ted Hammond, of Royston, took the title from fifty-two-year-old Dick Beedon, of Hemingfield. Nipsy was a variant of knur and spell peculiar to South Yorkshire and the championship spectators consisted entirely of miners in mufflers and caps. The match started with an argument. Ted objected to the construction of Dick's bat, a pick shaft two feet six inches long. Dick objected to the construction of Ted's nipsy—a small, pear-shaped object which was placed on an upturned brick, knocked into the air and hit as far as possible.

This argument resolved to the satisfaction of approximately half the spectators Dick took his strike. He began by dispatching officials to the far corners of the field so that they could spot exactly where the nipsy landed. But his optimistic foresight was unfounded. He did not knock the nipsy squarely and it travelled barely thirty yards. Ted followed and made an even worse show. He took a terrific swipe and missed completely.

This was only the beginning, however. Soon both contestants began to reveal their prowess at this ancient miners' game and the men in the far corners of the field were kept busy putting in pegs at what seemed incredible distances. Excitement rose, bets were laid and arguments flourished. The game went on for an hour or more and would probably have gone on longer if it had not been opening time. A tape measure was produced and Ted declared the new champion with a best hit of 178 yards and 4 inches. Ted attributed his success to his new brand of ivory nipsy, carved out of a billiard ball. Dick, who played with a wooden nipsy, continued to insist that Ted's nipsy was illegal.

There was the traction engine Derby at Pickering, a nightmarish event conceived for the prosaic reason of helping to pay off the mortgage on a bowling green and equip it as a children's playground. "We have a 'do' of some sort every year and we try and get fresh ideas", Mr Frank Hamilton, secretary of the Pickering Sports Committee explained. "Well we'd run sports and things before and the giant lollipop sucking competition had not enough popular appeal. So we decided on a traction engine Derby."

The brainwave was certainly a great success. Several hundred people turned up and saw four ancient engines pitching and rolling across a bumpy field, their funnels belching out not only clouds of thick black smoke but showers of sparks as impressive as Roman candles. A traction engine with its huge, sizzling boiler is a frightening vehicle at the best of times, looking like some vast mechanical monster which has escaped from a mechanical zoo. To see four of them racing with each other was a never-to-be-forgotten spectacle. The four engines had all been unearthed in Yorkshire and the oldest, Black Bess, was fifty-three years old and had been under a hedge for as long as its owner could remember.

The drivers warmed up their engines for nearly an hour before the race began—a terrifying procedure—but once the flag had dropped they all got off to an impressive start. Black Bess and Mary were soon outpaced, however, and Old Glory and Surprise waged a desperate duel for first place, Old Glory eventually winning in what was almost a photo finish. Her driver, Mr Ernest Mortimer, received a bottle of beer and a kiss from his wife as his prize. He attributed his success to his steerer, Mr Edward Wardrell, who, I discovered later, owned the field. "He couldn't help but win it", said the disconsolate loser. "He knew all the bloody bumps!"

Another odd sporting contest I attended was a marbles championship at Castleford's Reight Neet Aht. This was won by Lady Docker who, with her husband, Sir Bernard, came specially up from London in their famous gold plated Daimler to take part in the competition for the benefit of Castleford's cancer fund. The event attracted large press coverage and, I have no doubt, is still talked about in Castleford.

It was held at Castleford's festival hall and 800 ticket holders paid to watch it together with a few hundred more guests, photographers and pressmen. And outside in the street there was a vast crowd assembled to see the Dockers arrive and more policemen on duty than for a football cup tie.

It was a reight neet aht all right. It began, oddly enough, with the Castleford girls' choir in white blouses and red skirts rendering the Castleford anthem ("written in 1938 and seldom heard" an official told me) and went on fast and furiously until 2 o'clock in the morning.

Lady Docker matched her skill at flicking marbles against

that of ten Castleford mill girls—all attired in their best party dresses and looking as self-conscious as bridesmaids at a wedding—but it was obvious that however great the skill of her adversaries Lady Docker would win because the trophy consisted of a huge imitation gold marble on a stand bearing her name.

The vivacious Lady Docker was in her element and the Castleford miners and their wives just loved her. She was wearing a fabulous dress embroidered in different shades of blue sequins with an equally fabulous diamond pendant round her neck and diamond bracelets on both wrists. "Not a bit of gold anywhere" she told me. "Of course we have the car outside!" Sir Bernard presented the fund with a cheque for £1 000 to round off the night's proceedings and the miners went happily home with only their egalitarianism dented.

Piano playing marathon

I wrote about many other oddities but not all of them were sporting. There was nothing sporting, for instance, about Sandy Strickland's piano playing marathon. It was sheer masochism. Sandy, a young man of about thirty, played the piano non-stop for 104 hours at the Cambridge Road baths in Huddersfield and I interviewed him in the midst of it. He was wrapped in a blanket and wearing dark glasses and the audience consisted of two bus conductors and a woman cleaner, who had each paid a shilling entrance. His trainer, Mr Arthur Lea, wearing a blue sweater and grey flannels, introduced me. Sandy, strumming the keyboard of a grand piano, gave me a haggard nod. "I think I've got the flu", he said in a Lancashire accent. "And my wrists are swelling and I can hardly keep awake."

"And how", I asked, trying to find a suitable question for the occasion, "is the piano standing up to it?"

"Oh", he said, "the piano's all right. I tune it as I go along."

"I and my assistant do everything for him", Mr Lea explained. "He never stops playing for a second, night and day. People can come in and see him at any time. We give him food and drink and attend to his other requirements. We are both short of sleep but we don't mind. We will carry on to the end."

"And Sandy?", I asked.

"Oh we'll revive him with a foam bath", he said.

Sandy's "manager" and the brain behind the marathon was Mr Bernard M Woolley, who I found relaxing in the sunshine outside, looking fresh and prosperous in a smartly cut grey suit and brown shoes. I asked him if there was either point or purpose in getting someone to play a piano for 104 hours non-stop. I added that it struck me as sheer cruelty.

He looked rather injured. "It's all a question of sensation", he explained. "The public want sensation and today they're not getting enough of it. I'm going to give them sensation. This piano marathon is the beginning of a new era in British entertainment. It's going to lure people away from television."

He paused and looked at the notice board outside the baths, which contained the latest "bulletin". It announced that Sandy had done seventy-two hours and had only thirty-two hours still to do. It added laconically: "Falling asleep".

"My ambition", said Mr Woolley, who was far more interested in talking about himself than about Sandy, "is to be another Barnum. I have ideas. I have plans. I am bringing over a man from Austria who is going to fast for eighty-four days in a huge electric light bulb. And I am bringing a woman from the continent who is going to swallow live goldfish."

He brushed back his sleek hair. "I'm also trying to get hold of a whale. A huge whale. Something like Moby Dick. Talking of whales I made a bid for that queer fish they found off Madagascar—the coelacanth or whatever they call it. But they wanted it for research or something."

"To revert to piano playing, what does Sandy get out of the marathon?", I asked.

"Well", he said thoughtfully, "he gets the honour and glory. And also a percentage of the gate—and we have had 3 000 in at a shilling a time already. I've also received an offer to run him on Broadway. It will be the first piano marathon Americans have ever had. Of course to be a sensation over there will mean playing non-stop for a week—and here he's only doing four days and a bit. But he's got a good physique. And he'll be able to limber up on the boat."

His eyes sparkled as fresh ideas came to mind. "You know piano marathons are full of sensational possibilities. Sandy is trying to beat a record set up by a Frenchman. Now what I would like to do is to get them playing together. I could stage it in Leeds with an international jury. They could watch in shifts and see who collapsed first!"

"But", I said horrified, "what about the effects on their health?"

He looked at me keenly. "It would cost the taxpayer nothing" he said. "Any hospital bills would be paid by me."

Six months after this event I read that Sandy was staging another piano marathon in Castleford and I rang up Mr Bernard M Woolley, who lived at Bolton, to register a mild word of protest.

"You told me", I said, "that you were going to provide new sensations. You called yourself a modern Barnum. But what is there new about this?"

Mr Woolley explained, very indignantly, that he was Sandy's manager no longer. "I felt he was overdoing it", he said. "He has got a new manager. I am presenting the public with an entirely new sensation at Barrow-in-Furness."

"Ah", I replied, "it's the man from Austria you told me about. He is spending eighty-four days inside a giant electric light bulb. Or is it the woman from the continent who swallows live goldfish?"

Mr Woolley said these were old ideas. "It's another piano marathon", he explained. "But it's one that's entirely different. I've got the first woman marathon pianist in the history of the world. She's Musical Marie from Manchester. She weighs seventeen stones. She started playing in Barrow-in-Furness on Monday morning and won't finish until Saturday night. That's 132 hours non-stop."

I must have sounded disappointed. "And that's not all", he went on. "I'll back Marie against Sandy any time. Why don't you get hold of Sandy's new manager and tell him I challenge him to a sit-down duel? Maybe we could hold it in Leeds. Sandy and Marie playing together and a jury of pressmen to watch. And the one who collapses first is the loser!"

I could sense his enthusiasm mounting. "I'm prepared to back Marie for £500", he said excitedly. "I'm sure she'd win. She's got a wonderful temperament and suffers from insomnia."

I suggested that Marie should perhaps be consulted but he

said it was quite unnecessary. "She'd love it", he declared.

I agreed to put the proposal before Sandy's new manager in Castleford but said I still felt that piano marathons were a bit old hat. What about some new sensations?

"But I've already got some!", he replied. "I've a man in a barrel in Dublin who is fasting for six weeks. And a fat woman in Belfast who weighs twenty-two stones. And I'm still on the look-out for the world's largest whale."

He paused to consider some more of his current sensations. "And what about my spaceman?", he asked. "He swallows batteries and lights himself up inside. And he bends iron bars as a sideline. Don't you call that a new sensation?"

Sandy Strickland's new manager turned out to be Mr Leonard Coo. "My credentials", he told me, "are these—I was with Bertram Mills circus for twenty-three years and travelled all over the world. I have fetched giraffe women from Burma, plate-lipped women from the Amazon and a nine-foot giant from Texas . . . "

I explained that I was not wanting his credentials but his views on a challenge issued by Mr Bernard M Woolley. He became suddenly volatile but I cut him short. "No", I said hurriedly, "not your views on Mr Bernard M Woolley but your views on the challenge he has issued."

He paused. "My reaction to his challenge is this. I will back Sandy against Marie whenever he likes. And not for £500. For £1 000. Sandy could not lose. He taught Marie the job."

I suggested that Sandy with one marathon on his hands already should perhaps be consulted. But as with Marie it was considered unnecessary. Sandy it seemed was in splendid form. He had been playing at Castleford since Monday—and had had a lion watching him.

"A what?", I gasped.

"A lion", repeated Mr Coo. "Just a cub you know. Someone brought it in from a circus . . . "

I told him he should keep quiet about this. If Mr Woolley got to hear of it I had a shrewd idea what he would do. He'd have that lion playing a piano marathon for 200 hours—and it would be the greatest sensation of all time.

There was another follow-up to the piano playing marathon but I don't seem to have any record of how it turned out. It concerned a young Irishman called Kevin Sheehan whom I interviewed in Oldham about a year after talking to Mr Coo. He had the idea of making a public speech lasting from Monday to Saturday—127 hours non-stop.

"I estimate that I shall deliver about one and a quarter million words", he told me at his lodgings as casually as though he were about to address a Rotary Club luncheon. "I shall be sustained on liquid foods—chiefly soups and beaten up eggs—and the only time I will even pause will be to swallow them."

Mr Sheehan said he had got the idea from the piano marathons. "I put an advertisement in the *Stage* asking if any showman was interested", he told me. "I heard from a man called Bernard M Woolley and he is managing my venture. The public will be admitted at one shilling a time and I hope to make £200 or £300. But I'm more interested in speaking for six days than in money and if I make only £5 I shan't be disappointed."

"You mean", I said, "that what really matters is the honour and glory?"

"Exactly. Speaking non-stop from Monday to Saturday is a unique achievement—more unique, I think, than climbing Everest."

He had arranged his subjects for the week and was getting off to a cheerful start on the Monday with "Survival after death". Tuesday's subject was "If I were the world's dictator" and Wednesday's "Atom bombs." On Thursday he was moving on to "H bombs and flying saucers" and on Friday planned an esoteric dissertation entitled "Hypocrites all". He would finish on Saturday in the realm of metaphysics with "The conquest of fear".

Mr Sheehan said he wished to make one thing clear. An American lorry driver had actually talked non-stop for eleven days in 1934 but his record did not count because he had gone mad at the end of it.

Whether Mr Sheehan set up the record I don't know. Nor have I ever heard if Mr Woolley found his whale. Such is show business!

Canal journey under the Pennines

All Yorkshiremen have gone over the Pennines to Lancashire but there must be few who have gone under them by canal.

I did as the guest of the Docks and Inland Waterways Executive on a maintenance inspection of the Standedge tunnel on the Huddersfield narrow canal. Fourteen of us left the light and open air at Marsden by barge at 9 45 am and did not see it again until we emerged at Diggle at 12 40 pm. It was an eerie journey. We heard the ominous rumble of trains passing through the Pennine railway tunnel a few feet above our head and we got a backlash of their steam and water through the ventilation shafts.

As we made our way through the stoutly buttressed tunnel with only paraffin lamps and torches to light our way the divisional waterways officer, Mr C M Marsh, told me the romantic history of the canal. It had not been used by barge traffic since 1921 but back in the early part of the nineteenth-century it had been the main route for merchandise passing between Manchester and Huddersfield. That was before railways and lorries were invented and the only alternative was to transport goods by pack horse across a stony mountain track. The barges, or dumb boats as they were known because of the lack of any motive power, would stop at the entrance to the tunnel and engage "leggers" to push them through.

The "leggers" earned their living by sitting on the sides of the boat and pushing their feet against the walls of the tunnel, or alternatively against the roof. The boats were similar to the one in which we were travelling—about seventy feet long by seven feet wide—and as they could carry thirty or forty tons of cargo they must have taken quite a lot of propelling. Meanwhile the mate or someone had taken the horse over the top to join the boat at the other side.

Fording the Humber

Lord Noel-Buxton, a Socialist peer, did not use a boat of any description for very long when he crossed the Humber from Brough to Whitton Ness watched by an enthusiastic crowd of five or six hundred people. He walked it!

He made his much publicized walk to support his theory that the Roman legions forded the Humber on their way through Lincolnshire into Yorkshire—a theory already borne out by the fact that there were known Roman roads terminating at each side of the river. The journey necessarily began by boat because of the thirty-foot deep shipping channel dredged in modern times but once clear of it he walked the rest of the way across without much difficulty, accompanied by three interested aeroplanes and a hovering helicopter. He wore a life-jacket in case of emergency but the water did not at any point come above his knees. He had, however, to fight against a seven- or eight-knot current in places.

There was great excitement on the river bank at Whitton Ness when it became apparent that he was going to succeed in his venture and a group of press photographers struggled through ankle deep mud to meet him in. Lord Noel-Buxton said afterwards that it was clear that the ford completed the Ermine Street route from London to York and that the Ninth Legion moved this way from Lincoln to York in AD 82.

He was asked if there was likely to be any truth in the story that Dick Turpin had ridden Black Bess across the river at this point on one of his highway adventures. He said there was no reason to doubt it. "I think you could ride a three speed bicycle across in bottom gear", he said. He was also asked why it was necessary to walk across the river to prove there was a Roman ford. Would it not have been much simpler to use a boat and a piece of string with a weight on to indicate the depth? He gave various technical reasons why a piece of string could not be used. Besides, he might have added, the horde of pressmen and photographers would not have been in the least interested watching a man drop a weight attached to a piece of string.

Jehovah's Witnesses and Billy Graham

Perhaps the oddest oddities I came across in my travels were the Jehovah's Witnesses about whom I wrote a number of articles. Their peculiar religion is based on a literal interpretation of the more lurid parts of the Old Testament and its message is to the effect that Jehovah God is going to destroy the present world at Armageddon when forces "a million times more powerful than the detonation of one hundred atom bombs at once" (to quote their tracts) will be exploded, and to replace it with a new heaven and a new earth which will be perfect in every way. The date of Armageddon is not known but "will be realized within this generation". Those who publicly proclaim Jehovah's message will survive Armageddon and be raised from their graves if dead and live in glory, but those who don't "will be slain and lie unburied, the food of worms that will not die or cease from swarming over the odious carcases till they have eaten the bones clean".

I attended a number of meetings at various Kingdom Halls (as their churches are called) and talked to many Witnesses. I asked a number of them why they had become Witnesses in the first place and their reply usually was that they had bought some tracts at the door. When I pressed them I found in a number of cases a more compelling reason, however. It was summed up by a working woman: "When my husband died I could get no comfort from the Church but I did get it at Kingdom Hall. I was told that when Armageddon comes my husband will rise from his grave and come back to me. And it won't be long now." She said it with complete conviction.

Another oddity about whom I wrote a personal study was Dr Billy Graham, the American evangelist who toured Britain in the fifties and attracted huge audiences which displayed such wild enthusiasm that they threatened to outdo pop concerts. To see crowds flocking to a religious meeting with the same excitement as to a football match was a novel experience. People came by coach, by car and on foot and waited in long queues for tickets of admittance. Once inside they hung on the preacher's every word and hundreds flocked to the front of the hall when called to make a "decision" to surrender themselves to Christ.

Graham, a very affable and likeable man of thirty-six, worked up to this climax throughout his sermon. "I am going to ask you in a moment", he said "to come out of your seats, quietly and reverently, and stand in front of this platform. As you come you will say 'I know I have sinned against God but I will receive him this night as my Lord and Master . . .'."

The organ would begin to play and the choir would begin to sing softly and soulfully as the preacher went on repeating the appeal, with his hands clasped and his eyes closed. And up the people came, in ones and twos, then in threes and fours, and finally in dozens and scores. There were about 350 of them at the meeting I attended. Approximately eight out of ten were women and perhaps six out of ten were teenagers.

I asked Graham for his explanation as to why half a million people had been to hear him preach in the UK in a month—and why 10 000 of them had made decisions. He had a very simple answer. "The reason is God. God is conducting this crusade, not Billy Graham." He was certainly not a phoney as some people alleged but equally surely he was not a great preacher. He had the gift of the gab and all the histrionic tricks of the professional orator. He had mobile features, expressive eyes, an extensive repertoire of gestures and a dramatist's ability for building up suspense. He was often praised for the simplicity of his message but in my view he was not simplistic but trite. So trite that a lot of what he said was an insult to adult intelligence. There was no intellectual depth about his preaching whatever. But he was at least honest. "My methods", he declared, "are used for films, circuses and prize fights. Is there any reason why they should not be used to promote the Kingdom of God?" He was a phenomenon of the fifties and has hardly been heard of in this country since.

Dewsbury offer for Dome of Discovery

The events and people I have written about in my reminiscences of life on the *Yorkshire Post* consist of necessity of only a small selection from the hundreds of stories and articles gathering dust in my cuttings books. I have made little reference to the straight news stories which, in the early days in particular, occupied much of my time. A newspaper reporter's life is as varied as the weather and just as unpredictable. I went into the office expecting a quiet day at Leeds Assizes and found myself chasing up to Durham to cover a pit disaster at Easington colliery. I was switched from a leisurely investigation into life on a new Leeds corporation housing estate to an air crash in thick fog in the middle of the Pennines. I drifted aimlessly into the office on a summer Sunday afternoon to be sent dashing down to a train crash near Wilmslow in Cheshire. I had to cancel an invitation to speak at a ladies' luncheon club to cover a murder in Wakefield. Dramatic stories like these are the very essence of newspaper journalism and the good straight reporters are in many ways the most valuable men on the staff. The things I have been writing about are the feature writers' province; and the feature writers' articles are the icing on the cake.

I concluded my recollections of Batley with the story of the Batley municipal pianos. I will conclude my recollections of the *Yorkshire Post* with a story from Batley's neighbouring town, Dewsbury. I think it sums up the down to earth Yorkshire attitude as well as any.

It all concerned a Festival of Britain creation known as the Dome of Discovery. It was claimed to be the biggest dome in the world—365 feet in diameter and 97 feet high. It was constructed of aluminium and was one of the principal show-pieces of British craftsmanship at the Festival. The Festival guide book described it as "a structure as adventurous, fantastic and technologically triumphant as the history of British discovery itself". It was said to have an atmosphere of mystery and awe and its contents were described as "a memorandum on the pre-eminent achievements of British men and women in mapping and charting the globe, in exploring the heavens and in investigating the structure and nature of the universe".

The dome was visited by many thousands of people during the Festival and became something of a problem after the Festival was over. It was far too big to put in the British Museum, or indeed in any other museum. What, then, was to be done with it? Surely this unique symbol of British achievement in relation to the universe and its mysteries should not be merely dismantled and thrown away! Surely someone with some aesthetic sensitivity could think of somewhere it should go!

The problem was well publicized in the papers and various suggestions were put forward—such as transferring it to a permanent home on the site of the Crystal Palace or perhaps in Hyde Park.

Dewsbury had other ideas. A firm of blanket manufacturers offered to buy it as a storage shed for wool!

I rang up the firm, Wormalds & Walker Ltd, to see if this fantastic report was true. "I understand", I said—and how absurd it sounded—"that you are negotiating for the purchase of the Dome of Discovery as a wool shed?"

"Yes," a voice replied quite calmly, "that's right. We heard they didn't know what to do with it so we wrote to the Festival authorities and said we were interested in buying it. But that's as far as it's got."

I said I hardly thought it had been designed with wool storage in mind.

"Oh," said the voice, "that doesn't matter. There's plenty of room in it and it's got a roof on. It will be very useful to us. We are short of storage space."

I suggested tentatively that the aesthetic and cultural instincts of the nation might be a little taken aback by their proposal. After all, its contents at the Festival had been described as "a memorandum on the pre-eminent achievements of British men and woman in mapping and charting the globe, in exploring the heavens and investigating the structure and nature of the universe". Was it really appropriate that this memorial to British endeavour should finish up in Dewsbury as a wool shed?

The voice regarded this as completely irrelevant and said so.

"But where", I persisted, "do you propose to put it?"

There was a sigh of irritation at my obtuseness. "Oh," said the voice, in tones which suggested that domes of discovery might be significant in London but cut no ice at all in Dewsbury, "we haven't gone into that yet but we've got plenty of waste land round here."

There was nothing else I could say. So I rang up the Dewsbury borough architect to see what he thought about it. It would surely strike dismay in his heart. But, alas, Dewsbury is Dewsbury, even where borough architects are concerned.

"Well," he said, "they'll have to get a licence from the Ministry of Works. And then it will have to come before the Housing and Town Planning Committee. And then the Town Council will have to pass it . . . "

I gave it up in despair. As far as I know Dewsbury did not finally get the Dome of Discovery and what happened to it I have not the slightest idea.

Part three—The World of Wool

Top prices

I left the staff of the *Yorkshire Post* in pursuit of every journalist's dream—to own his own paper. With financial help from my father I bought a substantial shareholding in a local paper—none other than my old competitor the *Batley News*—and stayed with it for four years as editor and joint managing director. The other joint managing director was Miss G M R Roberts, the daughter of the former proprietor and editor, Rayner Roberts, a well-known figure in northern journalism in his day. Miss Roberts continued to run the paper very successfully after her father's death during the war but eventually it became too much for her and she sold it to a Halifax firm. I had known her all my life and she invited me to join her in buying the paper back.

But there had been many developments in the newspaper industry since Rayner Roberts had died. We were handicapped from the start by old machinery and had a rotary press which should have been in a museum years ago. There was only one man in the world who could make it run, our machine man, Jim Lyons, and even then it could print only eight- or twelve-page papers, neither of which was economic. We managed to make it pay but only just and after four years' unremitting labour we merged with our stronger competitor, the *Dewsbury Reporter*, and joined their board, on which we both sat until 1970, when I approached Sir Kenneth Parkinson, chairman of the *Yorkshire Post*, and the *Reporter* was sold to the *Yorkshire Post*'s parent company, the United Newspaper group.

When I left the *Yorkshire Post* my colleagues gave me as a parting gift a painting by Campbell Taylor called "Serenity". I was to reflect afterwards that that was the end of serenity for me! There was certainly none to be had on the *Batley News* and after the merger I moved out and became editor of the *Wool Record* in Bradford, a job I retained for three years before moving to London.

The *Wool Record* at that time (1960) was a thriving weekly trade magazine, carrying nearly a hundred pages of advertisements and circulating in eighty countries all round the world. It was universally respected by executives in all branches of the international wool trade and I looked forward to regaining serenity at last. One thing I felt I should at least be free of was the constant risk of libel actions which, I had found, was one of the many perils of editing a newspaper. So, on my first day as editor, I walked into the *Wool Record* offices at 91 Kirkgate, with a jaunty step.

The retiring editor, Ernest Brown, who had very kindly agreed to stay on for a time to show me the ropes, was deep in anxious conference with the chief feature writer, Royston Millmore. "I'm afraid we've got a problem", Brown greeted me. "There's a letter here threatening us with a libel action. As it's the editor who goes to jail I think you'd better have a look at it."

It all concerned an apparently inoffensive article written by Millmore who contributed among other things a humorous feature called Almost at Random under the pseudonym Jason—which, incidentally, is still running in the magazine and has a wide readership. Millmore had been making a little fun at the expense of man-made fibres which by now were being produced in large numbers and had become serious rivals of wool. He had referred rather disparagingly to what he thought was an entirely fictitious fabric called Flanlon. It was not fictitious and the manufacturers of Flanlon had been to see their solicitors. It was an auspicious start for the new editor!

Fortunately no one went to jail or even to court but it was a salutary reminder that even in trade magazines the printed word has perils of its own. As Fitzgerald puts it in Omar Khayyam: "The moving finger writes and, having writ, moves on; nor all your piety nor wit shall lure it back to cancel half a line; nor all your tears wash out a word of it." How often journalists wish it were otherwise!

The *Wool Record* was a tiny set-up compared with the *Yorkshire Post* although it was in fact part of a much larger company—the International Publishing Corporation. It dealt exclusively with news and developments in the wool textile industry and although international in its coverage was Bradford to the core in its character and outlook. The most important thing in the wool world, I quickly learnt, was not the balance of payments situation or the position of sterling or even the level of the stock exchange index. It was the price of tops on the Bradford market—and anyone who wanted to keep the *Wool Record* in business had never to forget it. The *Wool Record* top price quotations went out to the whole world every week and were basic to the *Wool Record*'s fortunes.

Ernest Brown, a plump, balding, rather Dickensian figure with an endearing personality and a puckish sense of humour, told me that when he had been made editor of the *Wool Record* many years previously he had met a friend in Market Street, Bradford, and told him rather proudly of his new appointment. He did not expect paeans of congratulations because Bradford after all was Bradford, but he did think he might get just a brief expression of good wishes. But no. His friend looked him up and down in silence and then said laconically "Well the first thing you must do, Ernest, is put your 64s tops up tuppence."

The Bradford market report (which summarized the state of the market) and the top price quotations were done together on Thursday morning by the editor and the chief trade adviser, who at this time was a well-known Bradford wool merchant called Dick Wharton. For the first few weeks I was merely a silent witness of this Thursday morning seance. It was far too technical and esoteric a business for me to meddle in. Wharton would bring in a market report which he had drafted the previous night and he and Brown would go through it, sentence by sentence, in the light of information which had come in that morning from a whole host of other advisers.

The two of them usually agreed in their estimate of the general tone of the market, but they were both perfectionists and wanted to get in every subtlety of feeling expressed by every one of the advisers. This was, of course, an impossible task but the two of them struggled manfully to find a formula of words which was all embracing enough and no parliamentary bill or international treaty was drafted with more care, reflection and consideration than the weekly *Wool Record* market report. Indeed it seemed to me that sometimes it was worded with such terminological exactitude as to be largely meaningless, or at any rate incomprehensible. I naturally did not dare to voice such sentiments but I gathered later that I was not the only person who held that opinion!

My brief as editor was to revitalize the magazine and bring it into the twentieth century—it was by now 1960—but any action I contemplated had to await Brown's departure because the shock of my changing anything in the *Wool Record* would have been too much for him. It had been the same for the last goodness knows how many years and would clearly remain the same for as long as he had anything to do with it. When I asked him why certain things were done in certain ways his answer was always the same "Oh it's always been done like that".

Not that Brown was unhelpful or unco-operative. He did everything he possibly could to assist me in learning everything there was to know about the *Wool Record* and his assistance was invaluable. But I was under forty and he was over seventy and we had very different ideas on what a modern trade magazine should look like.

Brown was a native of Bradford and had spent many years writing about the wool industry for the *Yorkshire Observer* and the *Telegraph and Argus*, Bradford's morning and evening papers. He had not been a journalist all his life, however, and at one time had occupied the post of secretary to the Lord Mayor of Bradford. He was a born raconteur and when the directors came up from London and he and I and other members of the staff had dinner with them at the Devonshire Arms at Bolton Abbey he would entertain the company with his most amusing repertoire of stories of civic life in Bradford.

The one I liked best was his story of a visit to the city by the late Duke of Windsor when he was Prince of Wales. The day's proceedings were brought to a stirring climax with a civic dinner in the City Hall and the Duke was placed on the right hand of the Lord Mayor. The Lord Mayor was a mill worker and was completely overawed by the occasion. And the Duke was not very talkative. They sat in complete silence for about five minutes and then, feeling that he must say something, the Lord Mayor turned abruptly to the Prince and asked "How's yer Dad?"

Another good one was his story of how the mayoral Daimler had to be stopped in the country on one occasion to enable the

Lord Mayor and Lady Mayoress in their chains of office to spend pennies by the roadside. But that one needs Ernest Brown to tell it and he, alas, has been dead for years.

The wool textile industry, Yorkshire's premier industry for several centuries, was not in bad shape when I joined the *Wool Record* in 1960. The Lancashire trade had been decimated by cheap imports from the developing countries but because it was more specialized the wool trade had survived almost intact. There were still hundreds of wool merchants and topmakers in the Bradford area and also hundreds of worsted spinners and manufacturers. Bradford was still considered to be a wealthy city and there were said to be more Bentleys per head of the population than in any other city in England.

But the writing was on the wall in the shape of man-made fibres and during the 1960s a tremendous contraction of the industry was to take place. Scores of old established wool companies were to merge in some form or other and scores of others were to go out of business altogether. This metamorphosis meant fewer advertisers and subscribers for the *Wool Record* and along with the rest of the industry it was to contract very severely. As I have said when I joined the *Wool Record* in 1960 it was carrying up to 100 pages of advertising a week. Today it is a monthly publication carrying about forty pages of advertising per issue. That is a measure of the decline of the industry in the past sixteen years.

But as I say in 1960 Bradford was still a prosperous city. The woolmen gathered in their hundreds on the floor of the Wool Exchange every Monday and Thursday and with the statue of Cobden, the apostle of free trade, looking down on them did business in wools, tops, noils and yarns running into millions of pounds. And what Bradford said today the wool world did tomorrow —from Sydney to Buenos Aires, from Capetown to Wellington.

It was this international aspect of Bradford which gave it an edge over Leeds. It is curious at first sight that Bradford should have become the capital of the wool world rather than Leeds, which was always a much bigger town. At the beginning of the nineteenth century—the century of the British wool trade's development from a localized cottage industry into a world supplier of textiles—the population of Leeds was 53 000 compared with Bradford's 12 000. And in the early years of the industrial revolution Bradford was much less important as a textile centre than either Leeds or even Halifax. A good deal of handloom weaving was done in Bradford but the cloth was not dyed or finished there but in Leeds, Halifax or Wakefield. There were cloth halls in these cities long before there was one in Bradford and the cloth merchants naturally congregated round them.

The reason why Leeds was eventually eclipsed by Bradford as a wool textile centre was because Leeds concentrated on the finishing and merchanting of woollen and cotton cloths, and began to develop a clothing industry, while Bradford concentrated on worsteds—which, as every Yorkshireman should know, are made from combed wool (tops) and involve a much more complex system of production than woollens.

This specialization in worsteds made Bradford the centre to which capital, population and enterprise were drawn, and whereas there was only one mill in the town in 1801 by 1850 there were 194, twice as many as there were in Leeds and Halifax put together. The worsted trade was given its biggest fillip by the development of machine combing—one of the last textile processes to be mechanized. The use of combing machines greatly speeded up the production of combed wool and also increased the yield—the amount of top obtained from the wool—and improved the quality of the noils—the short fibres extracted in the combing process.

People from many parts of Europe began to drift to Bradford toward the end of the nineteenth century and even in 1960 Bradford was still essentially a cosmopolitan city whereas Leeds was essentially metropolitan. And yet at the same time Bradford had many of the characteristics of a village. Its people were closely integrated by the wool industry and although it would be an exaggeration to say that everyone knew everyone else you could not go far in Bradford without bumping into someone you knew. I found a sense of community in Bradford that I never found in Leeds, and there was a sort of family atmosphere pervading the wool industry which was as distinctive as it was congenial.

Medals at the Midland

This was nowhere better illustrated than at the wool dinners at the Midland Hotel, now, alas, closed down. There were about four of them held every winter by different sections of the industry and they were the oddest mixture of pomp, splendour and down-to-earth common-or-garden "matiness" I have ever come across.

The pomp was awe-inspiring. It was *de rigueur* for all the top table guests to wear white tie and tails and the invitation stated that medals would be worn. And by jove they were! Hundreds of them. The Midland fairly clanked with medals. I had been attending public dinners in Leeds for ten years with never more than a dinner jacket but I had to see my tailor and apply for my war-time service decorations before I could put in an appearance at a public dinner in Bradford. I would not have dared otherwise to face the scarlet-coated toast-master who bawled out one's name at the reception and banged on the table for silence to announce that dinner was served.

I don't know where they got him from but the toast-master at the Midland dinners was the most commanding officer I have ever come across. He made the toast-masters at the Savoy and the Dorchester in London look like untrained amateurs. "My lords, ladies and gentlemen", he would declaim as soon as coffee had been served and he had terrified the three or four hundred people into silence with a great crashing battery on the table, "pray silence for the President, Mr So and So, who will give you the loyal toast." You jumped up at once, petrified that he might add "On your feet there, Boothroyd, and quick about it!"

That most famous of all Bradfordians, J B Priestley, must have had this Midland toast-master in mind when he wrote his inimitable essay on public dinners. The toast-master, he concluded, was the only person who enjoyed them. " 'My lords, ladies and gentlemen . . .' how he rolls it out, the ass! Why should we endure such misery for him and his 'pray silence'? Let him accept an invitation from the talkies and leave us in peace . . . they are our masters and they have us on toast. The time has come when their power must be broken. Let us all attend the last public dinner taking to it a plan of action. When the toast-master cries 'pray silence' let us all throw pieces of bread at him and sing comic songs."

But the tyranny of the toast-master was not the only special feature of the Midland wool dinners. Despite the stuffed shirts, the clanking medals, the fat cigars and the general air of opulent distinction of the top table there was at the same time an air of informality about the proceedings which I can only describe as "matey". The point was that the stuffed shirts on the top table were woolmen like the rest of them in the body of the room.

They may be titularly more significant in that they were the chairmen of the Wool Textile Delegation or the National Wool Textile Export Corporation or even the Worsted Spinners Federation or the Association of Exporters of Raw Materials and Yarns, but these grandiose labels remained on them only for a year or two. At the next dinner or the next but one they would be off the top table and back in the body of the hall.

There was, therefore, no point in affectation on the one hand or undue reverence on the other and when the chairman of the Export Corporation was proposing a toast and his pals at the back of the room couldn't hear him distinctly they would shout out "Speak up, Fred, we can't hear you". And if he spoke for what a down table consensus of opinion considered to be too long there would be a shuffling of feet, and if he did not take immediate notice of this an outbreak of barracking—sometimes so pronounced that it was rather like being at a Yorkshire cricket match at Bramall Lane.

Visitors to these dinners from the south of England were quite appalled by these demonstrations and the toast-master was, I expect, outraged. But the Bradfordians took it all for granted as an essential element of the Bradford scene.

Of course, not all Bradford woolmen were well-versed in dinner etiquette. Some were what are usually known as plain blunt Yorkshiremen and were apt to be a little bewildered by the pomp and circumstance of the wool dinners. A story is told of two wool merchants who were attending a Wool Federation dinner for the first time and were put a little ill at ease by the gleaming miscellany of cutlery on the tables and the elaborate nature of the table decorations. And they were mystified by the presence of finger bowls.

"What's this 'ere water for Fred?", one of them asked the other.

Fred examined it closely. "Nay, I don't know Joe. Happen we sup it—but I don't know when. Let's ask t'waiter."

"Nay, you can't do that Fred, not at a public dinner!"

"'Course you can, Joe. It hasn't started yet."

A waiter was hovering near and Fred summoned him with an imperious gesture. "What's this 'ere water for?", he asked.

The waiter, in that grandiloquent manner which these gentlemen have, explained that it was a finger bowl.

"Finger bowl?", repeated Fred. "But what's t'water for?"

"Well, sir, it's to wash your fingers in after you've eaten your asparagus."

Fred looked at him unbelievingly. Joe began to laugh.

"What's tha think tha's laughing at?", growled Fred.

"Nay, Fred lad", came the reply, "if you will ask damned silly questions you'll get damned silly answers."

Bradford characters

The Bradford wool trade has had its full quota of "characters" moulded in much the same way as those I described at the beginning of this book who flourished in Batley. They were self-made men of great determination and independence, great shrewdness and commercial judgement, who built up big businesses and big fortunes from very humble beginnings. In the story of Bradford's growth as the wool capital of the world four men stand out head and shoulders above the rest—Samuel Cunliffe Lister, who became the first Lord Masham, Sir Titus Salt, Sir Isaac Holden and John Foster. The mills they founded still flourish in Bradford and are the biggest in the district.

Lister was born of middle-class parents in the year of Waterloo and as a young man it was intended that he should enter the ministry. Instead he joined his brother who was a woollen manufacturer. With their father's aid a new mill was erected in Manningham and on his brother's death Samuel took complete control.

Although a highly capable and shrewd businessman his chief claim to fame was as an inventor. The first combing machine for producing the tops needed for worsted manufacture was invented in 1794 by Edmund Cartwright, who was of all things a clergyman, but it was a very crude piece of equipment motivated by a horse. Inventing a more practical combing machine occupied the attention of inventors and industrialists for many years after that and in addition to Lister such people as Collier, Heilmann, Donnisthorpe, Holden and Noble were the central figures.

But it was Lister who came to dominate the combing industry between 1850 and 1860, first by acquiring numerous patents for various combs, secondly by entering into partnership with two of the other key figures, Donnisthorpe and Isaac Holden, and thirdly by the establishment of a huge business controlling and virtually monopolizing for almost ten years the manufacture and use of combing machinery in Britain. This achieved he produced his own combs which he manufactured for £200 and sold to an eager market for £1 200, an enterprise which made him a fortune.

His restless, inventive mind made it impossible for him to rest on his laurels, however, and he turned to the problem of processing silk waste—for long regarded as a useless commodity. Bradford spinners of silk produced vast amounts of waste silk in making yarn but were unable to use it because of difficulties experienced during the winding operation. Lister laboured for six years to produce the right processing machinery, spending a quarter of a million pounds in doing so, and his patience was eventually rewarded. He proceeded to buy waste silk at one halfpenny a pound and convert it into fashionable fabric that sold as quickly as it could be woven. Indeed he had to seek new sources of silk and bought huge silk estates in the Punjab to cultivate his own supplies. In the late 1860s Lister turned his attention to velvets and soon made a reputation for weaving these fabrics. In 1871 his mills at Manningham were burned down and the present gigantic Manningham Mills covering twenty-eight acres, which dominate the skyline of Bradford from many different directions, were built.

Lister impressed his personality on the civic life of Bradford as well as being pre-eminent in the industrial sphere and was a prominent member of the Chamber of Commerce and a Justice of the Peace. He twice put up for Parliament but unsuccessfully. In 1887 he was appointed High Sheriff of Yorkshire and in 1891 was elevated to the peerage, becoming the first Lord Masham. He presented to the city of Bradford the fifty acres of ground attached to the Lister residence, Manningham Hall, which is known to all Bradfordians as Lister Park. He himself had acquired for £310 000 some

10 000 acres of land including Jervaulx Abbey chiefly in order to indulge his love for shooting and fishing. He continued to be an inventor until he was a very old man and his inventions included a patent air brake for railway trains. He died in 1906 aged 91.

Titus Salt, born in 1803, is most famous for his model village built around his enormous mill—the largest in Europe—at Saltaire in the 1850s. It comprised 850 houses, a school, an institute, a hospital, a church, almshouses and a beautifully landscaped park. He made his industrial fortune out of the manufacture of alpaca, a long stapled fibre of a soft and glossy nature obtained from the South American llama.

Salt had established himself as a spinner and manufacturer in Bradford and while on business in Liverpool in 1836 came by chance upon a consignment of bales of wool-like material from South America. No one seemed to know what they had been sent for and, his curiosity whetted, he took a sample back with him to Bradford. After testing it at the mill he bought the whole consignment—some 300 bales at 8d per lb. The transaction curiously enough was described by Charles Dickens in a weekly journal which he was then editing called *Household Words*. "Our friend Salt took it (the alpaca) up, looked at it, felt it, pulled it about; in fact he did all but taste it and he would have done that if it had suited his purpose, for he was 'Yorkshire'."

Salt believed that alpaca could be spun and woven into light, fancy fabrics which Bradford was beginning to produce in large quantities and he proceeded to manufacture such fabrics—not, however, without difficulties. But eventually he and John Foster of Black Dyke Mills, and another firm called G & S Turner of Great Horton, consumed over 90 per cent of the large quantities of alpaca imported into Britain. The new fibre, used in conjunction with either cotton or silk warp, became widely popular and rose in price from 10d to 30d per lb.

But Salt, like Lister, did not rest on his laurels. He continued to experiment with new fibres and turned to mohair, the hair of the angora goat. This venture was equally successful and together with John Foster and the Mitchell brothers of Bowling he eventually acquired and spun most of the mohair coming into Britain—and later exported great quantities of the spun yarn to the continent.

Again like Lister, Salt was prominent in the public life of Bradford, being first an alderman and in 1848 mayor of the city. He was also something of a philanthropist and at the time of the Chartist movement, when unemployment reached serious proportions in the textile industry, he was a prominent subscriber to relief funds and absorbed into his mill scores of handloom weavers whose occupation had ceased because of the advent of the power loom. He played a prominent part in establishing Saturday afternoon as a half-day holiday and was one of the first employers to organize a day's excursion into the country for his employees. In 1857 he became a Member of Parliament and in 1869 a baronet.

John Foster, son of a Bradford farmer and colliery owner, was the founder in 1819 at the age of twenty-one of what grew to be one of the most famous of West Riding worsted mills—Black Dyke Mills at Queensbury. Foster at that time was engaged in a variety of other industries including farming, shopkeeping and coal mining but they were all well integrated. In his shop he sold goods to the handloom weavers who worked for him on commission and also sold them coal from his colliery. And as at the peak there were 700 of them his turnover was considerable. In turn he sold the worsted cloth produced for him by the handloom weavers to the workers at his colliery!

The first power was not used at Black Dyke Mills until 1835 and in the years that followed they became a striking example of almost complete vertical organization—a great rarity in the worsted industry. The mills, in addition to spinning and weaving, had their own dye works, grease and soap works and combing and carding facilities. In 1835 the capital of the firm was £11 185. In 1867 it was £1 463 155. Production of worsted cloth had been geared to meet the demand in Victorian England for the bright lustre fabrics, notably alpaca and mohair, and in company with Salts of Saltaire, Foster had a virtual monopoly in this market.

Like Titus Salt and Samuel Cunliffe Lister, John Foster came to dominate the economy of the locality in which he lived and the small mountain township of Queensbury was equipped with houses, a library, a swimming bath and an institute. John Foster was also very interested in brass bands and the famous Black Dyke Mills Band was formed, entertaining the inhabitants of Queensbury on festive occasions.

Foster was a great individualist and paid little attention to his personal appearance. Many stories are told about him, none more characteristic than that concerning his purchase of a castle and estate at Hornby. He went to the auction in his usual scruffy state and after being the top bidder went into the best room of the local inn where the landlord was chatting with some of his more prosperous customers. He stopped Foster at the door and said bluntly "T'bar for you", indicating the situation of the taproom with a jerk of his thumb. Foster did not demur and the landlord later joined him in the lower regions and recounted some of the day's events. "They say that one of them wool chaps from Bradford has bought t'estate", he said. "So I look like having a new landlord." "Aye", said Foster casually, "I'm him!"

Isaac Holden, born in 1807, was the seventh child of a Cumberland lead miner and farmer and became head of the world's largest wool-combing company in the late nineteenth century. His development and introduction of combing machinery along with Lister was one of the main factors in Bradford's pre-eminence in worsted production. Holden was born in Paisley, Scotland, and having left school at ten, became an apprentice in the trade of shawl weaving. He studied diligently in his spare time and became assistant to a local lecturer in mathematics, taking up a teaching post eventually in Leeds. He later became a book-keeper at Cullingworth Mills, near Bradford, which had introduced some of the early Collier wool-combs without much success. He was very mechanically minded and at his employer's request transferred his attention from the books to the combs and succeeded in making them function satisfactorily. Later he was to develop his own wool comb which was to make him a fortune. In 1848 he went into partnership with Lister and moved to France, where in 1850 two large combing mills were opened. Several years later Lister sold his share to Holden and ten years later Holden returned to England and the combing company of Isaac Holden and Sons was formed in 1863. The company prospered and became the world's largest woolcombing concern. Holden became a Member of Parliament and in 1894, at the age of 87, received a baronetcy for his services to the country. Three years later he died.

Holden was a staunch Methodist, teetotaller and non-smoker

and was frugal in all his habits. His diet was said to consist of a banana, a biscuit, a baked apple, an orange and twenty grapes for breakfast and supper and three ounces of either fish or meat at mid-day. He was reputed to be one of the first men in the West Riding to install electric light and a telephone in his home and one of the first to enjoy the luxury of a Turkish bath.

But perhaps the most fabulous of all Bradford's wool trade characters was a man who made and lost a vast fortune more recently—William Clifford Gaunt. A well-known Bradford woolman called Alec Harrison wrote a series of articles on him in the *Wool Record* some years ago. Gaunt was a member of a family who had already made a big impact on the wool textile industry. He was the youngest son of Joseph Gaunt whose brothers, Isaac and Reuben, were already well established in the wool business. William started on his own at the age of twenty-one in a small office on the fourth floor of the famous Swan Arcade in Bradford, which Priestley has immortalized in his reminiscences "Margin Released". He had a capital, including overdraft, of £2 000. At the peak of his career it was estimated he was worth £15 000 000. He had no telephone in the office—this was in 1893—because he said he did not like talking to people through a wire—he preferred to meet them face to face. He used a neighbouring firm's telephone when he had to make a call and paid for the use of the instrument by giving them a turkey at Christmas.

He turned his original £2 000 into £27 000 in four years through buying and selling wool and then at twenty-five married the daughter of a woollen manufacturer and became a partner in the woolcombing business of Joseph Wilson & Co of Frizinghall. He also acquired one or two spinning plants and, thinking it would be advisable to have his own combs, built the large Valley Combing Mills for about £20 000. Later he bought partnerships in various spinning firms on the continent and by the middle of the first war had mills in Canada, the US, Australia, Germany, Belgium and France.

But the wool textile industry was not the only activity in which he invested. At one time he had £500 000 invested in London theatres, a large interest in a film company and a marine insurance company, and owned the sole agency for Packard cars in the United Kingdom. The folk legends say that he once bought the Savoy Hotel in London but this was not so. He always stayed at the Savoy while attending the wool sales in London and his son has told of his London routine. He would leave the Savoy at 7 30 am, walk to the Temple station and take the tube to Tower Hill where he would breakfast at a Lyons cafe with a roll and a cup of tea—"if the rolls had not arrived he just had tea". He would then walk to the docks and the show floors where the incoming consignments of wool were displayed.

So far as buying was concerned he was a man of instant decisions—and some of his decisions were pretty staggering. He is reputed to have bought the entire Punta wool clip on one occasion for £2 000 000 and the entire Buenos Aires clip during a slump for £1 000 000 on another. He was the first man in the wool trade to deal with the Bolsheviks in 1920. The Bolsheviks dearly wanted wool but had no sterling with which to pay for it. So Gaunt made a barter deal in which they paid him in jewels and Cossack saddles, or so it was said. Another of his big deals was to buy the entire stock of pieces from the UK Government's Disposal Board at a price of £5 000 000.

Like many makers of wool textile fortunes he was a simple man with limited horizons in everything else but business and lived to make money rather than spend it. His personal income in the early 1920s was said to be £600 000 a year, of which he spent only £2 000 a year including school fees. He lived adequately at Apperley Bridge and had a fine country house at Pateley Bridge, but he never went in for yachts in the Mediterranean or any extravagances of that sort. His wife liked the high life no more than he did and although they kept a housekeeper and servants at Pateley Bridge they did not go there very often.

His wealth represented the power to do still more business and it was that aspect of it which he valued. He carried very little money about with him and there is a story of him having dinner with the first Lord Barnby on the train coming up from London and finding that neither of them had enough cash to pay the bill. Fortunately the waiter knew them and allowed them credit. But like all woolmen he used huge overdrafts from the banks to finance his wool buying and he once claimed he had paid the banks £3 000 000 in interest.

He was always ready for a business deal of any description

and it was said that on one occasion he arrived at King's Cross to catch his train to Bradford to find that the dining car had been taken off the train because of a strike. He saw a man wheeling a food barrow along the platform and immediately made him an offer for its entire contents, which he got one of his clerks to sell to the train passengers on the journey north.

Gaunt crashed like many other textile men in the late 1920s and became penniless almost overnight when the banks foreclosed on him. But he did not drag others down with him. He never floated a public company and he reacted to hard times with courage and resourcefulness. He began all over again in the textile business and became a supplier of cheap three-piece suits which he had made up for him on commission in Leeds—from cloths he had had woven on commission in Bradford. The suits cost him ten shillings and were sold in London for twenty-five shillings. He still went to London a good deal, travelling at night because the fare was lower. Royston Millmore of the *Wool Record* recalls that when he was an apprentice woolsorter in the late 1920s he once bought a belted overcoat from W C Gaunt for £2. He remembers that Gaunt was very anxious to be sure that it fitted him and that he was satisfied with his bargain. Gaunt did not live long enough to rise to the top again but he did not die by any means a pauper.

Part four—Yorkshire Cricket

Herbert Sutcliffe—a boyhood hero

Someone once said that the English, not being a religious people, invented cricket to give themselves an idea of eternity. Yorkshire cricket is certainly one of the eternal factors in my life—a sort of thread which encompasses all my past and binds my existence together. I have been watching Yorkshire cricket very regularly since I was seven years old and neither time nor distance has separated me from it for very long. Certainly no Yorkshire recollections of mine would be complete without a section on cricket.

The remarkable thing about my cricket memories is their clarity and their agelessness. The Yorkshire cricketers who were the heroes of my boyhood are as clearly etched in my mind today as though I had seen them yesterday—and nearly all of them are now dead and gone. Not only their names but their faces, their figures, their styles, their mannerisms, and their characters are inscribed for ever in some corner of my mind which might be called Boothroyd's Cricketers' Almanac. I can see in my mind's eye Percy Holmes and Herbert Sutcliffe walking out to open the Yorkshire innings from the old pavilion at Headingley as vividly as I can see myself in the shaving mirror every morning—only they have not changed and grown older as I have done. Holmes, looking as R C Robertson-Glasgow, once put it, "as if he were off to Aintree or Harringay, merely incidentally in cricket flannels", and Sutcliffe "as if about to lay with a golden trowel the foundation stone of some hostel for deserving cricketers."

I can see Wilfred Rhodes digging his heels into the turf as he took his few steps up to the wicket to bowl one of the tens of thousands of overs he bowled for the county between 1898 and 1930. I can see the chubby figure of Maurice Leyland striking dismay into all types of bowlers with a bat which seemed almost as broad as his back. I can see a bandy-legged Emmott Robinson rubbing the new ball fiercely on his trousers before opening the bowling like a greyhound out of a trap at the pavilion end. I can see a tall, willowy, grave-faced Hedley Verity discussing tactics with his jester-ally behind the wicket—Arthur Wood who, when a batsman was hitting this great left arm slow bowler all over the field, told him not to worry because he clearly had the batsman in two minds—whether to hit him for four or six.

I can see the long, lanky, bespectacled figure of Bill Bowes ambling with deceptive indolence up to the wicket to bowl balls as fast and as menacing as any ever bowled for the county. I can see Arthur ("Ticker") Mitchell wearing his cap at an angle of forty-five degrees to his head, snatching up catches at silly mid off as miraculously as a magician producing rabbits from a hat. I can see an earnest and completely unpretentious Wilf Barber making nervous little pats and gestures with his bat as he completed one of his twenty-seven unpretentious but often invaluable centuries for the county. I can see a tireless George Macaulay putting everything he knew into every ball he bowled and inviting sympathy from heaven with the wild despairing agony of his appeals for lbw.

I know my first season as a Yorkshire cricket supporter was when I was seven because Captain Worsley (who later became Sir William Worsley and was the father of the Duchess of Kent) had just been made captain and the Yorkshire records tell me he was appointed in 1928. I know I did not see any Yorkshire cricket in 1927 because Major Lupton was the captain in that year and Roy Kilner, Arthur Dolphin and Abe Waddington were in the team—and I have no recollection of seeing any of them whereas I remember all the 1928 players very clearly—Holmes, Sutcliffe, Oldroyd, Leyland, Mitchell, Barber, Robinson, Rhodes, Wood, Macaulay and Dennis.

Another reason why I know I was seven is because I wrote a letter to Herbert Sutcliffe that winter congratulating him on scoring a century on a sticky wicket in the test match at Melbourne and the records tell me that happened on the MCC's Australian tour of 1928–9. That century represented for me the pinnacle of human achievement. Sutcliffe was not only the greatest batsman of all time—he was the greatest man of all time. Beside him such figures as Alexander the Great and Julius Caesar, not to mention Napoleon and the Duke of Wellington, were comparative nonentities.

I wondered what I could do to express my appreciation of his magnificent performance and decided to write him a letter. It took me hours to compose and I gave it to my father to post addressed Mr H Sutcliffe, Melbourne Cricket Ground, Australia. It was not a very literate letter but when I came across it many years later amongst my father's effects marked "D's letter to Herbert Sutcliffe—very funny", I experienced a momentary pang of pain. Very funny indeed! It was the most passionately sincere and profoundly earnest letter I had ever written in my life!

Sutcliffe's innings at Melbourne was later described by no less an authority than Sir Don Bradman as "the nearest approach to mastery" he had ever seen. So I was not a bad judge even at seven.

When the summer came round again and the cricketers were back from Australia I decided to become Herbert Sutcliffe myself now and again for I knew with certainty that nothing I could ever aspire to or achieve in life—be it the premiership or a fortune of millions—could ever give me anything like the satisfaction of being Herbert Sutcliffe.

So I plastered my hair down with brilliantine (fortunately it was black like his) and wore my long pyjama trousers over my shorts because they enabled me to put my pads on just as he did, with slight bulges of flannel between the straps. I then put my bat under my arm and donned my batting gloves as I walked out of the front door and down the path to the bottom lawn with my partner Jack Hobbs, my mind too concentrated on opening the England innings to notice the applause of the dense crowd.

On reaching the wicket I took my stance as elegantly as he did, with feet close together, and asked the umpire for leg and middle with just that touch of imperiousness which Sutcliffe's natural manner incorporated. I made my block hole unhurriedly and kept the bowler waiting while I looked carefully round the field and noted exactly where all the fielders were situated.

After a few fluent cover drives, leg glances and late cuts, with an occasional fierce hook, I raised my bat modestly to acknowledge the crowd's applause for my fifty, and a little later raised it a little higher to acknowledge the acclamation of my century. But even we Sutcliffes had to be out sometime and eventually I fell victim to a brilliant catch at the wicket, accepting my dismissal in the sporting Sutcliffe spirit without waiting for the umpire's decision. I walked back up the path to the front door as immaculate as I had left it, without a hair out of place, acknowledging the standing ovation with a modest wave of the bat.

The Sutcliffe of my boyhood fantasy (which was played out many times) was in fact no greater a performer on the bottom lawn than the Sutcliffe of real life was on the test grounds of the world. What intrigued me most about him as I grew older and took a maturer view of his talents was his incredible imperturbability. To say he was a man who was at his best in a crisis would be inaccurate. There never was a crisis so far as Sutcliffe was concerned. They were outside his philosophy. He was so supremely confident in his own abilities that there were never any doubts about the outcome of any battle.

This confidence is summed up by his remark after a thunderstorm had turned a good test batting pitch into a really sticky wicket. He was asked, records Peter Thomas in his excellent book *Yorkshire Cricketers*, what he thought about the prospects for Jack Hobbs and himself. "Oh we shall be all right so long as Jack doesn't get himself out" he is alleged to have replied. On another occasion, in a Lancashire and Yorkshire match, Sutcliffe was almost run out but the throw missed the stumps by inches. "Goodness", said the Lancashire captain, "that was a near thing." "I haven't the slightest idea what you're talking about, Mr Eckersley", he is said to have replied urbanely.

Yet again while fielding close to the wicket he received a tremendous blow on the kneecap from a ball that sent him staggering. Several of the Yorkshire players ran up to help him to his feet but, rising with obvious difficulty, he waved them imperiously aside, as though to say "We Sutcliffes don't suffer pain."

Although Sutcliffe presumably experienced emotion at the wicket he never showed it. He could be completely beaten by several balls in succession—an experience enough to harass the best of batsmen. But not Sutcliffe. After the ball had shaved his stumps for the third time he would lean nonchalantly on his bat while the bowler returned to his mark and would then prepare to receive the next ball as casually as though he had just hit three boundaries.

He was not always the quickest of scorers and there were occasions when he was barracked but he always appeared to be completely oblivious to such protests. A Lancastrian during a dull patch in a Roses match once shouted out "Come on Herbert! What does tha think tha are, a bloody war memorial?" But the spectator was not even given the satisfaction of knowing the batsman had heard the remark.

He was not a typical Yorkshire cricket professional by any manner of means. He came from Pudsey but he had the immaculate appearance of someone dressed in Savile Row and spoke with an accent which had distinct traces of what J B Priestley would describe as "la-di-da" and Emmott Robinson would have called "well off". He should really have been an amateur—except that in so many other ways he was so thoroughly a professional.

He was, indeed, on one occasion appointed captain of Yorkshire. A letter was sent to him in 1927 while he was touring in South Africa reading "Dear Herbert, At the committee meeting yesterday you were appointed captain for 1928 without your status being altered. It is hoped that this will be agreeable to you and that you will accept the same and be happy and successful in your new and honoured position. Best wishes, yours sincerely, F C Toone, Secretary." Sutcliffe replied by cable addressed to the president, Lord Hawke: "Official invitation received yesterday. Many thanks to you and committee. Great honour. Question carefully considered. Regret to decline. Willing to play under any captain elected."

Neville Cardus has summed him up in immortal prose in his autobiography and nothing can equal his description: "It is not known and will never be known what Rhodes and Robinson in their hearts thought of Sutcliffe, who made his hair resplendent with brilliantine and wore immaculate flannels and on the whole comported with an elegance which in the Yorkshire team was unique and apocryphal. He did not speak with the accent of Yorkshire but of Teddington. He would refer casually to the fact that he had yesterday 'mootered' down from Pudsey to London. Witnesses could be called to testify that at Lords Sutcliffe has held up fast bowlers in the middle of their approach to the wicket and with a wave of his bat has removed some obstruction to his vision in the pavilion, probably a peer of the realm, who has bent double and crawled away into invisibility while members have gone red in the face at him and said 'Sit down, sir, sit down!' "

There may well be batsmen still to walk down the pavilion steps at Headingley to cricketing glory but there will never be another Herbert Sutcliffe and as my letter to him forty-seven years ago was never posted let me take this opportunity of thanking him in print for all the joy he brought me between 1928 and his retirement in 1939. For I am glad to say that he is the one hero of my boyhood who is still alive, although now over eighty.

Maurice Leyland and other giants

A keen competitor with Herbert Sutcliffe as my boyhood hero was Maurice Leyland, who, unfortunately, it was impossible for me to turn myself into because he was a left hander and I was not. He was, in fact, one of the greatest left-handed batsmen the game has ever produced and his achievements for Yorkshire and England are certainly in the same category as those of Yorkshire's two primary batting stars, Sutcliffe and Hutton. Leyland scored eighty centuries in his career between 1920 and 1946 and I can still feel acutely the agony which quite a lot of those centuries caused me. I became nervous when he got into the nineties and when he got to ninety-six or ninety-seven I was almost a psychiatric case. I scarcely dared to watch in case he was out at this critical juncture and my heart was in my mouth until the century came. The surge of relief which that gave me has only been equalled in later life by one thing—the relief I feel when I sit down after making a public speech!

Indeed in some respects Leyland was more precious to me than Sutcliffe because I was not yet quite a cricket purist and liked to see sixes hit and the batsmen score runs quickly. Sutcliffe very seldom descended to the crudities of sixes and his scoring was often slow. Leyland hit sixes quite frequently and almost always scored quickly. They were not, of course, death or glory sixes like Captain Worsley's or the tail enders. They were beautifully timed and executed sixes expressing his batting artistry just as effectively as his drives for four through the covers which never rose an inch above the ground. He was an attacking batsman and always hit the ball hard even if it went straight to a fielder.

Above all he was a cheerful, good-natured, happy-looking cricketer. One somehow sensed his character and temperament by watching him at the crease and when I came to read about him in later life I was not in the least surprised to find my early assessment of him was perfectly correct. Maurice Leyland was one of the most popular men in cricket. J M Kilburn, who does not give praise easily, had this to say of him in his excellent cricket autobiography *Thanks to Cricket*: "Overseas or at home Maurice Leyland was the best of touring companions. He accepted obligation and inconvenience with comforting imperturbability. In the phrase of his time he was invariably ready to 'make one' when delegates were required for a social function or other representative occasions. He would go without demur to a race meeting or a municipal banquet, join a darts match or a fourball at golf. In all circumstances he would enjoy himself and let his enjoyment be known."

I noted a far-away look in his bright blue eyes when I last saw him at his home ground of Harrogate about 1966 and when he died on 1 January 1967, aged 67, I felt the same sense of personal loss one feels for a relative. I had not spoken more than a few dozen words to him in my life and yet I felt I had lost one of my oldest companions.

In the days of my boyhood, of course, all the Yorkshire players were demi-gods and to speak to any of them, even if it was only to ask for their autograph, was a thrill which lasted for weeks. I rarely asked for autographs, however, because I was put off the pursuit of them in my early days by Wilfred Rhodes, who did not suffer autograph hunters gladly. I once approached him with a school friend on his way into the Park Avenue ground at Bradford and we were told firmly to "hop it". I knew that if I asked Sutcliffe or Leyland for their autograph and was told to "hop it" I should never recover from the blow, and so I never exposed myself to the possibility.

All my early cricket watching was done with my father as guide and mentor and he often talked of players of an earlier epoch—Brown and Tunnicliffe, Lord Hawke and F S Jackson, David Denton and David Hunter, Schofield Haigh and George

Hirst. But the one who intrigued me most was a player of an even earlier generation, Louis Hall. He came from Batley and my father had actually known him as a boy.

Hall played for Yorkshire from 1873 to 1894 and must have been one of the most remarkable batsmen of all time. He went in first and was the king of stonewallers, rarely scoring at the rate of more than fifteen runs an hour. He carried his bat through a whole innings no fewer than fourteen times whereas his nearest competitor, Sutcliffe, did it only five times and Percy Holmes only three times. A Derbyshire bowler, George Davidson, once bowled him fourteen consecutive maiden overs and then retired, fuming and frustrated. He once took almost three hours to score twelve against Kent (including a runless spell of seventy minutes) and against Sussex carried his bat through an entire innings and scored only thirty-one.

Hall, as was appropriate for a Batleyite, was a life long teetotaller and non-smoker and was well known as a lay preacher in the West Riding Methodist chapels. His sober habits were said to be of the greatest value to Yorkshire cricket in an era when drunkenness on the field was not by any means unheard of. But how the spectators tolerated him I don't know.

My father recalled that on one occasion when he was stonewalling in his usual dogged manner a wag in the crowd shouted out to the man fielding close in at point "Get nearer to him, point, he wean't hurt thee if he hits thee wi' t'bat." He also recalled an occasion when the great W G Grace played against Hall in a match on his home ground at Batley. To Grace's utter astonishment Hall hit him for six out of the ground.

Another cricketer who came from Batley and who my father knew personally through his textile connections was Edgar Oldroyd, who batted number three for Yorkshire from 1910 to 1931. Oldroyd was also best known for his defensive play but he was not in the same street as Louis Hall. R C Robertson-Glasgow wrote of him as "one of those small, tough, humorous, militant men who make the comedy and the greatness of a country. They are to be found answering back something or someone which may or may not have existence; fate, a tax collector, Monday morning, a bus conductor, thirst or a Hyde Park orator. They bounce and argue down time's corridors and they generally win the battle."

Soon after the Second World War some friends of mine lived across the road from the Oldroyds in Horsforth and they became friendly with them. Apparently during the war Edgar had been a very keen air raid warden and used to pedal down to his post a mile or so away on a bicycle. In 1947 Mrs Oldroyd told them the story of Edgar's nocturnal adventure. He was roused in the middle of the night by a wailing noise. He bounced out of bed thinking it was an air raid siren, donned a tin helmet, got out his bicycle and began pedalling furiously off to his post—only to remember on the way that the war had been over for two years!

It was through my father that I first met the great George Herbert Hirst. It was at a charity match on the ground of the Dewsbury and Savile club of which my father's close friend, Henry Hill, was for many years president. Hill himself played for Yorkshire on a number of occasions at the turn of the century and he was instrumental in getting George Hirst, who had retired from cricket more than ten years previously and was now about sixty, to play for his team in a friendly match with the local police. The event was widely advertised and several thousand people turned up to see the great man in action. My father and I had seats of honour in the front of the pavilion and I was introduced to Hirst before he went out to open the innings with Henry Hill. To everyone's dismay Hirst was given out lbw in the first over. Hill was far more incensed about it than Hirst. "We get all these people here to come and see him and that blithering idiot of an umpire gives him out lbw" he said when he returned to the pavilion himself. "And what's more the ball was half a yard off the wicket."

White roses at Old Trafford

I watched most of my boyhood cricket at Headingley, Park Avenue, Bradford, or Bramall Lane, Sheffield. At these grounds I rarely missed a fixture and to say I knew every inch of them would not be an exaggeration. My father would occasionally take me to the other Yorkshire grounds where the county were playing and in those days they included Dewsbury, Huddersfield and Middlesbrough in their travels as well as Harrogate, Hull and Scarborough.

Unless the weather made cricketing out of the question we would be off about 10 30 on every Saturday morning on which there was a home fixture, complete with hard-boiled eggs, sandwiches and a thermos of tea, and almost always we stayed until the close of play and watched every ball that was bowled. My father had no time at all for the cricket spectators who spent half their time in the bar or refreshment room and left at the tea interval. And he was impatient of spectators who were not back in their seats promptly by the time the umpires came out after lunch or tea and disturbed our concentration by edging their way along the rows of seats in front of us.

He was, of course, a member of the Yorkshire County Cricket Club and we usually sat on the pavilion but occasionally he would elect to sit in the sun on the popular side, pavilions invariably being in the shade. At Park Avenue he had a penchant for sitting on the stand at the opposite side of the ground from the pavilion because he said it provided the best viewpoint. We would sit on long bench seats which were so high above the stand floor that my feet would not touch the ground and as there was a sheer drop of about twenty feet behind one, down to the concrete path beneath, it was a very precarious perch.

There was also the sight-screen to contend with. My father liked to get as close to it as possible so that he could be directly behind the bowler's arm or as near to it as possible. This was all right until the bowler decided to bowl round the wicket instead of over it. When this happened the sight-screens had to be moved a yard or two to ensure that the batsman was not unsighted. The sight-screens at Park Avenue were, and still are, as big as houses and it was always a tremendous struggle to move them at all, the unfortunate player on the boundary having to push and shove for all he was worth until someone in the crowd took pity on him and came on to the field to help him.

When this labour was over, and the batsman expressed himself satisfied, the result inevitably was that the sight-screen had been moved in our direction and now completely blocked our view. So we had to climb down from our perilous perches and move over to the other side of the screen, where my father would invariably complain that the view was not nearly as good, and if it was a Yorkshire batsman who had ordered the movement of the sight-screen he would be in bad odour for the rest of the day.

My father for some reason or other did not subscribe merely for one Yorkshire cricket ticket but for two or three. Each ticket admitted the member and a lady or youth under fourteen and when we arrived at Park Avenue or Headingley there was usually a string of untidy urchins hanging about trying to encounter some kindly member who was unescorted and would take them in free with his ticket. This was a practice frowned on by the club committee but my father was well disposed to youthful cricket followers and always made a habit of taking as many in with him as his tickets permitted. On one occasion he collected three grubby urchins at the members' entrance but the commissionaire at the gate would only let two of them in. "You've only got three youths' tickets and your son has got in on one" he pointed out firmly. My father, however, said that was not the case. His son was coming in with a full member's ticket. "He can't", snapped the commissionaire, "a full member's ticket is not transferable—and as he's under fourteen he can't have a full member's ticket." "Well, then, he can come in on this ticket" said my father, fishing in his breast pocket and pulling out another ticket. "This is a business house ticket and you'll see it is transferable." The commissionaire examined it and had to agree. "I've never seen one like that before", he commented.

The cricketing day was not always over when we got home. In early summer when the light was good he would tell me to put my pads on and we would go down to what we called the bottom lawn where we had a cricket net up from April to September and he would bowl to me for an hour or more. He had been a useful off-break bowler in his day and possibly he had visions that his son might make a Yorkshire batsman. What he failed to realize was that when I put my pads on and went down to the bottom lawn I was a Yorkshire batsman already. I was Herbert Sutcliffe again, armed with the latest repertoire of shots which I had been carefully studying earlier in the day.

But although it was always exciting going to Leeds, Bradford and Sheffield the greatest thrill of the season was going to the Roses match at Old Trafford. The matches were played alternately in Yorkshire or Lancashire at the Whitsuntide and

August bank holiday weekends and we rarely missed the Old Trafford fixture, usually going on the Saturday and Monday and sometimes on the Tuesday as well.

There was an atmosphere about the Roses matches in the 1930s which doesn't exist today. They attracted crowds as large as for Test matches against Australia and often when we arrived at Old Trafford after an exhilarating morning car journey across the Pennines we would find long queues at every entrance and it would take us half an hour to get into the ground. Sometimes the gates were closed altogether and thousands of people were locked out—but this grisly fate never happened to us.

My father's panoply of Yorkshire tickets admitted us to the pavilion (or one of the other stands in that vicinity) once we had paid our admission and he flourished them with unusual aggression just because we were in the heart of enemy territory. We were, of course, clearly indentified as Yorkshiremen by the large white roses which we sported in our buttonholes whenever we could get hold of any—it was sometimes a bit difficult when the match was at Whitsuntide because our home grown roses did not always bloom early enough—but my father just liked to emphasize the fact. For this was the golden age of Yorkshire cricket and we were usually the stronger team. Years later when Yorkshire were in eclipse the white roses and Yorkshire tickets were brandished less enthusiastically.

The drama started with the captains coming out to toss for choice of innings and rarely slackened all day. Gifted cricket writers like Neville Cardus have written volumes on the esoteric nature of Yorkshire and Lancashire matches and they really were quite different from any other match. Cardus has said it was like "a play and pageant exhibiting the genius of the two counties". He goes on:

"To watch it rightly you needed a clue; for years I myself had missed the point. There is slow play and slow play at cricket. There are batsmen who cannot score quickly because they cannot and there are batsmen who can score quickly but won't. In fact in a representative Lancashire and Yorkshire match of 1924–34 runs were severely discountenanced. No fours before lunch on principle was the unannounced policy; and as few as possible after. But fours or no fours, runs or no runs, the games touched greatness because of the north of

England character that was exposed in every action, every movement, all day."

The most enjoyable matches for us were naturally those in which Yorkshire did well and when I delve through my memories of Old Trafford these are the only matches I remember. The fierce partisanship of the whole occasion has obliterated every recollection of Yorkshire not doing well from my mind.

The match I remember most clearly was that played during the Whitsun weekend of 1933, of which I saw every ball. My father and I were in the crowd of 30 000 who saw Yorkshire make a pretty disastrous start with Holmes, Sutcliffe and Leyland out very early on. But Mitchell, Barber and Sellers saved the day and Yorkshire finished with the quite respectable total of 341. We motored back across the Pennines with reasonable satisfaction.

There was rain on the Sunday and when we arrived at Old Trafford on Whit Monday morning Lancashire spectators were full of foreboding in case the wicket was sticky. It was very sticky and George Macaulay, one of the most hostile bowlers in cricket, exploited it to such a degree that Lancashire were skittled out for 93 and had to follow on. They did no better in their second innings and before the close had been bowled out again for 92, Macaulay taking 7 for 28 in the first innings, including the hat trick, and 5 for 21 in the second. Twenty Lancashire wickets down in a day and a Yorkshire victory by an innings and 156 runs! It was the most exciting day of my life.

Winning, however, was not the only satisfaction to be gained from a Lancashire and Yorkshire match. Almost as much satisfaction could be gained by preventing Lancashire from winning and forcing a draw. This more recondite—some would say depraved—satisfaction was accorded us most generously in the first Roses match at Old Trafford after the war. It was an August bank holiday match and on the Saturday and Monday Lancashire completely outplayed Yorkshire, gaining a lead of 216 on the first innings. My father was so depressed about it that he initially decided not to go on the final day but, of course, he could not stay away and we were sitting miserably on the pavilion while five Yorkshire wickets crashed for 120 runs before lunch to put them in a completely hopeless position.

The home crowd were enjoying the debâcle immensely and the stout, red-faced Lancashire members who used to stand with their pints of bitter in their hands immediately in front of the pavilion entrance were deriving vast, sadistic entertainment from making derogatory remarks about the Yorkshire team in voices loud enough to agonize the ear drums of every Yorkshire supporter in sight. "No guts about 'em, no guts at all", one of them kept saying as the Yorkshire wickets clattered.

We listened to them in a growing desolation of spirit while our white roses drooped and I think we both prayed to the Almighty to make the impossible happen—as he sometimes did in cricket matches. Our prayers were answered. Maurice Leyland and Brian Sellers came out together after lunch and stayed at the wicket together for the whole of the rest of the day. Nothing Lancashire could do could shift either of them. They did not score many runs—but runs were meaningless anyway. The sole object of the grim battle was to prevent Lancashire gaining the victory they felt absolutely certain of at lunch time. They were Leyland's and Sellers' finest hours.

When the players finally came off the field the Lancashire faces at the entrance to the pavilion were as flat and dejected as their beer. "What was that you were saying about guts?" my father asked one of them as we set off jubilantly for home.

Sellers, Robinson, Hirst and Rhodes

Brian Sellers was captain of Yorkshire from 1933 to 1947 although no county cricket was played during the war. He typified the fighting spirit of the Yorkshire team in that golden age which brought them the county championship seven seasons out of nine between 1931 and 1939.

There is always dispute as to whether Sellers was a greater captain than the legendary Lord Hawke but there are certainly no other candidates for the honour. Sellers, with his square jaw and shambling gait, looked aggressive and there is no doubt was aggressive. His strict disciplinarian methods would unquestionably cause a strike, if not a riot, today. But in the thirties what the captain said went—and although at times he must have struck terror and anger into his team he always inspired respect. He was not a great cricketer but he was an immensely courageous one. He put his fielders suicidally close in at times but he always took one of the most dangerous positions himself—and never flinched in it.

He was not the only "character" in the teams of the thirties. Probably the most colourful character of the lot was Emmott Robinson, although how much of the colour was natural and how much was applied by his chief biographer, Neville Cardus, it is hard to say. Cardus has certainly made him immortal with his description of him as a "grizzled, squat, bandy-legged Yorkshireman, all sagging and loose at the braces in private life but on duty for Yorkshire liable at any minute to gather and concentrate his energy into sudden and vehement leaps and charges and scuffles. He had shrewd eyes, a hatchet face and grey hairs, most of them representing appeals that had gone against him for leg before wicket. I imagine that he was created one day by God sweeping up the nearest acre of Yorkshire soil at hand and then breathing into it and saying 'Now lad, tha's called Emmott Robinson and tha can go on wi' t'new ball at t'pavilion end'."

There is an abundance of stories about Emmott Robinson and no doubt most of them are apocryphal but one which has every hall-mark of truth is that about the university man. Robinson had little time for university men, particularly when they wore fancy coloured caps, and he positively bristled at the sight of one coming out of the pavilion. On this particular occasion the university man had not only a fancy cap but all the airs and graces which went with it and after bowling him a few balls which completely beat him and narrowly missed his wickets Emmott produced a real snorter which knocked his middle stump down flat. Facing the glaring bowler on his ignominious way back to the pavilion the batsman turned to him and said sportingly "Good ball, Robinson. Good ball." Emmott regarded him with undisguised contempt. "Aye", he said, "but it were wasted on thee."

Another story with rather less of the hall-mark of truth is that about the clergyman he once bowled out first ball. "Down goes thy bloody pulpit" he is alleged to have shouted triumphantly.

In the thirties as I have said the Yorkshire players were

demi-gods as far as I was concerned. The only one I ever remember meeting off the cricket field was Frank Smailes, who played for the county as an all rounder from 1932 to 1948. Smailes happened to be staying at the Park House Hotel at Blackpool where I had gone with my family for Easter and one day my brother and I were playing table tennis in the games room when Smailes came in. We rather fancied ourselves at table tennis and after he had watched us finish our match he said "I haven't played this game for ages. Would either of you care to give me a game?" As the elder of the two I at once agreed and actually beat him. It was one of my proudest moments!

After the war, however, I watched Yorkshire cricket as a schoolboy no longer. During the late forties and fifties I watched it as a journalist, sometimes on duty and sometimes off, and although I was never in any sense a cricket writer I often interviewed cricketers and wrote cricket sketches for the *Yorkshire Post*. This gave me an opportunity of meeting and getting to know some of the cricketers I had admired from a distance for so long, and it was a privilege I much enjoyed.

In 1949 I went to Silcoates school, near Wakefield, to see Wilfred Rhodes bowl a ceremonial first over on the school's new cricket field in a match between the school past and present and the Craven Gentlemen. He was now seventy-two years old and his sight was failing but he decked himself out for the occasion in white flannels and a Yorkshire cap and bowled six balls of impeccable length and direction to Brian Sellers, who was acting as captain of the Craven Gentlemen, to the plaudits of a large crowd. I interviewed Rhodes afterwards but he was not very talkative on this occasion and I was unable to get much out of him. A year or two later, however, I interviewed both him and George Hirst at their homes in Huddersfield—they lived almost within a six hit of each other—and they were both more forthcoming.

I went to Hirst's home first. He was eighty-two and a bent, frail little man, quite different from the Hirst I had seen at the Dewsbury and Savile cricket ground over twenty years previously. He told me he spent most of his time nowadays in an armchair by the fireside with his souvenirs in a cupboard behind him. He showed me them and there were silver trophies of all descriptions and enough mounted cricket balls to stock a shop, including half the ball with which Yorkshire dismissed the Australians for the record low score of 23. The inscription read: "Yorkshire *v* Australia, Leeds, June 1902. Yorkshire won by 5 wickets. Australia all out 23. Hirst 5 for 9. Jackson 5 for 12."

"They split the ball in half and gave me and F S Jackson half each" he said, handling it affectionately. "A great match!"

But although he was obviously nostalgic for his playing days which had finished thirty years earlier it was clear he did not live in the past. "I'm looking forward to the Australians coming this summer and I'll be at the Headingley test match in July, all being well. But don't ask me what I think of our chances because I don't know. And don't ask me for my views on modern cricket or cricketers because I haven't any—not for publication anyway! I had my day and I enjoyed it immensely but I'm best out of the picture now. If old cricketers can't enjoy the game without finding fault they want to stop at home."

He shook his large, oval-shaped head and his blue eyes twinkled. "But go and have a chat with Wilfred Rhodes. He can't see much these days but his views are as sound as ever. He was giving me a proper lecture only yesterday and I'll bet he'll give you one too!"

But Rhodes, who was seventy-five, was not to be drawn at first. "What's the good of me talking?", he asked. "I've had my day and I enjoyed it. My sight's gone now. I can't see you properly in that chair, never mind a cricket match. Folk will only say 'the silly old so-and-so—he wants to keep his mouth shut'."

But keeping his mouth shut about cricket, it soon became apparent, was very difficult for Wilfred Rhodes. As soon as he discovered I knew the difference between an in-swinger and an out-swinger (and in this respect, he informed me coldly, I was an improvement on the last journalist who had interviewed him—"T'chap knew nowt about t'game at all") I got the lecture Hirst had promised me. I was absorbed by a closely-reasoned and highly-technical discussion on the inadequacies of the leg before wicket rule.

He talked about the Australians and said that in test matches temperament was all important. "I never used to notice the test match atmosphere until I got back and played for Yorkshire again", he said. "Then I noticed the difference."

"There's another thing", he went on. "The Australians are better players off the back foot than we are. We are apt to over coach forward and under coach back."

He surveyed the matter from all angles and stood up to demonstrate more effectively. "The head wants to go out first, you see, and then the leg follows." I could see him in his mind's eye driving the ball crisply through the covers to the boundary and listening to the crowd's applause. "But no one wants my views", he said abruptly. "I've had my day."

He looked at me very keenly. "What did George Hirst tell you?", he demanded.

"He told me", I replied, "that you'd probably give me a lecture."

He smiled and a faraway look came into his eyes. "Aye", he reflected, "it's a great game. Now we were talking about back play weren't we? I remember once in Melbourne . . ."

I was very late getting back to the office that afternoon.

The incomparable Len Hutton

One of the brightest stars in the Yorkshire cricketing firmament between 1930 and 1960 was, of course, the incomparable Len Hutton, who after his retirement was knighted for his services to cricket. Hutton achieved just about everything a batsman could possibly hope to achieve. He scored no fewer than 129 centuries, he broke Don Bradman's test record with a score of 364, he was acknowledged to be the best batsman in the world after Bradman retired and he became the first professional ever to captain England—something which Lord Hawke had prayed to God would never happen!

Hutton was undoubtedly the most pleasure-giving batsman I have ever seen—and for comparison I saw Bradman get both his triple centuries in the Leeds test matches of 1930 and 1934. Bradman was an incomparable run-getting machine; Hutton was a supreme artist; he was style and grace personified and if I had a fairy godmother who would grant me one cricketing wish before I die it would be to see Hutton again execute one of his classic drives through the covers for four. Hutton's cover drives were more, far more than ordinary cricket. They were sheer poetry. They aroused in me the same aesthetic emotions which I imagine music lovers derive from a Beethoven symphony and art lovers from a Turner painting. His batting for me represented cricketing champagne of the finest vintage and I enjoyed every glass of it I ever had—and I had plenty.

I interviewed Hutton on a number of occasions at his home in Stanningley and in various pavilions throughout Yorkshire and I always found him most friendly and helpful—in contrast to some journalists who complained that he was stand-offish and inarticulate. What they interpreted as stand offishness was probably his natural reticence for I found him to be a cricketer completely without pretence or affectation. As for him being inarticulate this was probably his diffidence and modesty. He was reluctant to talk about himself and his achievements and was the antithesis of the brash type of Yorkshireman who likes to hold the floor.

I suppose the adjective "dour" could be justifiably applied to him because dourness is on the whole a praiseworthy Yorkshire characteristic and Hutton's brand of dourness was certainly not inhospitable. Neville Cardus has written that one of Hutton's most winning characteristics is his smile, "a smile with a twinkle in it . . . A Yorkshireman has his own idea of humour and Hutton, as great and famous as any Yorkshire contemporary, relished his laugh all the more because very often it came last."

Pudsey, his home town, was, of course, immensely proud of him although he was only one of a number of famous Yorkshire cricketers from that locality. Sutcliffe, of course, lived in Pudsey before moving to Ilkley and so did John Tunnicliffe, Major Booth and Harry Halliday. The civic dignitaries of Pudsey organized civic receptions for Hutton on two occasions, both of which I attended. The first was in 1951 on his return from Australia and the second in 1953 after he had captained the team which won the Ashes from the Australians in this country.

I described the latter as Pudsey's finest hour. "It was called a civic reception but it was more like a civic coronation. Several thousand people thronged the market place and the frontage of the gaily beflagged public baths and there were men selling favours and shouting 'don't forget your souvenir pictures . . . ' The Mayor, Alderman Walter Ward, described it as 'a gathering such as we have never had in Pudsey before' and Herbert Sutcliffe called it 'historic'. The MP for the borough, Colonel Cyril Banks, said it was one of the most exciting things that could happen to a Member of Parliament."

One of Hutton's many outstanding qualities as a cricketer was his courage. As opening batsman he received the full fury of the onslaught from two of the most formidable fast bowlers ever to play for Australia—Lindwall and Miller—and he received it without flinching. And this despite a war-time injury to his left arm which had to be shortened by surgery and left him vulnerable for the rest of his career.

Despite this some ignorant critics have accused Hutton of being "frightened of fast bowling" and in a speech on one occasion Hutton referred to this alleged fear. He said he had never feared Lindwall and Miller nearly as much as he had feared Bill Hudson, the demon bowler of Pudsey St Lawrence.

Intrigued by this remark I traced the Bill Hudson referred to and he turned out to be a fifty-three-year-old Pudsey coal merchant, standing six foot three inches tall and weighing sixteen stones ten pounds. He frightened me with a lump of coal in his hand, never mind a cricket ball!

"Can't you see I'm busy?", he snapped, looking down on me belligerently from the top of his lorry. "I've more to do than talk about Len Hutton."

"But, Mr Hudson", I protested, "you're the bowler whom Len Hutton feared more than Lindwall and Miller put together and yet few people outside Pudsey have ever heard of you."

He grunted non-committally and went on loading his coal from a wagon in the windswept railway siding. "He were t'only one I could bowl to", he ruminated, lifting a sack into position with effortless ease. "T'others wouldn't stand up to me—not even t'big uns."

He laughed grimly. "Mind you, I could chuck 'em down a bit in them days. I could throw a ball across the St Lawrence ground and twenty-four yards into t'next field. And I'm not saying I couldn't lay 'em out. There were often a couple lying dead in t'pavilion when I'd been on!"

"And yet young Hutton stood up to you?", I said, getting him back to the point.

He put down his coal, sat on his coal bags and prepared to

talk cricket at length. "Aye," he said reminiscently, "he did. And, think on, he were nobbut a lad of thirteen."

He shook his head in wistful admiration. "A wonder he was, a real wonder. He would hook balls into t'tennis ground off his chin. T'gardener would come next morning with half a dozen of 'em."

"How did it all start?", I asked.

"Well," he said, "it were this way. Leonard were only a schoolboy and the first and second team players—including his brothers—considered him a damned nuisance. They used to let him field for them but Leonard wasn't satisfied with that. He were no darned good at fielding anyway. 'Can't I have a bat?', he was always moaning. 'No tha' can't', they'd tell him, 'we've got to get our practice in for Saturday'.

"Well I reckon I took pity on him. Or maybe I wanted somebody to bowl to. I got old George—he was our groundsman until he was ninety—to put a special net up where I could bowl to him on his own. And then when we'd finished I'd buy him a fish and a penn'orth—because he was never flayed of owt. Mind you, I did used to try and bowl on the off."

"And then I suppose he got into the team?"

"Aye, it was about 1930. I had a bull-nosed Morris Cowley and because we were one short against East Bierley I went off to fetch him. He got 36. It was a good innings. But the best he ever played was his 115 against Bradford in the fourth round of the Priestley Cup. Far better than his 364 against Australia at the Oval. Think of it, fifteen years old and playing against veterans! There was a bowler called David Luckhurst and he was the best bowler in the district. 'I've tried everything I know on him, Bill', he told me. 'He's an absolute blooming master'."

Warming to his memories Mr Hudson went on to recall other great boyhood innings of the potential cricketing genius. "There was that 85 he got against Sydney Barnes. He wasn't sixteen then. I remember it well because I gave him a sweater—he'd only got one of his father's."

"And then", I said, "he played for Yorkshire and England?"

"Aye," he said, "he did."

"And yet some people still go on saying he was frightened of fast bowling?"

Mr Hudson gave a derisive guffaw and went back to work

again on his coal bags. "Him frightened of fast bowling!", he repeated ironically. "That's a laugh if ever there was one!"

Shy youth called Freddie Trueman

The other great star of the Yorkshire team in the post-war period was Freddie Trueman, no doubt one of the outstanding cricketing characters of all time. John Arlott has said in his book, *Fred, Portrait of a Fast Bowler*, which must rank as one of the best of all cricket biographies, that there are four Fred Truemans in one—Trueman the miner who set off from Maltby in 1949 with wonder and hope to play cricket for Yorkshire; Trueman the mature fast bowler, a sharply pointed and astutely directed weapon; Trueman the man, often tactless, haphazard, crude, a creature of impulse; and Trueman the public image, round the human core of which so many accretions of rumour and fiction have been deposited that the resultant figure is recognizable only to those who did not know him. "There is a histrionic streak in him", Arlott writes, "and if the men of his own county insisted on seeing him as the archetypal Yorkshireman they themselves wanted to be—blunt, honest, strong destroying bowler of high speed, smiter of sixes, taker of acrobatic catches, striker of wisecracks, cocker of snooks at authority—he was only too happy—in fact, compulsively eager—to play the part. . . . These four identities, too, are often completely contradictory. He can be uproarious but also—but not often—silent, moody; he can be generous—and mean; he could bowl his heart out or turn it in; he can be harsh—or gentle; he can be genuinely witty—and horribly crude; almost hysterically funny—and a complete bore; he can be intuitively understanding—and chillingly embarrassing; he can be arrogant—and as uncertain of himself as a schoolboy; he is pulled this way and that by his doubts and his emotions; he wants desperately to be liked and he is at bottom lonely."

I first met Trueman at the dinner held at the Grand Hotel, Sheffield, in 1949 to mark the centenary year of the Roses matches. The oldest ex-player present was seventy-nine-year-old E B Rowley of Lancashire, who had first played in a Roses match in 1896, and the youngest was eighteen-year-old Fred

Trueman, who had played in his first Roses match that summer. He was a shy, gauche, unsophisticated youngster who appeared to be completely overawed by the occasion and, as far as I could see, hardly opened his mouth the whole evening. I tried to have a chat with him while he drank orange juice at an interval but he spoke in monosyllables and gave me nothing worth reporting. I was to meet him on a number of occasions in the future but I never found him shy again!

My most vivid memory of Trueman on the field is of a test match against India at Headingley in 1952. India began their second innings at 3 pm on the Saturday with a reasonable chance of winning the game—England having led by only 41 runs on the first innings. There was a capacity crowd as Trueman ran up to the wicket in his usual aggressive manner to open the bowling at the Kirkstall Lane end. His first ball went straight through to the wicket-keeper. His second took a wicket. One of the Indian openers was caught by Denis Compton. The score board read 0 for 1. Alec Bedser bowled from the other end and took a wicket in his first over. 0 for 2. Trueman, stimulated as always by the tension, could not get back to his mark quickly enough. His first ball knocked the batsman's off stump out of the ground. 0 for 3 went up on the scoreboard.

The wild excitement and joy of the crowd was only matched by the blank misery of the normally cheerful little manager of the Indian team, Mr Pankaj Gupta, whom I happened to be talking to in the dressing room—I was interviewing him for a test match feature for the *Yorkshire Post.* "It's terrible, terrible", he told me, his face a study in horrified bewilderment. "I am very distressed."

But Trueman's slaughter was not yet over. The new batsman patted his block hole nervously as the bowler raced down to deliver his second ball of the over. He tried to drive it but missed completely and the ball again tore the off stump out of the ground. 0 for 4. Trueman had taken three wickets in eight balls and it was the most sensational start ever to a test match in England.

The crowd went mad. So did Mr Gupta. "Terrible, terrible, terrible", he repeated hoarsely. "This Trueman is terrifying them. The tour is going to cost £35 000 and there are four wickets down for nothing at 3 o'clock on Saturday afternoon. We shan't have a gate at all on Monday and Tuesday!"

But although Trueman maintained his fire the assault and battery was over and Mr Gupta got some gate money on the Monday after all.

As John Arlott says many of the stories about Trueman are apocryphal—but some are not. It is related that at the University Arms in Cambridge where he was spending the night with the Yorkshire team prior to playing his first county match against the university he was presented with a menu in French. "Ah'll have that for sweet", he is alleged to have said, pointing to the words at the bottom: "Jeudi le douzième mai".

Touring the West Indies under Len Hutton's captaincy he is said to have called an umpire who refused an appeal a "cheating black bastard". The umpire bridled naturally and Trueman hastily added "And there's no colour prejudice in it—if you weren't black I'd have called you a cheating white bastard."

En route to Australia he is said to have attended a dinner in Aden at which the local sheikh was present. One of the hosts pointed him out to Trueman and said he had 196 wives. "Has he?", said Fred. "Does he know that if he gets another four he can have a new ball"—a new ball at that time being due in test matches after 200 runs had been scored.

On the same tour Trueman is alleged to have said to the Reverend David Sheppard, the present Bishop of Liverpool and at that time a test cricketer, who had dropped a catch off his bowling "Kid yourself it's Sunday, Rev, and keep your hands together".

But the story which Trueman denies most firmly is that of the dinner given by the Indian High Commissioner in London to the English and Indian teams after the 1952 Test series. John Arlott tells it thus: "Fred as the outstanding success of the series was placed at the top table. He sat next to a high dignitary of the Indian Government who was deeply engaged in conversation with his neighbour on the other side when Fred, unable otherwise to attract his attention, gave him a nudge in the ribs and said "Hey Gunga Din, pass t'salt'."

The Roses dinner at Sheffield was an historic cricketing occasion. The tables were filled with past and present players in the Roses games—forty-one from Lancashire and fifty-two from Yorkshire. It is the only time I have seen cricketers themselves going round for autographs. Yorkshire's former captain, Sir William Worsley, then president of the club, was the chairman and he wound up the proceedings by presenting a flag to the Lancashire club to be flown at Old Trafford whenever Roses matches were played there. The flag contained a white rose and a red rose with their stems crossed and bearing the dates 1849–1949.

Scarcely a season between the years 1896 and 1949 was without its representatives. There were famous faces wherever one looked—Wilfred Rhodes, David Denton, Ernest Tyldesley, Emmott Robinson, Herbert Sutcliffe, Maurice Leyland, Cyril Washbrook, Reggie Spooner, Len Hutton, Percy Holmes, Harry Makepeace, Jack Ikin, C S Marriott and dozens more.

The speeches and the dinner table conversation flowed with reminiscence and many old battles were re-fought. Proposing a toast to the Lancashire County Cricket Club Lord Scarbrough said the matches had created in a rather material age a kind of chivalry between the two counties in which the characteristics of courage, energy and courtesy had been splendidly displayed.

He might have added that the characteristics of torpor had also been rather splendidly displayed and it was not inappropriate that the centenary Roses match at Headingley that year was one of the dullest ever. Five hours' batting on the Saturday produced 211 runs for Yorkshire and the crowd gave them the slow hand clap. But, as I wrote in the *Yorkshire Post*, expecting them to behave any differently in a Roses centenary would have been asking them to ignore a great tradition. It would have been like asking the organist to play ragtime at the harvest festival!

A dismal decade

The 1950s were a dismal decade for Yorkshire cricket—they did not win the championship once between 1949 and 1959 and it represented their longest period ever without that coveted award. There were three captains in that decade—Norman Yardley, Billy Sutcliffe and Ronnie Burnet—and only the latter achieved any success, the team regaining the championship under his leadership in 1959.

Yardley became one of the best player-captains Yorkshire

ever had when he succeeded Sellers in 1948 but he lacked Sellers' qualities of drive and leadership and from being the most efficient and well-disciplined team in the country Yorkshire became a house divided among itself—a rabble would really not be too strong a word for them. The dressing room was known to be unhappy and the cricket air was thick with rumours of feuding and fighting. One of the best bowlers and a regular test player, Johnny Wardle, was sacked for indiscipline and a number of others left without good reason—Alec Coxson, Brian Stott, Ken Taylor and Frank Lowson all retired from the game long before they should have done, one captain—Billy Sutcliffe—resigned and a captain presumptive—Geoffrey Keighley—withdrew before he was appointed. One of the county's best players, Willie Watson, left at the age of thirty-seven to play for another club. It seemed that even Len Hutton no longer enjoyed his cricket for he retired in 1955 at the relatively early age of thirty-nine.

Yardley must accept some of the responsibility for this unhappy state of affairs. He had a most pleasant personality but was far too casual and easy going to be a successful captain of Yorkshire. He was aptly summed up by one of his players, quoted by John Arlott in his book on Trueman, who described him as "too nice a chap to be the skipper we need". Another commented that the team had "too many captains".

In my view, and that of most Yorkshire members, however, the club committee were the chief culprits. Rightly or wrongly they were considered to be mainly old fuddy duddies still living in the past and entirely lacking in the qualities needed to run a successful county cricket team in the second half of the twentieth century. So far as the club's relations with its players were concerned it was considered that these, too, were rooted in the past and that one man who belonged by instinct and temperament to the 1930s had been given far too much influence over team selection and other practical matters in the 1950s and 1960s—none other than that great captain Brian Sellers. Sellers, it was believed, expected to assert the same disciplinary control over the players as chairman of the cricket committee in the sixties as he had done as captain in the thirties, and had not the flexibility of mind to recognize that times had changed. Professional cricketers in the 1960s no longer touched their forelocks respectfully but regarded themselves like everyone else in Britain as just as good as their masters.

This lack of confidence in the committee developed during the 1960s and there was blank dismay in the membership ranks when Ray Illingworth left to play for Leicester in 1968 because the club refused to give him a four-year contract. He went on to become one of England's most successful captains and led Leicester to championship honours seven years later.

The Brian Close revolt

But the censure of the committee reached its long-delayed flash-point in 1970 when the most successful Yorkshire captain since Sellers, Brian Close, who had led the team to the championship four times in eight seasons, was sacked in a manner which was considered to be disgraceful.

According to the reports—never denied—Sellers gave him fifteen minutes to decide whether to resign or be sacked. Even assuming the committee had adequate reasons for getting rid of Close this was no way to treat a brilliant cricketer who had given over twenty years' service to the county and the membership was incensed as never before in the history of the Yorkshire club. At a never-to-be-forgotten annual meeting of the club in Leeds town hall on 30 January 1971, an open revolt broke out and a vote of no confidence was passed by 570 votes to 507.

It was not officially a vote of no confidence as the chairman ruled such a motion out of order because the club rules required a fortnight's notice! The vote was taken on the motion to approve the annual report and accounts.

The only previous annual meeting of the Yorkshire county cricket club I had attended was in 1955 and it had been, as I am sure all previous annual meetings had been, a most decorous affair, held in, of all places, the Leeds city museum and attended by about fifty members. Every satisfaction was expressed with the way the affairs of the club were conducted and genial votes of thanks to the president, secretary and other officials were passed with unanimity and applause.

It was expected that there would be a much larger attendance than usual at the 1971 meeting because of the Close controversy and for that reason the main hall in the town hall had been booked. But no one expected over a thousand members to turn up, and even less did anyone expect the report and accounts to be thrown out.

The mood of the majority of the members was angry to say the least and although the committee, under a skilled chairman deputizing for the president, Sir William Worsley, did their very best to smooth things over a showdown was insisted upon and the committee were defeated.

Brian Sellers gave the reasons why the committee had dismissed Close—his opposition to Sunday cricket and his behaviour off the field were quoted, as well as his refusal to carry out the committee's wishes in team selection and in the "blooding" of new players—but Sellers' speech, although delivered with his usual pugnacity, did not give much satisfaction. Most people agreed with the leader of the action group formed by the rebels, Mr Jack Mewies, a Skipton solicitor. He said that what the action group complained about, and what he himself was deeply ashamed of, was not so much the dismissal of Close as the manner of his dismissal. To loud hear! hears! and applause he went on to say: "It is disgraceful that he should have been given fifteen minutes in which to decide whether to resign or be sacked. I think this committee is not fit to govern a club like Yorkshire and I move a vote of censure and no confidence in the committee."

Not even Close's best friends would say that he was an easy man to get on with and he said himself, apropos these events, that he was no angel. There had clearly been incidents in which he was culpable. One was in a match with Warwickshire at Edgbaston where Yorkshire were accused of time wasting on the field far beyond the bounds of tactical justification. Close was severely censured for his conduct after a formal investigation by the advisory county committee.

Another incident was at Old Trafford where Close was accused of swearing at the president of the Lancashire committee—he did not deny this in an interview on television and merely said that "something had happened" after the game when, in the heat of the moment, he had spoken to a man who had made some comment to him. But he insisted he did not know the man was the president of Lancashire and said that when he had discovered this he had written a letter of apology to him.

These incidents were no doubt regrettable but in the view of most Yorkshire members did not add up to an adequate reason for the dismissal of an exceptionally talented captain. The action group held a meeting on 14 February and decided unanimously to demand a special general meeting at which they would propose a vote of no confidence in the committee and call for their resignations.

But it never came to that. The committee made concessions to the action group by effecting various changes in the rules of the club and Sellers resigned as chairman of the cricketing committee. And that was about all. The fire of the action group seemed to fizzle out and the administration of the club went on much as before.

The loss of Close had, however, disastrous repercussions on the team's performance and the committee's report for the first season without him, 1971, began as follows: "It is with regret that your committee has to report that the season 1971 was without doubt the worst in the history of the club both from a playing and financial viewpoint." The team had dropped from fourth in the championship in Close's last season to thirteenth under the new captain, Boycott—the lowest on record since the turn of the century. Nor were the 1972, 1973 or 1974 seasons any better. Yorkshire were tenth in the championship in 1972, fourteenth in 1973 and eleventh in 1974.

The glory that was Yorkshire cricket had gone and watching Yorkshire in the 1970s has been a grim and depressing business. At Headingley, Park Avenue and Bramall Lane (until the latter's closure) the long suffering supporters have often looked more like mourners round the graveside than spectators round a cricket field. The talk has been constantly of the past. If only we had Close . . . Trueman . . . Illingworth . . . Hutton . . . Sutcliffe . . . Leyland . . . Bowes . . . Verity . . . Rhodes . . . Hirst . . . Denton . . . Jackson . . . Tunnicliffe . . . Haigh . . . Peel. The past was all glory and the further away it was the brighter it seemed to glow!

And when they have not been invoking the past Yorkshire supporters have been deploring the present. It has been depressing enough to listen to them at Headingley and Park Avenue but at Old Trafford it has been quite soul destroying.

"No, I'm not sitting with you, Fred", said a Lancastrian in a loud voice as he marched from the pavilion bar in mid-afternoon at the last Roses match I watched there, red of face and bright of eye and breathing beer and benevolence all round him. "I want a Yorkshireman to sit next to. I'm feeling like an argument. Now where's all these white roses?"

There was a general chortle of amusement. "There aren't none, Joe", said another Lancastrian. "They've all died." He pronounced it "deed."

Joe, however, identified a Yorkshireman a few rows in front of him by his blue and yellow tie and squeezed himself laboriously into the seat next to him. "Now then", he said belligerently, spoiling for a fight, "you've got a bloody awful team this season haven't you?"

He obviously expected a spirited defence of the Yorkshire team, but he didn't get it. The Yorkshireman looked at him glumly. "Aye", he said, "you're right. We have got a bloody awful team. We're all thoroughly ashamed of 'em. In fact I don't know what the hell we come and watch 'em for. We couldn't beat a team of old age pensioners, never mind Lancashire."

The Lancastrian looked at him in blank amazement. Never in all the long and glorious history of Old Trafford had such a terrible admission been elicited from a Yorkshireman before. It took the wind completely out of his sails. He found himself in the absurd position of having to defend Yorkshire against a Yorkshireman.

"Nay", he said slowly, "you've got Boycott haven't you . . . and your bowling's not too bad . . ."

The season of 1975—which is the last I can write about—saw a great improvement in Yorkshire's performance. They rose from eleventh to second in the County Championship table and hope was reborn among Yorkshire supporters. So, I think, was pride in the county as a whole. For although not by any means every Yorkshireman is keen enough on Yorkshire cricket to go and watch it the team's performances reflect sharply on the county's prestige and no true Yorkshireman can hold his head up high when the county team is near the bottom of the table. It is no exaggeration to say our cricket team is our ambassador round the world. And if Yorkshire cricket supporters still tend to look back rather than forward what a glorious heritage they have to look back on!

As Francis Thompson would have put it in his evocative verse if he had been a Yorkshireman instead of a Lancastrian:

For the field is full of shades as I near the shadowy coast,
And a ghostly batsman plays to the bowling of a ghost,
And I look through my tears on a soundless clapping host,
As the run stealers flicker to and fro, to and fro,
Oh my Sutcliffe and my Leyland long ago!